REFLECTIONS
OF A  MAN

LIFE AND TIMES OF
FLEET STREET'S
CHIEF ROTTER

JOHN JACKSON

To BARBARA
and our family

have rescued many bodies from the sea and I can tell you he didn't drown as there was no water in the lungs" I escorted Betty and Philip to officially identify Robert Maxwell.

It was certainly him and the one thing that struck me immediately was the position of his hands. His arms were bent upwards with his fists clenched, similar to the way a baby often sleeps. This was important to me as I will explain later.

We flew to the *Lady Ghislaine* and for the next few days it was a continuous round of interviews with coroners, lawyers, and police. I helped out at times by manning one of the satellite phones and fielded calls from Prime Minister Margaret Thatcher and US President George Bush Snr among others.

But Betty had just one thing on her mind – she was determined her husband's body would reach Jerusalem before sunset on November 9 for an arranged burial on the Mount of Olives. Arrival on the Sabbath, Saturday, was not possible.

One problem here was that a very big and heavy body, in a very big and heavy coffin would not fit into the Gulfstream. Betty said: "Robert will not mind if he is upside down, standing on his head, as long as we get there." The pilot said even if he did fit in the plane it might not get off the ground.

So son Ian Maxwell in London chartered a special jet to fly from Switzerland to Las Palmas for us all.

Meanwhile, daughter Ghislaine had arrived from New York. Now famous in her own right following her connection with American convicted sex offender Jeffrey Epstein, she was then the youngest of the seven grieving Maxwell children.

There were no public tears from Ghislaine and her mother Betty, but Philip was mourning in a different way. A very private man he asked me if we could have a quiet word. As there was a massive media presence on the quay alongside (packed with long-time Fleet Street buddies of mine) I managed to manoeuvre him away from the prying long lenses to a spot behind the funnel.

As we squatted on the deck he burst into tears and said: "My father hated me and I did not like him. But now I will never have

PREFACE

The helicopter lifted off the roof alongside the *Daily Mirror* building at London's Holborn Circus and through the grey November haze I looked down on the spot that had monopolized 30 years of my working life – Fleet Street.

Memories of fun and friendships raced through my mind as for that short time my thoughts zigzagged down what satirical magazine *Private Eye* calls The Street of Shame.

It was 2pm on Monday, November 5, 1991, and I had joined Betty Maxwell and eldest son Philip to fly to the Canary Islands, with the world having just learned that her husband and *Mirror* publisher Robert Maxwell was missing at sea. He had apparently fallen overboard from his yacht *Lady Ghislaine*, named after his youngest, and certainly favourite, child.

And in good Fleet Street tradition, I had been summoned from a splendid champagne lunch to head out on what became the last big news story of my career. As we headed off to Farnborough Airport to board the family's Gulfstream jet I could imagine the banter and boozing being enjoyed in the pubs below, between the Law Courts and Ludgate Circus.

As one of my many editors described it, the Fleet Street of those days was a 24-hour *village en fête*.

However, that was 30 years ago. The newspaper Fleet Street has gone, with offices scattered around the new high-rise London, I am well retired and journalism has changed completely. For me memories are golden!

The Maxwell demise story was certainly memorable. Halfway to the Canaries the Gulfstream pilot was told a body had been found in the sea. We were diverted to Las Palmas and allowed to taxi up to the hangar where the body was still in the air-sea rescue helicopter.

Betty refused to climb aboard to certify that it was her husband and said the body would have to be brought into a room nearby. This was done and after the air-sea rescue pilot had told us "I the chance to make it up with him." To his credit Philip held his emotions and shyness in check to deliver a splendid eulogy at the verging-on a State funeral in Jerusalem.

I ghosted Betty's tribute to her husband for the *Daily Mirror* and the speech Ghislaine gave from the side of the boat to the waiting media. She never faltered.

As we left the *Lady Ghislaine* for the last time Betty asked me to fetch Ghislaine who was lagging behind. I found her in the main lounge ordering staff to shred all important documents.

Then Betty handed me her handbag and said "guard it with your life". Much to the amusement of my mates ashore I walked down the gangplank handbag aquiver. Not until I read her biography *My Life With Robert Maxwell* years later did I discover I was carrying £30,000 in cash, her passport, credit cards and "precious life-savers".

On the flight from Las Palmas to Jerusalem colleague photographer Ken Lennox and I watched as the three Maxwells opened the rear door and sat by the coffin for a few moments, and Ghislaine placed some flowers on top.

For me I was a reporter covering the biggest story of the day, with much to recount in those pubs when home. Betty wrote later that during meal times on the yacht "I found John's stories both moving and amusing. He's a great raconteur."

And when I next met Ghislaine she came running across the editor's office to give me a hug and a kiss.

That was Fleet Street – and here's my story.

FUN, FUN, FUN

Journalism as a career has been fabulous. Life in the great days of Fleet Street could be frantic, fantastically competitive, often cruel. My son-in-law, after reading the memoirs of those times, now on a par with the dinosaurs, suggested that it showed a grittier, seamier side.

We never thought of it like that – to us it was just fun, fun, fun. We worked hard and played hard, knowing there would be a friendly face alongside the bar in whichever of the umpteen pubs on Fleet Street and its environs we fell into.

Every day was the equivalent of a well-contested rugby match. You would meet best mates on journalistic assignments everywhere, try your utmost to outsmart them and keep control of the action, aim to knock shit out of them, in the literal sense of course – then after the final phone call adjourn to the nearest hostelry for friendly refreshment, before returning to "the Street".

To begin at the beginning, I'm an unreconstructed English male of a certain age (all right then, 86) leading some members of my family to suggest I should give these memoirs the title "Anecdotage".

I realise my career experiences and attitudes to life are out of step with the greater awareness of my eight grandchildren and also the generation earlier, my four children.

However, this is my story of the Street of Shame as it was over four decades from the 1960s on: rumbustious, hard drinking (grandchildren, don't follow in my footsteps re the latter). A life of fun, friendships and travels on the road as an old tabloid hack with colleagues who were part of a journalistic family. Amid the jollifications we filled a newspaper which sold five million copies daily.

By God it was good – and frankly my dear, *je ne regrette rien.*

I got the message early on my very first job in Fleet Street. That morning, March 2, 1964, as holiday relief on the *Daily Herald* saw me dispatched with photographer Chris Smith on the biggest story of the day – a missing toddler in Stepney.

On arrival I spotted among the opposition the experienced John Smith, *Daily Mirror,* and then, help, the doyen of Fleet Street, the *Daily Mail's* Vincent Mulchrone. Both held out hands of greeting, with Mulchrone announcing: "Welcome, at 11 o'clock we take champagne."

He announced he had just heard that he had been voted the first ever Journalist of the Year, in the now common Press awards. So we drank champagne and after every glass I became more convinced this was the life for me.

A couple of hours later, fortunately, John Smith and the *Daily Sketch's* ebullient Vic Tredger hauled me off to the police station to catch up with the story. I made the front-page splash and congrats all round, which led to a staff job within two weeks. Mulchrone, of course, wrote us all under the table.

With no such accoutrement as a mobile phone in those days there was time to relax, unlike the immediacy of everything today brought about by the communications revolution. We thought life had come to an end when bleepers suddenly emerged on the scene, but even when their beep-beep caught you mid sip there was always the "problem" of finding a telephone with which to make contact.

As one hardened hack commented then: "They can always reach you, but they haven't a clue where you are."

In this day and age of instant communication, a simple press of a button on a mobile phone and you are through to your news desk.

I hark back to a cold January day in 1965 as I stood with the world's press in London's Hyde Park Gate, waiting for Sir Winston Churchill to die. With me was colleague Alan Dick, a wily old rascal who had been there, done it all, and got the tie (no such thing as common T-shirts in those days).

His philosophy as to what a reporter needed in order to be the complete on-the-road correspondent: "Dear boy, if you have a bidet and a telephone handy, you can reach every necessary part."

The only problem on that job, with the whole world beaming in on West London, was that tours of Kensington and Knightsbridge were needed to find a vacant phone box, and every hotel bidet was being used by photographers to process films.

Perhaps it was a conversation overheard between two of my great mates, photographers Kent Gavin (*Daily Mirror*) and Arthur Edwards (*Sun*), as they waited to take several hundred more snaps of Princess Diana, which summed up my philosophy at that time: "Not a bad life this. Fantastic fun. What is it, Gavs?"; "Fucking, fantastic fun, Arfur". They could not spell alliteration, but they had it in one.

Looking back over 70 years since I left school in North London to take my first steps into journalism, I can only boast that I have been very, very fortunate. But, as most people will agree, it is up to each individual to make their own luck.

I was certainly extremely fortunate to have been the right age in those happy-go-lucky days of the 1950s and 1960s when it was possible to up sticks and take off round the world, confident that when the coffers started running dry and you needed to earn money to keep travelling there was always some close-at-hand job ready to oblige.

Visas were never a problem, and the accompanying work permits, such a barrier these days, were a thing of the future. This allowed me to walk into on-the-spot staff jobs as a reporter on newspapers in Canada, Jamaica, New Zealand and South Africa; a brief interlude as a chef at the California Kitchens, an early fast food joint in Washington, DC; a responsible position as a treasury clerk with the Canadian Pacific Railroad in Vancouver, BC; and casual manual work ("seagulling" as it was called there then) on the docks at Wellington and Auckland, NZ.

But the biggest and most important decision, when Lady Luck stuck with me as I am sure she was aware it was a gamble I could not bear to lose, involved the one big chance to clinch a staff job with the *Daily Mirror*.

It was 1969 and the country's best newspaper was still enjoying the hangover of its huge circulation. No one ever left the *Mirror* as the staff was the best in the business and it was such a brilliant place to work. Any attempt to climb aboard, whoever you might be, was nigh impossible.

Working on the broadsheet *Sun,* the relaunch of the tired old *Daily Herald,* made it totally out of the question. The paper was owned by IPC, and it was an unwritten rule that no movement was allowed within that group. This meant I could not go to the *Daily* or *Sunday Mirror,* or *Sunday People.*

The death of the *Daily Herald* was marked by a lavish dinner for all staff at the Café Royal, where Mirror Group chairman Hugh Cudlipp bluntly summed up its demise:

"The *Daily Herald* was formed by the labour unions to serve the labour unions, and it has done a good job for 50 years. But recent surveys have shown its readers are the wrong age, the wrong sex and they all live in the North East.

"And nowhere today can we find advertisers willing to try to sell Tampax to old men in Newcastle."

Five years later when Cudlipp decided to sell our *Sun* for a song to Rupert Murdoch, to make way for the tabloid *Sun* we enjoy today, that barrier was lifted. Every member of the editorial staff was told they could transfer to the new paper, or attend an interview for one of a few vacancies being opened at the *Daily Mirror.*

The attraction for the vast majority was the compensation payment (four figures for the longest serving) which became payable if you went with Murdoch – leaving one company to join another. For me there was no need for thought. I had always wanted to work on the *Daily Mirror*: here was a chance, so all my eggs went in the one basket – and to hell with the payoff cheque.

Not even pleading phone calls from the first news editor of the new *Sun,* my old buddy and long-time *Mirror* man Brian McConnell, could sway me. Pioneering editor Larry Lamb phoned to stress he would like me on the staff.

My *Mirror* meeting was with news editor Roly Watkins, renowned for his interviewing technique of declaring how he saw his reporting staff as an orchestra, and often disappointing young hopefuls with the decision: "I see you as a clarinet and that part of the wind section is full at the moment".

Fortunately, I knew I might circumvent the musical aspect by hitting home how Roly and I had started at different times on newspapers in the same town, Birkenhead. Reminiscences and old names did the trick.

So on August 23, 1969, a letter fell through the door of our Twickenham home from *Daily Mirror* deputy editor Geoff Pinnington. It offered the job I had always coveted, with the same £2,595 annual salary I was on at the *Sun*. He stressed that an early decision would be appreciated. I headed straight for the typewriter.

This also brought Brownie points as a follow-up welcoming letter from Roly Watkins was generous with praise: "Let me say we were all delighted to hear you are joining us. I reckon I shall not easily forget that you were the first of the *Sun* chaps to make a decision and not to make an each way bet!"

There was never any chance of that. For the record, just four reporters were offered *Mirror* jobs and two declined in favour of Murdoch money. Sadly two of the four, Mavis Davidson and Jim Render, died very young and were unable to enjoy the fun ahead. For me, the most fulfilling 24 years of my working life had left the launching pad.

Here I will look back on 57 years in the life of a general reporter, who covered every type of news assignment but pioneered, then specialised in, the news side of sport. The latter took me to 22 Olympic Games (12 Summer, 10 Winter), 10 soccer World Cups, 55 Wimbledons, England cricket tours of West Indies and South Africa, five Commonwealth Games, plus a host of FA Cup Finals, European Championships in athletics and football, and other top sporting events.

Just mention John McEnroe, Paul Gascoigne, Ian Botham, Daley Thompson, and anyone would realise there is the odd tale to tell.

As a news reporter I covered the lot, from the death of Winston Churchill to being flown out to the Canaries to find, then help bury in Jerusalem, my paper's publisher Robert Maxwell; Nelson Mandela's release from prison; earthquakes in Algeria and Romania; a farting/burping reception from Sid Vicious, Johnny Rotten and the other Sex Pistols; watching a man sentenced to be hanged at the Old Bailey; asked to witness an execution in New Zealand; to a series of libel cases with the brilliant George Carman QC; a politically incorrect dwarf throwing championship; murders, mayhem, bombs, banquets, politics, personalities, demonstrations, dog shows.

I can honestly say that there was rarely a morning when I failed to wake without tremendous enthusiasm for what the day might hold. Simply because I did not know where I might finish up, whom I might meet, what story I would be tackling. And if it was a dull news day, there were always those pubs and mates.

I do not intend to go into newspaper politics and the many problems that troubled the industry during my time. These have been well documented by commentators far more prominent than me.

And I am certainly not one of those old hacks who continually assert "We had the best days. It's not the same now." I am sure the "game" is just as much fun today, despite the communications revolution which allows TV and radio to inform the world before the pen, notebook and tape recorder brigade can start filing. Mind you, the accountants are now the rulers, which can only hamper good, keen reporting – and the necessary long lunches!

My chronicling here will spare no blushes, but one area will remain locked away in the memory bank. There will be no tell-tale stories (and I have many) of those unofficial indoor Olympic frolics or unreported fumblings far from home, no doubt enjoyed (certainly from the recounting next day) by colleagues still alive.

This is not a kiss and tell book, for I have witnessed the terrible hurt that playing away causes. I have only ever had one office fling and I have been married to her for 61 happy years. Boozing, bad behaviour, and straight bloody fun, yes; bonking no.

I watched with amusement at separate times as two well married fathers battled agonisingly about seriously abandoning everything at home and staying on in New Zealand with the crumpet (as it was called then) they had found to comfort them on the other side of the world, at the 1974 Commonwealth Games in Christchurch.

Mind you, no one knows better than me the fatal attraction of those Kiwi girls. My story would not be the same without my wonderful lifetime companion Barbara. Full details later.

A well-known name managed to miss the Ben Johnson banned drugs saga at the 1988 Seoul Olympics, as he was on a lone assignment to a local lovely's apartment, with his bleeper switched off to avoid interruption; a photographer sent on an urgent Middle East assignment on Christmas Eve was being seen off at Heathrow Airport by his very disappointed wife and children when he spotted a recent girlfriend checking in alongside him "as a surprise" – dressed as a nun.

A tabloid hack felt so alone at a World Cup he paid for the amply proportioned barmaid at his office pub to fly out and "care" for him; a sports columnist spent the night with a young Tokyo geisha girl, then found to his horror everyone knew about it on his return to the Press Centre. The girl's mother had gone searching for him as she wished to return his wallet, which she found by the bed.

When deciding to refrain from elaborating on those tales of naughtiness away from home I am reminded of the reminiscences of Ian Christie, an old drinking pal when he was film critic for the *Daily Express*. In an earlier life he had been a fulltime clarinet player with top trad bands, during those halcyon days in the 1950s when traditional jazz was the rage. Crazy times! Music with a tune, which you could actually tap your feet to. Oh happy days!

He played for a long time with the Mick Mulligan Band, the singer with which was the incomparable George Melly. Now it is no secret that George enjoyed sexual romps on both sides of the AC/DC line. When he decided to write a book about his days with the band (to follow such tomes as his memoirs of naval life,

entitled *Rum, Bum and Concertina*) he kept away from overnight
gig frolicking which would embarrass the past and present
married men.

The book was named *Owning Up*, but as a result of this
thoughtfulness Christie suggested it was actually *Clamming Up*.
This meant no mention of an "I'm bored, so I'm going to have a
wank" incident on the band bus, which reached the point of no
return while stopped at traffic lights in downtown Newcastle,
much to the amazement of passengers on a double-decker bus
which pulled alongside.

Fleet Street housed one big family, and finding members was
never hard. A short stroll down, without venturing into the
hostelry-lined side streets, would offer you 15 pubs. There would
always be a familiar face, between The George at Temple Bar and
the Punch Tavern on Ludgate Circus. You soon came to know
the plusses and pitfalls.

The beer in the top bar of the Cheshire Cheese was a favourite
(especially as Ron the barman, once he knew you, would pour
a pint but charge for a half. Good man.), but you had to be
wary about crossing Fleet Street to the Falstaff as the old biddy
of a landlady would throw you out if she sensed you had been
drinking in a rival establishment; say something out of place in
Ye Olde Bell Tavern and you would be barred from using the one
telephone on the stairs behind the bar.

Each office had its own regular drinking hole: the *Daily
Telegraph* strolled next door to the King and Keys; the *Daily
Express* had tiny Poppins, with a tortuous climb to its single
loo; Murdoch people used to prefer the Tipperary. Off Fleet
Street were the *Daily Mail* locals, "Aunties" (Rose and Crown),
"Mucky Duck" (White Swan), The Harrow; the *Daily Mirror,*
had the "Stab in the Back" (White Hart), "Barney Finnegans"
(Red Lion), with Winnie's No 10 in earlier days, and marvellous
Vagabonds later.

The Stab, as the *Mirror's* "branch" office was known, was in the
1970s a rollicking establishment reminiscent of Ye Olde Music
Hall, with features editor Des Lyons on the piano and Ginger Lil

from the canteen belting out Cockney and other pub songs.

When at work Ginger Lil's soprano tones could be heard from her seat behind the till. Behind me one morning a printer in overalls complained quietly that the two slices of white bread with his breakfast fry-up were covered in green mould.

Brandishing the bread aloft Ginger Lil was immediately in full voice: "Flossie, if I've told you once I've told you twice, this must be used for toast only."

Vagabonds, run by former Scotland Yard detective John Mulally, was the go-to place in the 1980s whatever the hour, for journalists, sports stars, pop musicians, lawyers and policemen.

And then there was always El Vino, with its club-like atmosphere where oik-like behaviour was frowned upon just as women had to wear skirts, always sit down and could not buy drinks. Long lunches were the norm and – well, long. And there are many legendary reports, if remembered. El Vino often, when closing time was 3pm, catered for first sessions, with the glass raising then moving 100 yards to the Wig and Pen. I remember such an enjoyable occasion in the company of writer Kingsley Amis.

When it came to fine dining the go-to restaurant was the Gay Hussar in Soho, favourite haunt for journalists, satirists, and mainly left-wing politicians, who enjoyed gossip and how to bring about the socialist millennium with the Hungarian menu – goulash, Bulls Blood wine, etc.

Barbara and I were regulars for almost 50 of its 65 years existence, even when its clientele changed with Fleet Street's finale and the move by newspapers to Canary Wharf and Wapping. You could always guarantee that lunchtime bonhomie, with, of course, glasses of Hungarian barack (apricot schnapps), might often be interrupted by the arrival of the dinner crowd.

When on the road the ideal companion was one of the *Daily Mail's* star reporters, Richard "Dickie" Herd. Always immaculately dressed, with a floral buttonhole, his greeting, whatever the job, was "I've arranged lunch". A nasty murder in

Maidenhead wrote itself after a splendid repast at one of those very expensive restaurants in nearby Bray.

But Dickie excelled himself in 1981 when we were covering the British Open Golf championship, which for once was in the south at Sandwich, Kent. On the final day, with American Bill Rogers a certain winner, I negotiated the country lanes for an early arrival to find Dickie already enjoying a liquid breakfast.

"Jacko. I've arranged lunch." What a surprise, but where in such a remote spot? "Boulogne." Mon Dieu!

Well, Dickie, Bob McGowan of the *Daily Express* and I managed to board the hovercraft at Ramsgate but Dickie was not best pleased when the captain welcomed us on "this service to Calais". A splendid dinner made up for a missed late lunch.

Operator connected calls to news desks to "explain" the necessity for an overnight stay in Sandwich had to be handled carefully, especially with "*Un moment, s'il vous plait*" continually butting in. "Bloody crossed lines…"

But for me, the 13-hour lunch at English Harbour, Antigua, in 1986 tops the lot. My wonderful companions were Blowers and TC, cricket commentators Henry Blofeld and Tony Cozier. Some details are still very hazy!!

When it comes to talking shop, there are not many professions able to silence journalists. I would like to think that this is because we have had an exciting and varied life and have the gift of re-telling our experiences with humour and interest.

We certainly meet famous people, get in free to cover popular and interesting events, and travel extensively at others' expense, in a way not open to the average person. Every story reminds a listener of another, and so it goes on.

Always garrulous, I seem over the years to have entertained people around the globe with my anecdotes, prompting the usual advice: "Why don't you write a book?" The answer so far has been a combination of laziness and lack of time. Now, at last… so here we go, on with my reminiscences.

I have tried hard to maintain a sense of readable order,

allowing the book to flow like the conversation when a gaggle of hacks gather at the bar. Each yarn is prompted by the one preceding, without the spoken "that reminds me of...; have you heard ...?; let me tell you about...".

Newspaper hacks are a special breed, and never change. I would love to minus a few years and get myself back on the duty roster again, certain that necessary new techniques could be learned as rapidly as the old ones.

I, by choice I might add, remained a good old-fashioned hack with never any ambition to climb the executive ladder and find myself behind a desk. I never wanted to be in a position where I would have to send reporters on assignments I wanted to do myself.

Out on the road was my forte, well away from the stress, strain and often annoying commands from junior executives whom you felt were where they were because they couldn't make it in your shoes.

I was christened Chief Rotter by rivals, a title I cherished and which, to this day, still prompts calls and e-mails from younger "rotters". (Rotter was the term for news reporters who ventured into the world of sport and covered the "real stories".)

I will concentrate on the fun side of what was the best job in the world. Even as my well-stamped passports (we always needed two because of diplomatic difficulties with visits to South Africa and Israel, even Northern Cyprus) announced that I was reaching "wrinkly" status, the enjoyment never faded. Many a young reporter would comment, after receiving an ear bashing from some news desk underling: "I don't know how you continue to be so enthusiastic."

Perhaps I was helped by a permanent overdose of self-confidence. There is nothing more satisfying than having the chase for a story, filing what you believe to be readable copy with all the salient facts, then waking in the morning to learn you have been "given a good show" in the paper, with a prominent by-line.

My philosophy was simple: receive a hard time from your

superiors and get nothing in the paper – fine them on expenses; find yourself flavour of the moment with a front-page splash or good chunk of the paper – give yourself a bonus on expenses.

You couldn't lose, especially in those halcyon days when the 10th floor of the *Mirror* building was known affectionately as "the bank in the sky". Robert Maxwell sadly sussed it out rather rapidly when he bought the *Mirror*. "The gravy train has hit the buffers," he declared. Bastard!

I also maintained that if I was competent enough to have been sent on the story, then I should tell my news desk what they were going to get, rather than ask what they wanted.

This confidence had grown from one of my first jobs on the *Daily Mirror,* when I phoned in from a political rally (a "joyous" occasion when eggs aimed at hated MP Enoch Powell, shortly after his infamous "rivers of blood" speech, missed and splattered the shoulders of my colleague John Pilger), explained what I had, and wondered how they would like the story slanted.

Gruff, but brilliant night news editor Dan Ferrari (whose youngest son Nick, LBC star, has certainly proved a chip off the old block) told me in a few curt words: "If you didn't know what the *Daily Mirror* wanted we would have never employed you."

OLYMPIC DREAM

The Olympic Games have been a dominant part of my sports news working life. To be at every day of one Games is a dream. To be there for 22 means the heavens have exploded. I was the lucky one, clocking up the memories over five decades, watching the cream of the world's athletes striving to go "Faster, Higher, and Stronger". This involved 15 countries on four continents.

There is nothing to compare with an Olympic Games. To witness the variety of sheer emotions that combine to make this the greatest show on earth, cannot be bettered. I know people who have regularly opened special savings accounts with the aim to attend just one Games. Piggy banks have been slowly filled over years with the same dream in mind.

Just to be in the main stadium for the Opening Ceremony is enough to prompt a lump in the throat of the hardest individual. Never mind the thrill of witnessing gold medal performances, the moment the Olympic Flame enters the arena can be a real tearjerker.

And medal ceremonies always bring tremendous pride for winners and compatriot spectators alike. But one of the first I covered brought more fists than fanfares,

It was at the weightlifting at the 1960 Rome Games. Tan Howe Liang won a first ever Olympic medal for Singapore when he took silver in the lightweight division. Due to bad organisation and timekeeping in those early days the medal ceremonies were held during the early hours of the morning, after that day's session of action had finished.

Needless to say, every member of the small Singapore team was present as the familiar anthem struck up for the Soviet gold medallist, and the three flags were slowly raised. Then all hell was let loose!

For sliding up the Singapore pole was the Japanese flag – just 15 years after World War II which saw Singapore occupied and horrendously treated by the Japanese. The Italian organisers could not find enough words of apology.

Nowadays the soccer World Cup is often described as the world's biggest sporting event. What nonsense, and I say that as someone who covered them during the four decades when they alternated between Europe and South America.

How can a bunch of overpaid men, many of whom can only claim their main brainwork is situated south of the ankle, who are in action never more than twice a week and represent just 32 countries, attempt to surpass the sheer variety and magnitude of the Olympic Games?

It all started for me in the most extraordinary way. After several days covering the wrestling and weightlifting (the only consolation was that the grunting and groaning took place outside in the magnificent setting of Rome's Basilica di Massenzio, alongside the Colosseum), the first interview at my first Olympic Games brought me face to face with the man who was to become certainly the greatest sports personality of his generation and maybe of all time. And he introduced himself to me.

This came about on a sunny August afternoon in 1960, with the XVII Olympiad well underway in the Italian capital, when a Yorkshire lass named Dorothy Hyman won the silver medal in the 100 metres track event.

This was quite something for Great Britain (the gold medal tally at these Olympics was confined to 50km walker Don Thompson and 200m breaststroke swimmer Anita Lonsbrough) and a major story for British news agency Reuters, with whom I was working. (Barbara was in the same office as a member of the Australian Associated Press team.)

I rushed down to the Olympic Village, as usual taking my life in my hands as a pillion passenger on one of the Vespa scooters which served as the official transport for the press. The problem was that they were driven by Italian sailors, mostly natives of Naples, who not only hadn't a clue where they were going but had a habit of standing up to whistle and gesture to every attractive young lady – and there has never been a shortage of those in Rome.

Once inside the Village I was faced with the problem of the segregated areas. Until Mexico in 1968 there were always two separate Olympic villages, one for men and one for women. (I could never understand why women could enter the male domain but no man was allowed near the female section!)

While pondering how I could get a message into the British women I spotted a tall, handsome couple walking towards me, hand in hand. I immediately spotted that the woman was the USA's Wilma Rudolph who had won the gold in the same 100m event.

I asked her whether she had seen Dorothy and she replied that she knew she was in the village and volunteered to fetch her. But added: "On one condition: while I'm away you must look after him."

Now "him" was a tall young man who I could spot instantly needed no looking after. He launched into non-stop chat, virtually forcing me to brace myself for the periodic jab in the chest. He assured me: "She's the greatest sprinter in the world and is going to win the 200m (which she did). And I'm the greatest boxer in the world and you're going to come later this week to see me win my gold medal (which I did).

"My name is Cassius Marcellus Clay."

This meant little then, but the continual use of the word greatest would give it away instantly now. Of course, "him" went on to wow the sporting world as Muhammad Ali.

Four years later at the Tokyo Olympics I was assigned to the boxing. I covered 232 fights for the Associated Press but it was the one Games where the usually dominant Americans were out punched – except for one man. His wild celebration after winning his country's only boxing gold medal saw him fall out of the ring on to my typewriter.

"Hi, I'm Joe Frazier," he said.

I am sure I was never mentioned in their conversations but the three Ali-Frazier heavyweight fights in years to come, culminating with the Thrilla in Manila, were the fiercest on record, from which neither man fully recovered.

In between these two titans I found myself closeted with another about-to-become-a legend. This was at the 1962 World Cup in Chile, and his name was Pele. Recognised as the best player in the world after his teenage exploits at the previous World Cup in Sweden, Pele was injured and did not play in Chile. So he enjoyed beating me at table tennis on many a morning in the heavily guarded Brazilian camp.

With no English he rarely spoke, except occasionally through the team's Dr Hilton Gosling. But I discovered an extra reason to name him as the world's greatest ever footballer (ahead, for me, of Maradona, Di Stefano, Puskas, Messi, Platini, Ronaldo et al) – few people knew he was Brazil's reserve goalkeeper.

My stories from all the many great sporting events could fill several volumes, as they did over a period of time in the then Sports Journalists' Association bulletin.

Here is a flavour of those earlier writings, reproduced as they appeared in that publication.

★★

When pioneering the news side of sport I often became the story. Veteran football writers still hail me as "Ring of steel" or "Dead dog Jacko", referring back to my exclusives at the 1974 and 1982 World Cups.

The latter, when I found a dead dog amid the squalor on the beach outside the hotel chosen for the England squad near Bilbao, prompted then manager Ron Greenwood to wittily suggest I was the only person to travel by air with "excess doggage".

But this Spanish spat could not compare with the major aggravation following my innocent look-ahead piece before the 1962 World Cup in Chile. At one point the tournament was threatened as the Mexican team delayed their departure, then talked of withdrawing altogether because of my predictions.

An Associated Press correspondent, I was assigned to the plum group based at the coastal holiday resort of Vina del Mar. I had reigning champions Brazil, an aged, but still star-studded Spain (Di Stefano, Puskas, Del Sol, Santamaria et al), Czechoslovakia, who progressed to the final with Brazil, and Mexico.

From the wonderfully named Hotel O'Higgins I filed my preliminary piece suggesting that Brazil, even without an injured Pele, should retain their title, the Czechs were strong outsiders, Spain had the big names but elderly tired legs, while Mexico...

I had canvassed local opinion, including the well-informed Austrian manager of the O'Higgins, where the Mexicans would be staying, which agreed, as I reported, that Mexico could not win an egg cup.

But I stressed they would be striving on the PR front to impress FIFA and all officialdom, as they were desperate to be awarded the 1970 World Cup.

In international news agency jargon I was told by the head office in Santiago "you are scoring well in South America" – major splashes in Brazil, Chile, Argentina, and, rather differently, Mexico.

A very worried hotel manager showed me local reports of Mexico's anger. He was particularly perturbed as the whole team was booked to stay at Hotel O'Higgins. Three words stood out: "John Jackson idiota". I was certainly front page news in Mexico City.

It appeared the Mexicans were so angry with my prediction that a hastily called meeting of their football hierarchy discussed whether or not to withdraw totally from the World Cup.

Finally, a day late, they decided to travel.

Prominent English sportswriters Brian Glanville and Desmond Hackett watched as the local media watched me. A soothing pisco sour, the local jungle juice, was necessary.

The Mexican team bus arrived, but only three men alighted – the manager, the captain, and the suave, English speaking Mexican FA vice president Peter Pons. My name was shouted, the captain muttered in Spanish "Jackson is a dirty name in Mexico."

Pons, or Mr Ponce as he soon became because of his aggressive attitude, said a few words – then they threw me, with little ceremony, into the hotel fountain.

They never forgave me. A man pulled a knife in the O'Higgins lift; in Santiago another approached as I hailed a taxi and shouted: "You are John Jackson. I am a Mexican and you can go to hell." When the Mexicans surprisingly beat Czechoslovakia 3-1 the players celebrated - by throwing me in the fountain again.

Two years later at the Tokyo Olympics I covered the FIFA meeting when Mexico was awarded the sought after 1970 tournament. I approached a happy Peter Pons: "Mr Ponce, you owe me a pisco." He smiled, held out his hand, and agreed.

There were absolutely no hard feelings when I covered the 1968 Mexico City Olympics and 1970 World Cup.

★★

Tragedy struck early at my first of 10 Winter Olympics. It was Innsbruck 1964 and luge was making its debut at a Winter Games. Just as with women's boxing and its introduction at London 2012, there was serious discussion about it being far too dangerous.

And on the first day of training I was on hand to witness the death of a British competitor.

The Austrians opened the Igls track despite it lacking the certainly improved safety requirements of today, such as protective lip covers over the treacherous ice bends.

Subsequently, on his first practice run two weeks before the Games opening, Britain's Kazimierz Kay-Skrzypeski, a 50-year-old Anglo-Pole, misjudged a bend, shot into the air, and hit two policemen before smashing into a tree. He died in hospital a few hours later.

From the chaotic scenes on the edge of the ice run, I followed the ambulance to the downtown hospital. There was no question, as now, of waiting outside for an official statement. As I spoke

English I was taken without hesitation past a stretcher bearing one of the badly injured policemen and into, wait for it – the operating theatre. My colleague AP photographer also.

The scene that greeted me would have been hilarious if it had been a Hollywood script, and not so tragic. Kay-Skrzypeski was obviously minutes from death, while leaning over him was the British team doctor, who soon revealed he had been rudely summoned from a very liquid lunch.

On spotting me he stopped tending the patient, ripped off his gloves, held out his hand with the greeting: "Great to see you again, old boy. It's been a couple of years since we had that pleasant session at Perth (1962 Commonwealth Games)." It was obvious the doctor had moved quite easily from Swan lager to Austrian schnapps.

As he outlined that nothing could be done for the dying man, the photographer, a hard-nosed German, was standing atop a trolley snapping pictures of the near corpse. His shot filled the front page of that evening's local newspaper.

The athletes already in the Olympic Village turned out in force to pay tribute to their dead rival. And little did they know they would be repeating the process a few days later, with this time the Australian flag being lowered to half mast. And another Alpine tree was left with heavy bruising.

The 1964 Innsbruck Games were hit from the start by a total lack of snow. In those days there were no artificial snow machines, so battalions of Austrian soldiers were drafted in to transport lorry loads of the white stuff from the nearby Brenner Pass. This meant the ski runs were hand-laid, to a certain width.

I was also present when the downhill skiers started practice runs and, sadly, 19-year-old Aussie Ross Milne flew off the narrow course and, literally, went both sides of a tree. Two deaths were not the ideal start to my first Winter Games.

There had to be a consolation. And none better than when I next stood at the bottom of the bobsleigh run to hail the gold medal for Great Britain won by our two-man team, Tony

Nash and Grenadier Guards Captain Robin Dixon, now Lord Glentoran. That night brought many an excuse for celebration schnapps. And the team doctor was there.

★★

Daley Thompson will go down in history as one of the greatest athletes the world has seen, certainly the best this country has ever produced. It takes some all-rounder to win back-to-back Olympic gold medals and break the world record four times in the most gruelling of events – the decathlon. Despite the fact that his fame was achieved at the two Games, Moscow 1980 and Los Angeles 1984, which were boycotted in turn by the super-powers, his performances were outstanding.

But when it came to public relations Daley was a non-starter. When competing he could run, jump, throw like a true champion, but one of his favourite activities was to tell the media to take a running jump. His behaviour in this and other areas often won over some public support but at times he overstepped the mark.

When he won BBC Sports Personality in 1982 he shambled forward on live TV, wearing a track suit and muttered something which sounded like "I need a shit". But nothing really can compare with my intervention at a crowded press conference in Los Angeles when Daley suggested he was going to have babies with Princess Anne.

It all came on the day when Daley won his second decathlon gold and celebrated in his own controversial way. He brandished a T-shirt which suggested that "The Second Greatest Athlete In The World Is Gay" – a reference to America's sprinting maestro Carl Lewis, who won four golds at those Games. On the victory rostrum Daley stuck his hands in his pockets and whistled during the playing of God Save The Queen.

Then came the press conference in a massive tent, attended by several hundred journalists. Strict instructions were given that no one could speak until a microphone was handed to them. Sadly, sporting press conferences can often be dominated by nonsensical questions, usually from Americans. ("Daley, today you jumped 2.03m in the high jump. If you could go again would you try to jump higher?")

Standing near my mate Jeremy Thompson (then ITN) I decided I couldn't stand anymore of this banal quizzing, so shouted: "Daley, the first person to congratulate you on the track was Princess Anne. What did she say to you?"

"She said I was a jolly good looking fellow," replied Daley, who I am sure was pleased to have a non-decathlon question thrown at him.

I kept going, despite calls from the organisers to wait until a microphone had arrived.

"Yesterday you said that if you retained your Olympic title you intended to take a rest and have babies. Who are you having these babies with?"

To a stunned audience the reply came: "You've just mentioned the lady."

No stopping me now so I hit back: "What does Captain Mark Phillips (Princess Anne's then husband) think about this?"

"He hopes they're all white."

Needless to say apoplexy set in among the press chief and his microphone bearers, and with no help from colleagues my line of questioning was halted. But as it turned out, Daley decided he had had enough and headed for the exit near me.

As he pulled up alongside I told him: "That's your knighthood gone." To which he replied: "I guess so."

At that very moment he was stopped in his tracks when a television camera and microphone was pushed in his face and a reporter said: "Station ABCD San Diego. Daley Thompson tonight you must be a very happy man?"

Daley, who had a habit like other great sportsmen – John McEnroe and Ian Botham, when young, come to mind – of clicking his brain from lunatic to sensible, adopted a very serious tone. He had spent six months leading up to the Olympics training in San Diego.

"Daley Thompson today you won a gold medal for Great Britain but would it be fair to say that a portion of it could be shared with the people of San Diego?"

Sensible Daley replied: "Yes I must thank all the people of San Diego for the help, kindness and courtesy they have shown me. Without them I could not have won and, yes, I devote a part of my medal to them."

Once again the same question: "Daley Thompson, tonight you must be a very happy man?"

Click and brain was back in lunatic mode.

"Yep," said Daley. "I haven't been so happy since my granny caught her tits in the mangle." The TV interview was terminated amid shouts of "cut".

Two years later, at the Commonwealth Games in Edinburgh, he was up to both his winning and controversial tricks again. He won another gold medal without too much trouble.

But the Games were sponsored by Guinness, and Daley took offence to this. Each athlete wore a bib with their number under the name Guinness.

On the first day of the decathlon my photographer colleague Monte Fresco spotted through his long lens that Daley had blacked out the word Guinness. In order to ask him about this I had to wait for a lengthy time while he trained on the practise track in preparation for the second day of competition.

He finally strode off, holding a bottle of Coca Cola to his lips. When I asked why he had removed Guinness from his bib, he snarled: "I don't drink the stuff, so why should I advertise it?"

Daley was then well known, and no doubt well remunerated, for his TV commercials advertising the drink Lucozade. I replied: "As you advertise Lucozade, why are you drinking a big rival Coca Cola?" With that he threw the bottle on to the ground and strode off.

Daley Thompson has become a great sporting ambassador for

this country and does an awful lot of good work to help children and budding athletes. The world would be a sadder place without his like, whatever mode his brain is in.

★★

When Hollywood beauty Ali McGraw took my arm and whispered "Hi star" I simply preened, but when Don Howe, the then England football coach, shouted across some foreign hotel lobby "If I ever see you on my f...ing TV screen again I'll..." I knew I had made the big time.

And all because on a quiet day at Wimbledon in 1977 I ventured out to discover how the filming of Players was progressing.

The movie, starring Dean Martin Jnr and Ali McGraw, had been given permission to film at the All England Club before play started (always 2 pm in those days). It told the story of how a young Californian tearaway was guided to the Wimbledon championship – interspersed with the odd love tangle with my new co-star.

They were filming on the roof of the then players' lounge when I approached a man with a clipboard. Immediately came a booming megaphone query from director Robert Evans above: "Have you got those goddam reporters yet?"

Clipboard aquiver the aide replied: "I'm talking to a real reporter." With the answer: "He'll do, bring him up."

That is how I entered the world of Hollywood. I was handed a piece of paper marked Reporter One, with my lines for an interview with Argentine star Guillermo Vilas. I had to ask about his tactics when he met the Dean Martin character in the Wimbledon final, and in J. McEnroe-speak he would reply: "Why should I tell you, you'll only put it in the paper?" I was to counter that that was my job.

I stood in front of this mammoth camera, with Vilas and his film manager Ion Tiriac leaning against the railing.

"Lights, cameras roll." I took a deep breath and asked Vilas: "How will you play Christensen in the final?" Vilas replied: "The same way I played when I last met him."

Hang on, that's not the script I had. In desperation I nudged Reporter Two alongside me but all that happened were frantic cries of "cut, cut". A few more takes and my Hollywood career was off and… ending. At least Ali McGraw was pleased: "Hi star. I've just seen the cuts, and you're great."

There was no invitation to walk the red carpet at any premiere, but I soon realised I was becoming well known by England's international footballers. Hotels abroad felt that as it was a film about sport it was ideal for their guests' private viewing. Kevin Keegan was one who occasionally observed: "Oh, not you again."

Don Howe, a great player who became a good coach, was not best pleased, however. I had known him since meeting at the 1962 World Cup in Chile and although we always got on, he did not want my ugly mug on his TV every time he went abroad. "I will not be responsible for my actions if you appear in my bedroom again," he observed.

I did point out that it could be worse. He could be seeing a re-run of a Jim'll Fix It when I was helping a precocious 13-year-old who wanted to be a reporter, taking him to a football pools reception to interview the big winner and presenter, comedienne Marti Caine.

And then appearing live on BBC TV with the then well thought of Jimmy Savile to present the coveted Jim'll Fix It badge. Stardom can be difficult, but who cares when Ali McGraw and Marti Caine like you?

★★

How times change! As Lewis Hamilton and Max Verstappenl rev up their bitter rivalry on the world's Grand Prix circuits, four elderly gentlemen speedsters could have pondered what happened to the term "sporting".

Sir Stirling Moss and Sir Jack Brabham were deadly rivals on the same racetracks; Tony Nash and Captain Robin Dixon, now Lord Glentoran, were the speediest in a bobsleigh. But when faced with an emergency they all knew immediate help would be at hand – from their main competitors.

It all happened nigh on 60 years ago, when people were definitely a lot nicer to each other. My mind goes racing back to a boiling hot afternoon on a disused airfield outside Auckland, New Zealand, and a freezing morning on the snowy slopes of Igls, near Innsbruck.

First, in 1959, came the 6th New Zealand Grand Prix, which I was covering for the Auckland Star's Saturday night green-un, the 8 O'Clock. Around 100,000 people gathered at the Ardmore track for a rare glimpse of the world's best racing drivers. There were two qualifying races, with the fastest 12 lining up for the final.

The plan was for all the big-name visitors to qualify easily. But, oh no! Just 400 yards from the chequered flag, the greatest of them all, Stirling Moss, came to a sudden halt with a broken half-shaft and was forced to push his Cooper home in last place. The crowd clearly did not want a final without Moss.

So, Bernie Ecclestone-like, the organisers suddenly "revealed" that overseas drivers qualified automatically. So why bother having qualifying? But Moss didn't have a spare half-shaft.

As if nowadays Mercedes bosses wandered over to Ferrari to blag a few tyres, Moss cheekily sauntered across to Jack Brabham, easy winner of the first race in another Cooper, and shouted: "Got a spare half-shaft I could borrow, old boy?" The answer came back loud and clear from the Australian three times world champion: "Too right, mate. Help yourself."

You've guessed it. Moss won the final easily with Brabham roaring home second – to comment: "That's what chums are for."

Five years later at the 1964 Winter Olympics, I was the Associated Press man shivering at the bottom of the Igls two-man bob run reporting a rare British success. Garage owner Tony

Nash and army Captain Robin Dixon were leading after the first run, but all betting was on Italian maestro Eugenio Monti.

British delight was shattered when the pair discovered they had a broken axle bolt. With no back-up facilities, a withdrawal looked likely.

But all bobsleighers are great buddies (probably because you have to be totally bonkers to enjoy careering out of control down an ice chute), and Monti immediately removed a bolt from one of his sleds to let the Brits continue.

Yes, it happened again. Nash and Dixon won gold for Great Britain, while Monti had to be content with bronze.

Robin Dixon became the 3rd Baron of Glentoran and told me years later that his love of bobsleighing revolved round three factors – excitement, adrenalin flowing, and CAMARADERIE.

Note to Hamilton and Verstappen: Jack Brabham's sporting gesture meant Auckland's local hero had to be content with third place. His name was Bruce McLaren, founder of Team McLaren.

★★

When the Winter Olympics come around every four years there is always worry about lack of snow and other problems. All that is needed is a call to Calgary to recommend the best formula for success.

Without doubt, the immediate reply will be: "Get yourselves an Eddie."

The 1988 Calgary Winter Olympics will always be remembered as the Eddie "The Eagle" Edwards Games. Even today, 32 years on, Eddie memorabilia is a big seller in Calgary stores. And all for a man who not only came last in both ski jumping events but finished with total points less than half those of every other competitor.

For us scribes, with the difficult task of seeking the remotest evidence of British success, the 25-year-old, short-sighted

plasterer from Cheltenham was manna from heaven. Skier
Martin Bell finished 8th in the downhill, a record for a British
male, and received little more than a paragraph and line in the
results section.

Meanwhile, Eddie's exploits attracted page after page, with the
Daily Mirror illustrating my despatches with a graph showing that
if the competitors had jumped from the top of St Paul's Cathedral,
Finnish gold medallist Matti Nykänen would have hit the Law
Courts while Eddie would have been lucky to reach Ye Olde Bell
pub at the bottom of Fleet Street.

Eddie Edwards, whose thick lenses always steamed up in mid-
air, admitted that when he first ventured to the top of a ski jump:
"I looked down and was so frightened that my bum shrivelled
up like a prune." But he kept at it and made the Olympics as the
British ski jumping record holder, albeit at the time he was ranked
55th in the world.

At the Calgary closing ceremony the Games president told the
watching world: "At these Games some competitors have won
gold, some have broken records and one has even flown like an
eagle" – and 100,000 spectators spontaneously chanted "Eddie!
Eddie!" It was the only time in the history of the Olympics that
an individual has been mentioned.

From the moment Eddie landed in Calgary it was pure farce.
For his first press conference he arrived at the media centre
without his pass, so was refused entry. He told about his glasses
steaming up, having to wear six pairs of socks to make his boots
fit, repairing his helmet with sticky tape, and so on.

One American journalist muttered loudly: "Is this Mr Magoo
for real?"

His two events were the biggest in town, with thousands of
spectators whooping and hollering as Eddie clambered up to the
starting point. He didn't jump, he simply plopped.

One Norwegian judge complained: "My 10-year-old
granddaughter could jump further." And other such comments
prompted the entry requirements to be immediately toughened so

no future Eddie could compete.

But as winner Nykänen stressed: "Don't you dare laugh at Eddie until you have the guts to do what he is doing."

One man who will never forget Eddie The Eagle is Simon Clegg, later chief executive of the British Olympic Association, who in Calgary found himself "minding" Eddie. This included taking him to Los Angeles where his fame had alerted the top Johnny Carson TV show.

★★

There is no doubt that having English as your mother tongue when travelling the sporting world makes you extremely lazy - but there can be great fun listening to foreign mates struggling with the intricacies of our language.

I still laugh at the problem faced by one of my oldest buddies, star German sports scribe Ulrich Kaiser, when trying to give instructions to a Wimbledon taxi driver, despite the fact it happened over 50 years ago.

Ulrich, sadly no longer with us, and I chortled our way around world, although he was someone who did not suffer fools gladly. When the teenage Boris Becker won Wimbledon for the first time he twice rudely blanked my press conference question asking what the Duchess of Kent had said to him when presenting the trophy.

Ulrich hit back at him in German, advising that "being an arrogant German was not a sensible start to his career". Boris immediately turned to me, gave some splendid quotes, and has never ducked a question since.

When Ulrich and I left Frankfurt for the 1972 Winter Olympics at Sapporo in freezing northern Japan, he was dressed in a complete set of fur hat, coat, gloves and boots. Well prepared, but no one had told us we were having a full night stopover in Bangkok.

When this apparition in fur appeared at the top of the plane steps in a temperature of 45 C there was instant panic among the Thai ground staff. A limousine duly appeared, and a baffled Ulrich was hustled into it. He had been mistaken as the Soviet ambassador.

Ulrich duly became Germany's foremost sports columnist and was the first to see that Bernhard Langer offered the chance to specialise in covering golf. He wrote a book entitled What Would Have Happened To The World If Stalin Had Played Golf?

In the Wimbledon press box he was the only writer to have a personalised seat – reserved for the Ulrich Kaiser Syndicate.

But it was our first Wimbledon in 1964 that brings back the smile. They were the halcyon days when players, press, umpires et al socialised together without thought. And on the first Friday evening the umpires traditionally held a splendid party in the Fred Perry bar at the nearby Dog and Fox pub. Nothing was called out as drink flowed freely.

Ulrich's English was adequate and he seemed to understand when I told him that after he had finished filing he should ask a taxi driver to take him to the Dog and Fox. "Ja, Ja, Dog und Fox. I understand. Kein problem."

Hours later a very red faced Ulrich arrived. What had happened? "Taxi driver got very angry with me when I asked him twice to take me to the Focking Dog."

But it was in the same Wimbledon Village pub that another German colleague brought a stunned silence. She was explaining that a friend had found himself in a Centre Court seat with limited visibility but a steward pointed out that if he moved quickly there was a better position further down.

"He was so happy he quickly tossed himself off and went down to it," she said. There was no answer to that, whatever your native tongue.

★★

In those halcyon days before big showbiz personalities were surrounded by agents and large security men, it was great fun while covering a major sporting event to fall upon an offbeat news story.

Calming down Louis Armstrong in Chile, having a necessary pee alongside Bing Crosby at Wimbledon, fighting off drunken crooner Eddie Fisher at a Winter Olympics, helping Rod Stewart recover from a fatal shoot-out in Buenos Aires, walking into Bob Dylan when chasing a "naughty" snooker player, and cosying up to the adorable Audrey Hepburn alongside the skating rink in Grenoble – the list is long.

I was standing at the Wimbledon champagne bar, (maybe the adjoining hot dog stand?) when I spotted Bing Crosby ambling unrecognised through Gate 5. To my welcome he muttered: "Those goddam scalpers" - but refused to stop walking.

Fortunately, he needed a pee. A man renowned for his meanness, he faced the wall and complained at length about the ticket tout who had forced £5 from him. "Goddam cheating scalper," he kept repeating.

A few nights later he walked from the Savoy Hotel to the old Sun's local Endell Street fish and chip shop. "I hear it's cheap," he told me.

While chasing such stars as Pele, Puskas, Di Stefano, Garrincha, at the 1962 World Cup in Chile, I was told to divert to Valparaiso and find Louis Armstrong. Soviet president Nikita Krushchev had suddenly invited Benny Goodman to Moscow. Would the great Satchmo follow?

Early warning from band members Trummy Young and Billy Kyle reported that "Pops", another man known to be tight with money, was fuming after checking the hotel bill as he didn't trust his manager.

So for me there was no flashing smile but a simple "I'll take my horn and play for Krushchev or anyone." But when my colleague photographer appeared, on came the smile and flashing teeth, he posed – while whispering to me: "Ham all the way boy, ham all the way."

Dealing with a drunken Eddie Fisher at the 1964 Innsbruck Winter Olympics was difficult. I met him on arrival to ask why he was refusing to give then wife Elizabeth Taylor a divorce. "Let's have a drink and talk about it" was his command.

The following night, as an AP man, I was doing the running on the important Soviet Union vs USA ice hockey match, with my New York sports editor taking copy personally.

Suddenly my descriptive prose was interrupted by my very sozzled new Hollywood friend shouting almost nose to nose: "Come on John, come and sit in the VIP box between me and the Shah of Persia." Copytaker was totally baffled, and not pleased.

Rod Stewart, a cheerleader with Ally MacLeod's disastrous Scotland at the 1978 World Cup, was dining at a Buenos Aires restaurant when two chaps decided to stage a hold-up. A simple press of an under-desk button brought the police in seconds. They proceeded to shoot the robbers dead through the window.

I arrived to wade through broken glass, and Rod decided an early breakfast was the answer. Another person careful with money meant I had to pay – but he did invite me to "recover" with him in Rio de Janeiro. Work beckoned, however.

A shy Bob Dylan, on his way for lunch with local resident Fergal Sharkey, did a runner when I walked into him while door-stepping a North London home where snooker player Ray Reardon was playing away with a girlfriend.

There was the odd more memorable moment. None better than at the 1968 Grenoble Winter Olympics when the delectable Audrey Hepburn asked if she could sit next to me at the figure skating training. Bliss!

★★

The sad death of prominent journalist Steve Parry on the eve of the Beijing Olympics rekindled fond memories of the most famous of his predecessors as sports editor of Reuters, the man who introduced my wife and me to the magic of the Olympic Games at Rome in 1960.

Vernon Morgan was of the old school. Having sat alongside him on many occasions, when his booming copy dictation almost made the telephone redundant, I know how he would have announced this sudden death: "On this penultimate day before the opening of the Games of the 29th Olympiad we bring the sad news...." They don't write intros like that anymore.

Morgan was the kindest of men, always eager to offer advice and a helping hand to us young whippersnappers. Football writing doyen Brian Glanville and agency veteran Morley Myers are among many "big names" who thanked him for that vital first leg-up.

Avuncular, with a throaty chuckle Morgan was a prominent athlete in the 1920s and retained friendships from those fun days. None closer than with Harold Abrahams, whose Olympic gold medal exploits were portrayed in the film Chariots of Fire. This in turn allowed me the privilege of socialising with Abrahams in many parts of the world.

Morgan competed for Britain in the steeplechase at the 1928 Amsterdam Olympics and won a bronze medal at the first ever British Empire Games at Hamilton, Canada, in 1930. With Reuters at the 1936 Berlin Games he found Hitler "a very sociable chap, and Goebbels gave some good parties".

It was Morgan's everlasting ties with his Oxford University and athletic chums that prompted me in later years to tell the British Olympic Association that their press liaison techniques, especially at the Olympics, were pitiful. The message was eventually taken on board and I acted as the BOA press officer in the Main Press Centre at the Sydney and Athens Games.

My first encounter with the ridiculous BOA system came at the 1962 British Empire and Commonwealth Games at Perth, Australia, where I was a member of Vernon Morgan's small Reuters team. Unknown to me, Morgan was also press officer for the English team, having been appointed by his fellow Oxford

Blue, the BOA's general secretary Sandy Duncan. A ludicrous situation.

When I picked up a cracking tip that former British star runner Gordon Pirie, then working in radio, had offered England's teenage high jumper Linda Knowles money (a heinous crime in those true amateur days) to tell all on air, I reported back excitedly to Vernon Morgan. He proposed I get a quote from the England camp.

Sandy Duncan viewed the allegation seriously and said he would consult his press adviser Vernon Morgan. Morgan gave him a quote over the phone, which was relayed to me. I then returned to Vernon Morgan, read out "his" quote, and he said it was a good story. Crackers!

Six years later Vernon Morgan retired, tears rolling down his cheeks, as the flame died at the Mexico City Olympics. I sat in front of him with another Fleet Street great, George Whiting.

★★

Since I bade farewell and closed my memory bank at Athens in 2004, Olympic flames have continued to be lit. I doubt my absence was noticed. After all, our Queen, with other royals, Spain's King Juan Carlos and Norway's King Harald, Emperors Hirohito and Akihito, a gaggle of Presidents (De Gaulle, Brezhnev, Reagan, Mitterand, Clinton), and other heads of state, never bothered to say hi when it was their big day and I was close by.

Overall, I don't miss anything, as the fun factor has diminished rapidly over the years, due mainly to the instantaneous demands of new technology, the often absurdly strict security, and tightened newspaper budgets.

A lot of races have been run since the steamy Roman summer of 1960 when around 1,000 journalists (minuscule by present numbers) were billeted in basic accommodation in two monasteries, Domus Pacis and Domus Maria. If you needed a quick interview after a race you simply walked on to the track and grabbed the always breathless, but usually cooperative, athlete.

After the exciting 10,000 metres at Tokyo 1964, I accompanied a baffled Ron Clarke from the finishing line. The bronze medal Aussie, who will go down in history as the greatest long-distance runner never to win a gold medal, had been overtaken at the last by Native American Billy Mills, who streaked down the final straight as if it was the 100 metres final.

An American journalist shouted: "Did you take Mills into your pre-race thinking?" Replied Ron: "No mate, 'cos I'd never heard of the bastard." Such spontaneity is very rare in today's cattle pen, called the Mixed Zone, where many athletes simply ignore shouted questions, or at the ridiculously controlled press conferences later.

The one time I beat this latter system came when Sally Gunnell won the 400 metres hurdles at Barcelona 1992 - right on deadline in London. From the *Daily Mirror* night editor came the command that I had less than 10 minutes to stand up the front-page splash headline, already written. When told what that headline was I shuddered somewhat.

Fortunately, the press conference was announced almost immediately and as the three medallists were led in I shouted, much against the rules, and before she had sat down: "Sally, have you just proved that Essex girls do come first?"

Her confused yes was well received in London. The following day, with the headline "Essex Girls Do Come First" taking prominence on newspaper stalls, Sally admitted she had been so taken by surprise that she forgot to mention she had lived most of her life in Hampshire.

At Mexico City in 1968 British TV decided for the first time to have a reporter at trackside to race on with a live microphone to capture the immediate thoughts of medal winners. The idea was short lived, as the first man to be asked how he felt, as he lay gasping on the track after the gruelling 10,000 metres at high altitude, spluttered one simple word: "Fucked".

It was at Tokyo '64 that I actually marched into the Opening Ceremony. I was keeping an eye on the boxing draw, especially for the US big medal hope Joe Frazier.

The draw was made immediately before the Opening Ceremony so I was pounding a typewriter when the festivities started. When I finished the athletes were still marching into the stadium past my AP office. I happened to be wearing a bright red shirt and was quick to spot that the Japanese contingent, as hosts the last to enter, had blazers in the same colour.

I tagged on behind and once inside the stadium peeled off to the side, from where I had the perfect view. I hate to think what could happen to anyone trying that now.

Mind you, a few days after the opening of the 1996 Atlanta Games police revealed that a man with a gun had been found sitting close to the press enclosure, with a perfect view of President Clinton. A local reporter observed: "Hey, you don't have to be Clint Eastwood to hit the president from there. How the hell did he get in?"

The police chief thought for a while, then replied: "He arrived early."

Although it may sound strange when you consider the horror that happened later, security was very tight around the Olympic Village at Munich in 1972. One restriction introduced by the German organisers involved the press having to give a minimum of 24 hours' notice when wanting to interview an athlete. This was ridiculous as most stories can't wait that long.

Nothing happened until a few days before the opening when all competitors and journalists suddenly received invitations to visit Dachau concentration camp. The only countries that took any notice and attended were the Soviet Union and Israel – the latter only days away from losing 11 team members in the Black September terrorist attack.

It was at the nightly press conference later that another Fleet Street stalwart, J.L. Manning of the *Daily Mail,* asked a totally stunned press chief: "Herr Klein, can you reveal why it is much easier for us to get into Dachau concentration camp than the Olympic Village?"

The 24-hour rule was dropped immediately by officials so conscious that the Games were Germany's big chance to re-enter the family of nations after the atrocities of World War Two. It would be unfair to say Black September benefited from this, for they simply clambered over the wire fence.

Tuesday, September 5, 1972, is a day I will never forget. Woken early I managed to sneak into the Olympic Village as the hostage situation progressed but had to leave to file copy. Later I rushed to Furstenfeldbruck Airport where the planned escape saw the terrorists blow up their helicopter, then returned for the disastrous 0400 press conference where Bavarian officials gave incorrect reports of terrorists escaping down the autobahn.

A few hours later I automatically dressed in a suit and went to the memorial service in the Olympic Stadium where IOC president Avery Brundage inexplicably brought up the subject of Rhodesia (before it became Zimbabwe) which had been expelled by the IOC after complaints from black African delegates.

Totally inappropriate, as he gazed at the eleven empty seats to honour the dead Israelis.

IS THERE MUCH MORE OF THIS?

Technology is the area which has changed out of sight. For years it was the combination of telephone and telex that ruled, both of which needed vital cooperation from local operators. Telephoning copy could be long, expensive and agonising, especially when you had copytakers in London who did not know the difference between decathlon, dressage and double sculls. Oh how the expletives flew!

My favourite came in 1962, at the then called British Empire and Commonwealth Games at Perth, Australia. The wrestling finals were held at the Perth Tennis Club and agency reporters were given a telephone on the front row of the tiny Royal Box.

Of the eight finals the last gold was won for England by a lad from Liverpool, while the others all went to Pakistan, courtesy of seven railway porters from Lahore.

This was big news for the Agence France Press correspondent sitting next to me, a hard-bitten Aussie who was grabbing any work after being sacked as a prominent Melbourne crime correspondent, for spending, unknown to his office, every day at the races. It was the old story: when the course Tannoy announced there was a call for him it was always a police contact with that day's story. The last call was from his editor.

At the wrestling he was hampered by a very bad phone line, and a succession of disinterested copytakers. So the grunting and groaning in the ring was continually drowned out by this Aussie voice shouting: "Railway porter from Lahore... La-hore... what? No, not as in whore... Jesus, La effing hore."

It came to a head when, with him crouching below the parapet in order to hear better, I was asked to move a few seats away to make way for a Royal visitor. So after another session of "La effing hore", he sat upright, sweating profusely, glanced to his right, and found himself staring into the face of the Duke of Edinburgh, tearful with laughter.

Without a thought, our correspondent grabbed the phone and

shouted: "Now you've lost me a knighthood, you deaf bastard."

Telex entailed copy being typed, then handed into the dispatch area where it was added to a pile. There was never any problem peeking at a rival's exclusive. At the 1968 Mexico Olympics, another Fleet Street rascal, Maurice Smith of the then *Sunday People,* waited until the last moment to file his biggie for Sunday – an explosive suggestion of an affair between two possible British medallists.

After a daily paper man had spotted it and expressed "unfairness", pressure was put on Smith to spike the story, which he did with a nonchalant shrug. He took no chance with the instant replacement. He phoned from a quiet spot his report that the British section of the Olympic Village was known as the "Olympic brothel". Smith lay low for a few days.

There were of course copy filing disasters. At the 1972 Winter Olympics at Sapporo, Japan, the 84-year-old amateur-to-the-core American Avery Brundage sensationally ordered that the world's top skier, Austria's Karl Schranz, be booted out of the Games for admitting he took money from ski companies (as did every other skier competing).

Schranz had also said some rude things in print about Brundage. This was a fantastic story for Austria. A massive crowd and ticker tape parade greeted Schranz's return to Vienna, the largest demonstration since World War II.

As I bashed out my 10-paragraph *Daily Mirror* story I spotted old friend Michael Kuhn, from Austria's *Kurier,* frantically typing nearby. He was grabbing every piece of available paper, most of them Olympic handouts.

Together we walked to the telex office where the operators, none of whom could speak or read a foreign language, were brilliant, and fast, at simply transcribing what was placed in front of them.

On collecting my finished telex, typed perfectly, I found an almost tearful Kuhn struggling with his length of paper, almost enough to wallpaper a small bathroom. "I'm finished, I'll be sacked – it's all in French," he whimpered, having said earlier he was right on deadline.

A quick check revealed that the operator had been handed his sheaves of copy the wrong side up. So back in the excitement of his Vienna office the sports editor was suddenly confronted with yards of copy outlining in French that "Emperor Hirohito will arrive at Sapporo railway station at 2pm and drive by car to the Opening Ceremony…" The Sapporo press handout had been sent in full.

A worried Kuhn, arranging for the right side to be sent, was comforted by a return telex message which read: "Okay you've had a few schnapps, but your French has improved."

A new era dawned at Seoul 1988, which were soon dubbed the Tandy Games. Many of us had these new-fangled machines, complete with couplers, special cards and complicated sending procedures. When everything worked, it was magic, but….

It would be no exaggeration to say that the night air in the Press Village was frequently interrupted by the shrieking of rude words, and the crash of Tandys exiting windows several storeys high.

The one time my Tandy worked perfectly helped me cover the 1990 rebel cricket tour of South Africa. This allowed daily reports of noisy "Go home, Gatting" demonstrations by angry anti-apartheid protestors, a succession of unfortunate verbal faux pas by captain Mike Gatting (he described the angry mobs as "a few people singing and dancing"), and finally the biggest story in the world – the release from prison of Nelson Mandela.

We had witnessed the immense anger in Johannesburg, Pretoria, Kimberley, Bloemfontein, Pietermaritzburg, and Durban before returning to Johannesburg for the first unofficial Test match.

Sitting in the press box in the famous Wanderers ground on the warm afternoon of Saturday, February 10, the silence accompanying another English batsman dragging his bat back to the dressing room was shattered with a cry from the man from Reuters: "Mandela will be released from prison tomorrow afternoon."

Telephones were seized and in my case calls went from my office in London to the home of *Daily Mirror* editor Roy Greenslade.

Totally unaware of the news that thrilled all mankind, Mike Gatting was at the time making his way slowly down the long, covered walkway and across the field to the crease. His arrival there coincided with the phone being answered in Brighton by the editor's wife, colleague feature writer Noreen Taylor.

She immediately exclaimed: "Isn't it wonderful?" To which I am afraid I replied: "No it's not. Gatting has just been bowled first ball." She quite rightly told me to behave myself.

With *Sun* cricket correspondent John Etheridge and the *Daily Star*'s Bob Driscoll I flew to Cape Town and was outside the Victor Verster Prison on a treacherously hot afternoon as Nelson Mandela walked to freedom, hand in hand with his wife, Winnie.

If I had ever had the honour of meeting the great man, I could have told him that in the melee his car grazed my foot. It was something special to be in the crowd when he arrived back in Soweto to a tumultuous reception.

Mandela's release brought my memory full circle, for 27 years earlier Barbara and I were living in Johannesburg when Mandela was arrested nearby. We had sailed from Wellington, New Zealand, to Cape Town. On arrival we bought a battered Austin A30 and drove the then possible Garden Route taking in Port Elizabeth, the Transkei, Durban, Pietermaritzburg, and across to Johannesburg.

I worked on the sports staff of the brave, anti-apartheid *Rand Daily Mail*. The horrors of apartheid were everywhere but I felt no danger as I manoeuvred my office scooter to football matches in suburbs Boksburg and Benoni.

The only nastiness came when I covered the national wrestling championships in Pretoria. Needless to say, it was an all-white event with announcements, hand-outs, and general chatter in

Afrikaans. I couldn't understand a word but a friendly rival on
the *Johannesburg Star* had the decency to help me out.

The questions I have been asked a thousand times are, of
course: "Which was your favourite Olympics? Which were the
most memorable events?"

There have been so many unforgettable performances I would
need too much space to do them all justice. Here are just a
few: Mary Rand and Ann Packer (Tokyo '64); teenage wonder
gymnasts Olga Korbut (Munich '72) and Nadia Comaneci
(Montreal '76); double gold rivalry, Sebastian Coe and Steve
Ovett (Moscow '80); attending all of Steve Redgrave's five
rowing golds (Los Angeles '84 – Sydney 2000); ice skaters John
Curry (Innsbruck '76) and Robin Cousins (Lake Placid '80);
swimmer Mark Spitz' seven golds (Munich '72); basketball's
Dream Team (Barcelona '92); tragic Zola Budd (LA '84); brilliant
Michael Johnson (Atlanta '96) and Cathy Freeman (Sydney
2000); finally my farewell with double gold Kelly Holmes
(Athens 2004).

But my one standout memory would be the wonderful
Torvill and Dean ice dancing *Bolero* success at Sarajevo in 1984.
In Communist Yugoslavia there was initial fear that the strong
Soviet competition could pip them to the gold.

A moment of relief on this front came when a few days before
the Games, the *New York Times* ran an exclusive front page
headline reporting that Soviet leader Yuri Andropov had died.
Would the Soviet team be recalled in mourning?

I ventured in to the *Tass* office, voice of the Kremlin, to
confront Sergei, an old friend from many Olympics, for the
answer. There had been no comment from Moscow so I asked:
"Is he dead?"

As inscrutable as ever he replied: "Only 90 per cent."

He had died, but the athletes stayed to compete – and Jayne
Torvill and Christopher Dean stunned them and the world with
a performance which prompted every judge, several from the
Eastern bloc, to award them a perfect 6. At home in Britain the

BBC live broadcast attracted 24 million viewers.

And ironically, at the celebration party later, I was quizzed about my favourite Games by someone who has been to a fair few herself – Princess Anne. At that time Tokyo, Lake Placid and Moscow stood out.

My answer now would be: "I think it easier to start at the beginning of the alphabet and name the two that were undoubtedly the worst – Albertville and Atlanta." The French had an excuse for the below par Albertville, but in Atlanta it was the greed of the corporate sector who put money before medals and national pride.

Albertville drew the short straw because of personal vendettas and intrigue at the highest level of the International Olympic Committee.

1992 had virtually been sealed as the year when the Winter Games would go to Germany (either Garmisch Partenkirchen or Berchtesgaden) and the Summer Olympics would return to Paris after 68 years.

But the then newish president of the IOC, Juan Antonio Samaranch, said he had promised it to his home city of Barcelona. The committee's long time general secretary, former French swimmer Monique Berlioux, was fronting the Paris bid.

The President pulled rank and a deal was done. Barcelona would be chosen, while France could have the winter event. Germany was abandoned, and Albertville had to prepare for a major sporting extravaganza it had not sought.

So it's all over! But the memories!

HERE WE GO

News executives could conjure up very strange ideas! How about:
"Old boy, could you arrange for us to laser I Love You on the
moon for St Valentine's Day?" True!

Their command of geography often went haywire, with the
favourite standby assurance: "It's only that far on the map."
"Once you have finished filing from Athens, could you pop up to
this decent yarn in Tromso?" is the sort of thing I mean.

There was dear old *Mirror* news editor Tom Hendry,
a desperately keen story digger and far too nice a man to
continually bollock, who took a call from top reporter Ted Oliver
volunteering to head for China at the time of the Tiananmen
Square massacre: "Good idea, but when you get to Beijing, how
long will it take you to reach Peking?"

What many observers may construe as my lack of ambition
(or, in truth, the certainty that I would have made a disastrous
executive), was countered by the chap who started on the
permanent night shift, sat alongside me for years, and ended by
sending me around the world.

Richard Stott joined the *Daily Mirror* a few months before me.
We had met before when he was doing casual shifts on the *Mirror*,
and I was the cocky done-it-all staff man on the broadsheet *Sun*.
One memorable Easter when we followed Michael Foot, Canon
John Collins, Vanessa Redgrave, Tariq Ali, and the usual cast of
Ban the Bomb revolutionaries on the annual Aldermaston march,
I showed my immense knowledge by helping him find the
nearest telephone.

This just happened to be in a small room at Heathrow Airport,
alongside the then Queen's Building, or Terminal 2 as it is now
known. The result was his sports car was towed away, with more
than his day shift payment required to get it back, while my old
Standard Vanguard was left unhindered on a double yellow line.

If I had kept a crystal ball in the glove compartment I might
have shuddered when looking into the future. Fortunately,

Richard and I continued to be the closest of friends for 38 years until his very untimely death, after a brave fight against pancreatic cancer, in 2007. He was a few days from his 64th birthday, and far, far too young to die. The very generous obituaries in all the major papers, plus the outpouring of grief from Fleet Street generally, showed what a loss it was.

We always had a special relationship. He and his lovely wife Penny even apparently conceived the idea in 1971 that their first child, Emily, should be born on my birthday. Sadly, Richard died on our eldest son's birthday.

I always say that Stott and I remained buddies despite him moving rapidly to 5-star general, while I wandered along happily as lance corporal unpaid. He was a Fleet Street editor a record five times -- *Daily Mirror* twice, *Sunday People* twice, then *Today.*

He was one of a few *Mirror* executives who later stood up to Robert Maxwell and prevented many of the old rogue's choice of stories damaging the paper.

On one occasion when Maxwell ordered that Tom Hendry and I be fired, over a minor misunderstanding regarding the boycott of the 1986 Edinburgh Commonwealth Games by African nations (Maxwell had promised two million pounds to save the event but, in the end, handed over just £250,000) Stott told him: "You can't fire Jackson. He could be the best centre forward Oxford United has ever had."

"Really?" Nothing was heard again re any firing from the then chairman of Oxford United.

It was a great shame that Rupert Murdoch found it necessary in 1995 to close down *Today,* as Stott was guiding it to the million a day circulation mark with clever support of the Labour Party.

It could have taken great credit for helping Tony Blair into 10 Downing Street and would have gone from strength to strength. With Alastair Campbell as political editor, we certainly had a good start on most rivals.

While Stott and his predecessors kept control on the *Daily Mirror* bridge, the motley crew in the engine room persevered with two simple aims – first and foremost to ensure the paper continued as the leading tabloid, and enjoying life to the full while doing so.

Two fellow stokers stand out and I could not consider writing any reminiscences without mentioning Ron Ricketts and Frank Palmer. Sadly, like Richard Stott, neither lived long enough to enjoy retirement, with Ricketts heading off to the newsroom in the sky a year after the two of us had been fired together by the dreadful David Montgomery, who had seized the helm after the death of Robert Maxwell.

In fact, March 17, 1993, told everything about the old *Mirror* and the arrival of Montgomery to send the newspaper we loved pirouetting downwards. Four of us – Robin Parkin, Alastair McQueen, Ricketts and I – had 110 years of service between us but Ulsterman Montgomery decided he could buy that experience by offering low wages and short contracts to youngsters who were keen but green. And all on St Patrick's Day.

Ricketts is no doubt still violently wagging his finger at horrified angels, and certainly Robert Maxwell if he has ventured downstairs to find him, to stress his frustration at news desk commands he had received over the years.

Perhaps his attitude is best summed up by his intention to write a book on the subject, entitled *Wankers and Weasels*. When I suggested W H Smith might baulk at this, he toned it down to *Wallies and Weasels*. But he was determined to retain his title for the sequel – *Urban Pygmies*.

On one occasion he regaled colleague John Penrose (who later married another former *Mirror* chum, Anne Robinson) with a tirade about news desk personnel.

Leaping about the Ricketts' council maisonette at the Elephant and Castle he shouted: "Sometimes I am so angry by the time I reach home that I want to kick the cat." With that, his daughter Tracy interrupted: "Dad, we ain't got a cat."

Ron did have a dog, however – "called Peanuts, after my fucking salary".

He waged a perpetual war with a succession of news editors, and none more so than Alan Shillum. To me, Shillum was a very good boss, a man who would fight to the hilt for his reporters, whatever the problem, as long as they were honest with him. For Ricketts he fulfilled all the roles – wanker, weasel and wally. And the feeling was mutual.

It came to a head one afternoon when Ricketts applied for a special day off, several weeks ahead. Instead of having a quiet word with Shillum or his secretary, he typed a memo, then walked a few feet to plonk it down on the secretary's desk. In turn it was moved another couple of paces to Shillum. The charade continued with Shillum loudly dictating the one-word reply: "No".

Total apoplexy from Ricketts sitting behind me. Meanwhile, on the news desk John Penrose expressed his opinion that Shillum had been somewhat harsh as Ricketts had applied in April for the day off in June, to celebrate his silver wedding.

"That's the problem. He has known for 25 fucking years this was coming up, but he has only given me six weeks' notice", said Shillum.

I owe Ron a lot. As a result of him spending many a lunchtime in the pub yacking on boringly about the benefits of AVCs, the additional voluntary contributions to your company pension, several colleagues and I signed up to invest the maximum "just to shut him up".

How right he was – and I have enjoyed a healthier pension for the last 28 years.

Both Ricketts and Frank Palmer were working class boys who had entered journalism by the traditional route, working their way through local papers to the nationals. As a result they were brilliant reporters, and both staunch battlers within the National Union of Journalists and the office chapel for better pay and conditions for editorial staff, at a time when the printers and electricians were skinning the golden goose.

Palmer ran his own freelance agency as Palmer of Lincoln,

before joining the *Daily Mirror* as its East Midlands correspondent based in Nottingham. We scribes were "real people", a fact he would continually underline for his great mate Stott, who was slowly climbing the executive ladder to "wankerdom".

When accountants started to take over, Palmer was an early casualty with the withdrawal of his mobile phone. This proved disastrous a short time later when a British Midland airliner approaching East Midlands airport crashed alongside the M1. Palmer was first on the scene from his home nearby, but was forced to leave to file his first edition copy from a public phone box. On his return a wider police cordon had been established so he was unable to continue his eyewitness accounts.

From that moment on, each time he ventured away from Nottingham on a story (virtually daily) he would send the news desk a postcard: "Am in Little Bogtown Under Sea, please contact by pigeon".

Disillusioned by these cuts and attitude Palmer took the generous Maxwell shilling when first offered to some *Mirror* oldies and commenced a new career writing crime novels. He was extremely successful and I would like to suggest it was because his principal character was Det. Insp. "Jacko" Jackson. His superior was a little fat man named Scott (as near to former editor Stott as he dared go).

One prominent journalist who will remember Palmer's antics is Lorraine Candy, whose obvious talent took her right to the top, editorship of *Cosmopolitan* and other glossy magazines. As the very bright young reporter Lorraine Butler, who had success written all over her during the days I worked alongside her on the *Daily Mirror* and *Today,* she was earnestly bashing her keyboard to complete a feature deadline when she was interrupted by a very noisy Palmer on a visit to the London office.

His programme always followed a similar pattern: a visit to Stott's office where gins and tonic were served in pint pots, somehow his shoe would often find itself flying through a window and dropping to the roof of the Rotunda restaurant below, and throughout Frankie would berate everyone in his

Lincolnshire accent about being "Loondon wankers who should get out to meet the reeeal people."

Butler sat outside the editor's office and when the remains of this pissed district man emerged to address the whole office, she asked him very firmly to be quiet. "Who the hell are you?" replied this gibbering wreck, dragging on the ever present cigarette. "One day I will be a literary lion, and you will want to interview me. And I'll tell you 'Fook off'". I am sure Mrs Candy could have handled any such problem.

Palmer's literary notoriety brought him an invitation to appear on Radio Nottingham's version of Desert Island Discs. He chose eight Lonnie Donegan records, which so impressed the producer he allowed Frank a ninth.

Pubs were an integral part of our lives. When out on the road working on whatever story, the first place you visited in search of your mates from the opposition was the natural meeting ground, the pub closest to the action. When it was time to send over copy, in those days when such luxuries as mobile phones were straight out of science fiction, it was invariably the pub where you sat down to write and take your turn on the nearest telephone. And once back in the Street of Shame there was always the "need" for a livener to discuss recent adventures.

The value of the pub meeting place was highlighted in 1970 when the Palestinian freedom fighter Leila Khaled was being held following several airliner hijackings. She was at Ealing police station in west London waiting to be exchanged for hostages taken in earlier terrorist actions. A plane was ready at Northolt to fly her to Damascus.

I was the *Daily Mirror* reporter door-stepping Ealing nick, while my colleague photographer Albert Foster was at Northolt. Of course, we had no way whatsoever of contacting each other.

As usual on such events the pack took turns for refreshment at a nearby hostelry. You can imagine the surprise when a few of us had our drinks break interrupted by a telegram boy (remember them?) who wandered into the pub and shouted: "Telegram for a Mr John Jackson."

Usually, telegrams were something one saw mainly at weddings when the best man read out the messages of best wishes which had arrived from parts afar. This telegram was simply addressed to "John Jackson, in the nearest pub to Ealing Police Station". And it read: "Khaled expected to arrive Northolt 4 pm. Cheers, Albert." Albert, in turn, would have needed a public telephone to send the telegram.

One other telegram I can remember was from the singing heartthrob of the time, Tommy Steele. He was involved in a publicity stunt to do with the disappearance, then discovery in Leicester Square, of a large statue of Charlie Chaplin. When we all sat down for a coffee in Covent Garden later Tommy refused to give his age. I told him: "Come on Tommy you are the same age as me, 43". Next day I received a telegram which said simply: "Touche, Tommy Steele 42."

Youngsters in my day who set their sights on a career in journalism started on a local weekly paper to learn the basics, then progressed slowly through the evening and local daily options before hitting the big time with a national.

It's very different now with university graduates successfully popping straight into top writing jobs, and, of course, star sports people who hang up their playing gear and are handed a laptop and a regular back page column. None of them, in my opinion, will ever be real journalists. (Cricketer Michael Atherton is the one exception.)

When I ventured in later years into travel writing, I wondered why I was never really accepted by fellow national travel editors. It soon became clear that the majority had never stood on a doorstep in their lives, with their entire career depending on handouts and freebie trips from gushing PR companies. There are numerous examples of these "editors" totally ignoring major news events which broke near a glamorous location they had been flown to, with real reporters having to jet in from head office.

My progress was weekly magazine, twice-weekly local paper, top provincial daily evening, numerous dailies abroad, then Fleet Street. In retrospect the drudgery of collecting names of mourners at funerals (standing at the door of the church hoping they had business cards to drop into my motorcycle helmet), scribbling down every minor case in the magistrates' court, collecting pick-up pictures of people killed in road accidents, listing details of all weddings that week, and suffering the nonsense trotted out at local council meetings, could be fun.

The main attraction of this progress, which was never appreciated at the time, was that the bigger the paper, the better the salary – and a marked decrease in your workload.

Such advice could have a backlash, once the brashest of local lads had risen to the top and become a household name. Ian Wooldridge, the brilliant sports columnist on the *Daily Mail* and a close buddy and travelling companion over 40 years, could recount a classic example.

Piers Morgan, not my idea of a *Daily Mirror* person (before, of course, he moved on to his own brand of super stardom) but who must be congratulated for much of his strategy in pulling the paper away from the abyss into which it was plummeting under the editorship of such buffoons as David Banks, marked his first editorship, at the helm of the *News of the World,* by bidding farewell to one of the most respected sports editors in the business, Bill Bateson.

At a very boozy farewell lunch, Wooldridge addressed the throng with reports of how he continued to receive numerous letters from school leavers asking his advice about the best ways to enter journalism. He repeated the routine of starting with a weekly and working up slowly. The vast majority received a helpful letter from the star writer, which they no doubt filed away proudly, but on occasions "when they appeared to be very bright, and a cut above the average," he invited them to lunch in London.

"And today I mourn the occasion I took young Piers Morgan to lunch," said Wooldridge.

I was a staff reporter, in chronological order, on *The Scout* magazine; *Birkenhead Advertiser* then *Birkenhead News; Orillia Daily Packet and Times,* Ontario, Canada; *Auckland Star,* New

Zealand; *Manchester Evening News; Hamilton Spectator,* Ontario,
Canada; *Daily Gleaner,* Kingston, Jamaica; *Auckland Star,* a second
time around; *Rand Daily Mail,* Johannesburg, South Africa;
Daily Herald; original broadsheet *Sun; Daily Mirror.* In between
I worked for Reuters and Associated Press as a freelance at big
sporting events, then finished my days as a travel editor, a position
shared with my wife, Barbara, on *Today* newspaper then the
Sunday Post, Dundee.

On *Today,* editor Richard Stott came up with the brilliant idea
of "Around the World with the Travelling Jacksons". I am sure he
knew we would do a good job and be an asset to the paper but,
as ever, the offer came in blunt fashion: "You're always on bloody
holiday, so you might as well write about them."

This allowed Barbara and me, plus our children Catherine,
Nicholas, Stella and Thomas, to travel extensively in order to fill
a double page spread each Saturday. It was tremendous fun while
it lasted.

Travel has always dominated our lives - and drained away our
savings. Before children started arriving in 1967, with the fourth
in 1972, we had enjoyed adventurous trips by public transport
through South America and Africa, delivered a 12-seater Cadillac
from New York City to San Diego, and sailed the Pacific.

And we can remember well where we were on November
22, 1963, the day President John F. Kennedy was assassinated –
marooned in no-man's land between Sudan and Uganda after
been deported at gunpoint from Juba as we were journalists. A lift
on a soap truck back to Nairobi saved us.

Later highlights were the Trans-Siberian railway, Moscow to
Beijing, with two stopovers in Siberia; long drives in Australia,
New Zealand, Argentina, Chile, India, Egypt, Turkey, Morocco,
South Africa and Syria, followed by the Karakoram Highway
in Pakistan; island hopping across the Pacific from Valparaiso to
Auckland; and tours of Iraq and Iran, entering Baghdad on the
first anniversary of the 9/11 attack, and six months before the
outbreak of war.

As an indication of my standing in Fleet Street in those good old days, I will mention three people who as young things on the way up sought guidance from old Jacko Jackson at what turned out to be crucial times in their careers. Perhaps some people might read this and demand an apology!

The first happened in 1967 when I was sent to cover an unexciting Red Cross press conference at an office near Victoria Station. A feisty young redhead and I exchanged glances of excruciating boredom, and after a further display of bandages, splints and neck braces, connived to slip away together for a required freshener in a nearby pub. She represented the North London New Agency, so was working for my old mate John Rodgers. Over a welcome half of bitter, she said I was the ideal person to give her advice.

A few days from then she was having an interview with the *Daily Mail,* and somewhat feared what she might have to face. I had been down that road (with total lack of success), so was able to forecast: "You will have no problem whatsoever. You will be met by news editor Jack Crossley and his deputy Charlie Wilson, who will take one look at you, turn you round and march you to the *Mail's* favourite watering hole, the Mucky Duck. Simply be yourself and you will wow them."

Grateful for this hopeful confidence booster, she drove me back in her smart little green MG sports car to my Covent Garden office. All went well, in the end, for her, despite the initial interview being aborted as Crossley and Wilson were "delayed at lunch". She got the job and phoned to say thanks, then, what seemed no time later, she announced she was marrying Charlie Wilson.

Over the years we ran across each other in Fleet Street pubs (she did like a drink in her younger days, as she readily admits), and often on stories. During the famous reappearance of John Stonehouse, the former Cabinet Minister who had faked his own death, she and I managed to be the first to interview his secretary, and mistress, Sheila Buckley.

Later still she became an assistant editor on the *Daily Mirror* and was in the editor's chair on the Sunday I delivered an exclusive which caused mayhem in the football world (a description of the England team's chosen hotel and environs for the 1982 World Cup near Bilbao, which featured pictures of a dead dog on the beach opposite - mentioned in the Sports Journalists' articles above - and the discomfort of the room later shared by Kevin Keegan and Trevor Brooking).

She pulled out every stop, to the extent of removing a special centre-spread feature, to make sure I received the maximum space possible.

Her name? – ANNE ROBINSON.

The second advice seeker I found disappearing into his umpteenth pint of the day as he slumped over the bar in one of the later Fleet Street dives – the underground City Snooker Club behind St Bride's Church. I asked this usually bubbly industrial correspondent of the *Evening Standard* why he was so morose and he slurped: "Jacko, I've been offered a regular column but I know I can't handle that – hic! Help me."

In my sternest voice I virtually commanded: "Bollocks. 'Course you can. Get off your fat arse and get up those steps and ask when you can start." He did.

His name? – RICHARD LITTLEJOHN.

A casual whisper over my shoulder in the *Daily Mirror* newsroom one afternoon in 1985 prompted the third youngster to pick my brains: "Jacko, can we have a conference quickie over the road? I need your advice."

I should explain that the The Stab was linked by a covered road bridge across New Fetter Lane. A totally, warm, dry route, far too close for comfort, offered the ideal opportunity for scribes to sneak across for a crafty glass of refreshment when all department heads were summoned to the editor's office for the twice daily planning conferences – hence "conference quickie over the road". Other needs were heart starter and liveners.

My young colleague took up his usual stance at the bar – permanent cigarette in one hand, and almost permanent pint in his other. It was at the time that Eddie Shah was busily recruiting for the launch of his *Today* newspaper. I was told in confidence that my drinking companion had been offered a good job as a news desk executive on what would be the *Sunday Today.* Should he go?

My response was immediate and emphatic: "No, no, no. Under no circumstances, no." I explained that I knew he was highly regarded and had a great future at the *Mirror,* a very big ship, so why abandon everything and take a chance on a small vessel which could soon sink?

He thanked me, returned to the office and walked straight into editor Richard Stott to hand in his notice. His career at *Today* was short lived but he did progress to bigger things.

His name? – ALASTAIR CAMPBELL.

Although we were all sorry to see Campbell leave, the one consolation was that Stott managed to persuade fellow reporter, and Alastair's greatest pal, John Merritt, to abandon the road to *Today* and stay with us big shippers. The two of them had graduated through the *Mirror* training scheme together and were great additions to our London newsroom.

Merritt was a man who exuded fun, who shone in all company, and never gave any hint of the illness that would soon kill him. He did eventually move on to *The Observer,* then tragically died at a very early age from leukaemia. A dreadful loss to us all, shown by the massive turnout for his memorial service at Fleet Street's own St. Bride's Church.

In giving a masterly eulogy – a very difficult task when you are talking about your closest friend – Campbell listed the practical joking escapades of his mate then finished, in tears, with the story that has prompted him to run the London Marathon to raise money for leukaemia research in the memory of Merritt.

Campbell has never hidden the fact that he boozed himself into a nervous breakdown, and needed sound advice from great friends like John Merritt, former Labour leader Neil Kinnock, and, of course, his long-time partner Fiona Millar, to heave himself back on the rails.

With him recovering, and Merritt dying, they joked at the latter's bedside. Merritt held out his clenched fist to hand over a present. Campbell took it and found himself holding some marbles. "This is to make sure you never lose them again," Merritt said.

A year or so later I should have made a mental note in my "this could be interesting in the future" compartment when Alastair had returned to the *Mirror* as deputy political editor. One evening I was struggling with a routine, but still possible front-page story, which could not be completed without a quote from the then shadow minister, Tony Blair. I just could not get hold of him by phone, which was unusual as Blair was always ready to speak.

It was one of those aggravating occasions when the time was dragging into early evening, but the job had to be completed. I spotted Alastair walk through the door and shouted something like: "Where is that bastard Blair?" He queried why I wanted to know, thought for possibly three seconds then replied: "Here is his quote."

When I suggested it could be dangerous to use it without checking, Alastair brushed this anxiety aside with the comment: "He'll agree it okay. I am seeing him in about an hour and will tell him what he said to the *Mirror*." It made the front page.

This moment came flooding back 15 years later when Barbara and I received a letter headed 10 Downing Street, and signed Yours ever, Alastair Campbell, Chief Press Secretary. He had written: "It would have been great to meet up with you and all the *Mirror* crowd, but sadly it can't be. However, Fiona and I send our warmest wishes for a delightful occasion and look forward to celebrating your Golden Anniversary."

This invitation involved the other side of my life – my marriage to Barbara. The occasion was our 40th or Ruby Wedding anniversary, and of course *Mirror* chums would dominate the guest list with family and close friends.

If I was lucky with my job, I was mega-fortunate with my choice of bride. Without Barbara I could not possibly be the contented soul I am today.

We have always been a great partnership, but as in so many happy marriages, particularly then, it was mainly the wife who made all the sacrifices. A superb journalist whom I met when she was an 18-year-old cadet reporter on the *Auckland Star,* and who prompted me to rush halfway round the world in order to prevent some other scoundrel making overtures, Barbara has kept the whole show on the road.

We were married on May 7, 1960, with Barbara aged 19, and after covering the Olympic Games in Rome together, spent seven adventurous years travelling the world. To start we drove overland from Manchester to Istanbul and return in a Morris Minor 1000 van, sleeping in the back for six weeks. Quite a trip!

My luck in finding such a marvellous lifelong partner came shortly after arriving by ship in New Zealand in June 1958 after my sojourn in Canada. I immediately applied for a job on the *Auckland Star,* the city's evening newspaper, but met a stern rejection from assistant editor Ross Sayers.

With a few chums who had shared the voyage on the Orient Line's *Orsova* from Vancouver to Auckland, via San Francisco, Honolulu and Fiji, I hitch-hiked down to Wellington where we chaps got jobs working on the docks, mainly humping sides of lamb around with strong Hungarians, recent refugees from the 1956 revolution in their faraway country.

Lodging courtesy of the Salvation Army, then called Peoples' Palaces in New Zealand, it soon became clear it was time to move on, probably across the Tasman to Sydney. This meant a return to Auckland, where I adopted the old "nothing ventured, nothing gained" philosophy and paid another visit to the *Auckland Star.*

This time the same Ross Sayers, soon to be recognised as not the greatest newspaper executive on the planet, said yes, and I was hired as a general reporter on a splendid weekly wage of NZ£25, then on a par with sterling.

Nothing much happened in Auckland in those days so the first chore for the news desk was to cut out all stories worth following (more like repeating) from the morning *New Zealand Herald*, and dispatching wodges of cuttings to each reporter.

The delivery was undertaken by the young cadet reporters, and with Lady Luck still giving me a helping hand my first batch was delivered by a very attractive 18-year-old Barbara Johnson. As she walked away, with my eyes following every movement, I whispered to my colleague Ted Daly: "Hopefully, she's mine." It truly was love at first sight.

(Ted Daly was perhaps the best on-the-spot reporter I ever encountered. Someone who had left school at 14 to become a journalist he later returned to England and we worked together again on the *Daily Herald* and broadsheet *Sun*. He finished his Fleet Street career as the late-night man on the *Daily Express*.)

From that moment on the Jackson charm went into overdrive to try to lure Barbara away from some boring sports sub-editor whose one advantage was that he drove an Inspector Maigret-type Citroen.

This was not easy as I could only produce a 1930 Austin Seven, which usually needed a push-start, which I bought from a fellow hack for £30. (He was the type of businessman who demanded he take my trusty Olivetti portable typewriter as guarantee until I handed over the final £10, as I had only £20 to my name when I bought it.)

The first possible opening came with the annual Auckland Press Ball. Barbara and boyfriend were booked as a couple but I had no partner. I decided on a plan, which today fills me with some horror.

I wandered down to Auckland bus station and kept a close eye on the more attractive young ladies alighting from such exotic suburbs as Papatoetoe and Otahuhu. One stood out and I hurried brazenly to her side and enquired: "Would you like to come with me to the Auckland Press Ball." Shamefully I cannot remember her name, but she hailed from Sunderland and said she would love to. Different days! Harassment charges would probably follow today.

On the night I made sure we were always close to Barbara and thought I had made a breakthrough when Mr Silly offered Miss Sunderland and me a lift back into Auckland in the Citroen.

But the bastard had different ideas. He dropped us as far away as possible – the equivalent of Hackney if we lived in Ealing.

But something clicked, for Barbara soon ditched the Maigret motor for my Laurel and Hardy Austin Seven. And I spared no expense or careful planning in arranging our first date – to see a Norman Wisdom film. I'd won her over, and there was no way I ever wanted to lose her. It was August 28, 1958.

A year later Barbara decided to achieve her lifelong ambition and booked with her parents to sail to England, ironically on the same ship, *Orsova*, which had brought me to their shores. It was hard to watch her sail away from Auckland's Princes Wharf, but we had arranged to meet up again at the Rome Olympics the following year.

I was then living in digs in the Auckland suburb of Herne Bay, sharing a room with a charming Maori postman named Croydon. That was his first name, for who needs a surname when you are called Croydon – unless it's Bus-Garage?

With our different hours we rarely saw each other but with Barbara gone two days we went to the cinema to see *Room At The Top*. Croydon was quick to spot I was pining, but my demeanour got worse with the film, British and set in Bradford where both my parents were born.

"I just can't let her go," I exclaimed. Croydon understood: "Go chase her, mate."

The following day was Saturday and as usual I worked on the late evening sports edition, the *8 O'Clock*. My assignment was a hockey match in Onehunga.

I couldn't really concentrate on face-offs, penalty corners, etc as I knew that the *Orsova* was docked in Sydney Harbour. I made a flash decision. I arranged with a young freelance to cover for me and hared back to the Central Post Office at the bottom of Auckland's famous Queen Street.

I asked to be connected by shore-to-ship telephone to the *Orsova* but was told it was impossible at that time as no contact could be made (remember this was 1959) until the ship had sailed through the Sydney Heads out into open sea.

Finally, I was put through on a crackly line and asked to speak to Barbara Johnson. A few moments later there was this distant "Hello".

I shouted down the line: "Will you marry me?" And much to my joy the reply came back "Yis" (she still had a Kiwi accent then).

(I should point out that if you ever want to bring a crowded Post Office to a standstill and total silence, I recommend my little effort from a standing phone on a counter.)

I told Barbara that she still had five weeks on board, via the Suez Canal, and that I would be waiting at Tilbury when she disembarked. I gave a month's notice at the *Auckland Star* and set about gathering enough money for the air fare back. Ted Daly showed what a great mate he was by lending me £50, then adding an extra £50 as a wedding present.

The journey home took me by TEAL (Tasman Empire Airlines) to Sydney. There I changed on to a Qantas Super Constellation for Hong Kong, via Port Moresby, New Guinea and Manila. But this was slightly delayed when we lost one of the four engines and made an emergency landing in Brisbane.

The following day we got to Hong Kong, with minutes to spare for me to board a BOAC Comet to Rome, via Singapore, Colombo, Bombay, Bahrein. Then it cost me an extra £5 to enjoy the luxury of a first Pan American Boeing 707 to Paris. Followed by BEA (British European Airways) to London, a few hours before the *Orsova* chugged into Tilbury.

Ten months later we were married, with me on the *Manchester Evening News* and Barbara spending the time living with my parents in Solihull, working for the *Birmingham Mail* and Rover cars. (Barbara simply went from Johnson to Jackson, but together we have totally cancelled out the saying: "Change the name not the letter, change for worse not for better.")

Our wonderful adventure through life together had begun.

When we decided to start a family (Barbara has always said it was my idea, and she is probably right), we were blessed with two boys and two girls in five years. Barbara managed to keep her hand in with freelance writing from home, but the children always came first.

The four framed photographs of them in graduation gowns from their top universities (Sheffield, London, Manchester, Bristol) are proof of her devotion. All four, two of whom followed parents into journalism, now have their own happy families having produced five grandsons and three granddaughters.

When able to return to fulltime journalism Barbara filled several positions within the *Mirror* group, including cookery writer working for the executive she christened "My Mrs Terrifying", a title which has often been thrown back at Anne Robinson. Richard Stott, then *People* editor, later rode to our assistance and appointed her as agony aunt *Dear Barbara*.

Among the distress of many very sad letters this did allow one moment of extreme comedy. A very lucrative role for agony aunts can be the recording of comforting advice lines for troubled souls who prefer listening on the telephone to putting pen to paper.

One year a not uncommon internal battle of words had got nasty at a meeting of Yorkshire Cricket Club. So it was decided that members could vote by choosing a telephone number – eg 1234 if you agreed with Geoffrey Boycott, or 5678 if you were for Freddie Trueman.

But somehow British Telecom managed to get their lines crossed. So those who voted for Boycott found themselves listening to *Dear Barbara* explaining all about premature ejaculation.

Needless to say, editorial conferences were greeted with such comments: "If anyone should know about premature ejaculation, it's Barbara."

Later Barbara and I were lucky to venture into travel writing, after dragging the children to camping sites on the Black Sea in Romania, to dude ranches in Texas, a Yugoslavia/Croatian island every Easter, Christmas in New Zealand, and rail journeys through the Soviet Union, India and China,

I am very conscious that in this day and age, Barbara might well have rebelled at the "homebound housewife" role I accepted as natural. My frequent comment when leaving on a glamorous assignment that "it just happens I am the male of the species" would be rightly dismissed as fatuous and not tolerated in these changed times.

I regret that I ever uttered such a harmful remark, but you must remember that I am talking of a time when women were a minority in the world of Fleet Street, and there were certainly no female editors.

I am also only too aware that a comment I would make on the few occasions when times were awkward – "I can always find another job, but I cannot get another family" – would not be as flippant in present day circumstances, with such good jobs more difficult to come by.

I repeat, I have been a very lucky man – wonderful wife, smashing children and grandchildren, and a career that I loved and which allowed me to maintain a brilliant family life. Holidays were important, and I was a master at manipulating the duty roster to full advantage. Why not - work hard, holiday hard, you only come this way once.

In retirement I have endeavoured to compensate Barbara for the days when she coped with family life alone while I enjoyed my job to the full with, of course, some long periods away from home. Not that I have ever been a golfer, or patronised a local pub, or enjoyed regular long lunches with the chaps.

When I do now have such a lunch (probably no more than four times a year) I do get the understandable comment; "Don't be late. I've had years of this."

Barbara and I are enjoying a splendid retirement, still travelling on our own with Barbara continuing her outstanding abilities to arrange our itineraries, with me on hand as the technician with laptop, and paymaster.

We celebrated our Diamond Wedding during the coronavirus lockdown, but after 60 years together this brought no problems. And on we go.

We have always been a close family, strengthened by our clever children producing delightful grandchildren – William, Mia, Oscar, Harry, Ned, Jacob, Martha and Edie.

AND THAT REMINDS ME

A favourite story involves Chris Lander, one of the gentlemen of sports writing who lived life to the full, plus some. Sadly, Crash (gedditt?) died aged 58, but as his best mate Ian, now Lord, Botham said at his funeral: "Crash always said he was on the torpedo but would be off the bastard before it shot out of the pod."

Lander covered cricket and rugby in the liver punishing, women chasing days when the seasons did not clash. Once world travel became faster, he was confined to cricket full time, with two long stints on both the *Daily Mirror* and *Sun*. It was after finishing a tour in New Zealand that Crash decided to take a few days R and R in Fiji before returning home.

Walking past the *Mirror* sports desk I was hailed by sports editor Don Bate. He showed me a telex message from Crash which said he would be delayed a few days as he had been involved in a traffic accident and would need to recover from a few minor facial injuries.

As we wished him well, a sub editor handed on a piece of Reuters agency copy which, datelined Suva, Fiji, read: "Fijian heavyweight boxer ___ was yesterday sent to prison for beating up London sports journalist Chris Lander, whom he found in a nightclub with his arm around his fiancé." That was Crash. There'll never be anyone like him.

For me, my Fleet Street years and travels around the world were male orientated. When I arrived in the early 1960s there was at least one national daily which did not have a single woman general reporter. This was never the case on the *Daily Herald,* old broadsheet *Sun* and *Daily Mirror* where I plied my trade with formidable early trail blazers Paula James, Maggie Hall, Joan Smith and Mary Malone.

In the late 1960s BBC TV brought together some Fleet Street women for a round-table discussion about whether they could cope in a man's world. There was the *Daily Telegraph's* Gerda Paul, never seen without a sober handbag and string of pearls, the bubbly Sally Moore of the *Daily Mirror* who would prompt feminist shrieks of protest today as her great talents (she was possibly the best telephone interviewer I have ever worked with) were often confined to the weekly Shopping Clock, or dressing up as a Playboy Bunny for some page lead stunt, and the indomitable Clare Hollingsworth, a veteran who will always be classed as one of the great war correspondents.

When asked how women could possibly handle the situation in a war zone (are you listening Kate Adie, Orla Guerin et al?), Hollingsworth, with memories of the Second World War, Korean conflict and the then still raging Vietnam War, retorted: "Some problems. When you are stuck in a canoe on the Mekong River for several days, the knickers are inclined to get a little stiff."

One of the first drinking companions I soon latched on to was the wonderful Ann Pacey, highly regarded film critic of the *Daily Herald*. Other than the fact she was great company, we shared our birthday. Our office was in Endell Street, on the fringe of Covent Garden when it was still one of the most famous markets in the world. To wander through the hustle and bustle of the crowded streets after finishing a dog-watch shift at 4 a.m. was pure magic.

Pubs stayed open all night, and although you were supposed to be a genuine market worker in order to get a drink, this did not stop Pacey and others mingling with the likes of Richard Harris, Peter O'Toole and fellow actors for all-night binges. And dear old Pacey was never backward in coming forward when it came to describing any "afters".

She had a flat in nearby Gray's Inn Road and on one occasion I was present when understanding neighbours did express some concern, all be it with mild amusement.

As one elderly lady explained: "Dear Ann. We have become accustomed to young men calling at your flat at all hours, but at around two a.m. today a charabanc pulled up and several males of all ages trooped upstairs. It wasn't the numbers – it was the fact that some were carrying footballs."

A quick explanation: in those days in the late 1960s there was a traditional Maundy Thursday football match between the London and Manchester offices (no papers published on Good Friday), alternate years in each city. On this occasion the London match and late-night drinking had lingered so long that the drive back to Manchester was unthinkable, so good sport Pacey had them all doss down in her flat.

But the true Pacey came out when I found her one afternoon staring into a large gin and tonic in our office local, The Cross Keys. I knew she had just returned that day from the Cannes Film Festival so inquired how it had gone.

"Brilliant, Jacko – I was fucked by Hollywood great ..."

As she glimpsed upwards with a sly smile, I noticed some redness around her left eye, so wondered how that had come about. "Simple. I was pissed, he was pissed, and while he was on top of me fumbling about I joked: 'You've got your wrong side to camera.' And he thumped me."

Another Covent Garden story involved colleague and Pacey pal, Allan Hall. At times diary editor and feature writer, he later collated all his knowledge gathered from Fleet Street drinking establishments (by day) and Covent Garden pubs (by night) to become a respected wine critic and later wine merchant. One night I was beavering away on the night news desk when I received a call from Allan, who was probably no more than 200 yards away in some watering hole.

"Dear Boy, the situation is looking extremely promising at the moment, so would you do me a great favour? Phone my wife and say I have been sent to Belfast and will obviously have to stay the night." I duly passed on this message, which was gratefully accepted by the nice Mrs Hall.

Mission successfully accomplished, a whistling, still tipsy Allan wandered into the office early next morning, obviously heading for a crafty kip in the diary room.

Instead, he was grabbed by a delighted news editor, handed a wad of Press Association copy and told an office car was waiting to rush him to Heathrow Airport where he would collect a ticket for Dublin – and there write a long feature on the breaking story of the day.

Ho hum, thought Allan while waiting at Heathrow with a muzzy brain, must phone the wife. With no recollection of earlier arrangements, he said: "Hello darling, I'm on a rush job to Dublin and will be overnighting. Sorry."

"Where are you now?" was the natural inquiry from her-indoors.

"Well, Heathrow, of course."

"But why come back from Belfast to go to Dublin?"

"Belfast...?

That story could be added to the collection of "bad luck" situations, which for me will always be headed by the misfortune suffered by a top TV press officer. A great lad, happily married, with whom I shared many a necessary vodka at the 1980 Moscow Olympics, found himself in charge of a large group of competition winners heading for a free week in the sun at the expense of his company.

On his own admission, he did stand at the front of the plane on boarding, studied the talent (as was his wont), and chose her with the come-to-bed eyes/got to be a cert/no obvious companion in 12F. The pair, on all accounts, appeared to enjoy a very pleasant trip getting to know each other well, before going their separate ways on return, never to make contact again.

The scene then moves forward several months and our happy-with-his-lot executive arrived home from work, early, not having had a drink all day and looking forward to a quiet evening *en famille*.

His "Hello, darling. I'm home," as he closed the door, was greeted by a rolled up bundle of magazines flying through the air and hitting him fair and square on the back of his head. "Page 33, Clarksons travel brochure," was the only response from the kitchen.

His mystified search turned up a page of pictures featuring the hotel which hosted his competition party. And there alongside the pool was our man, clearly spread over Miss Attractive from 12F wearing a skimpy bikini.

It was as a result of joining Allan Hall and Ann Pacey in The Cross Keys for a farewell ale in the summer of 1968, before they ventured into the Covent Garden gloaming, that I embarked on one of the more interesting long-haul adventures. With us was another great colleague, sportswriter Jack Wood.

For many years he had combined the golf and boxing reporting jobs but one morning, after covering top boxing title fights around the globe, he awoke with the decision (and probably a massive hangover) that the sport was obscene, should be banned, and he refused to witness another thrown punch.

I mentioned that I was leaving next day for the Olympic Games in Mexico City, and he embarked on a rambling suggestion of how I should stop in Bermuda and have a drink with his old friend, George Bird, the golf professional at the Castle Harbour Hotel. I politely thanked him and said I would note the name.

Next morning, I boarded a packed BOAC Boeing 707 for the flight, which in those pre-Jumbo days stopped at Bermuda and Bahamas en route to Mexico City. The BBC Olympic team was on board with commentator David Coleman immediately in front of me, Frank Bough and others nearby.

I was the middle seat of three, two rows from the rear. Occupying the aisle seat was a frail elderly gentleman who turned out to be Philip Noel-Baker, Nobel Peace Prize winner and a competitor at the 1912 and 1920 Olympics.

With the plane full and the door at the front about to be closed I was delighted to note that the one empty seat was by the window alongside me. Good for a sleep. Then suddenly, loud voices alerted all eyes to a tall man being helped along the plane by two uniformed stewards.

Oh God, he must be sitting next to me! Obviously drunk, he was ushered into our row. Noel-Baker, deep in a book, was only able to partially slide up on to his feet. I decided to stand on my seat.

"Put it there, buddy," said chatty, obviously American chummy as he pinned me up under the luggage rack. "My name is George Bird, golf professional at the Castle Harbour Hotel."

Flabbergasted, I gasped: "You're the man Jack Wood told me to call."

"Jack Wood, Jack Wood," he snarled with the sort of behaviour that would not let him near a departure gate these days. "Who the hell do you think has just got me monumentally pissed?"

With that he slumped in his seat, and before the engines had started had scribbled three notes which he loudly ordered be taken instantly to the pilot. They all carried the same request: "When you get through flying this thing, come straight back and marry me to the gorgeous blonde stewardess."

(In those days there were rumours, always refuted, that airline pilots and ship captains could officiate at wedding ceremonies while travelling.)

As the engines roared for take-off, George Bird fell completely silent, almost as if he had been struck by a poison dart. And I am not ashamed to admit that I have thought about what happened next during each take-off since, and there have been a great many.

Bird remained as if in a trance until there was a ping, and the No Smoking sign went off. "Okay, we are safe now," he muttered coherently, before reverting to his loud pissed state. It was not that he wanted a cigarette. He explained: "I flew Flying Fortresses during the war and I know that the most dangerous part of a flight is on take-off and the pilot is not in complete control. When the smoking sign goes off, you know he is back in charge."

I have found that encouraging, even in this day and age when the No Smoking sign never goes off. If you listen carefully, you can often hear the ping.

As for the Castle Harbour Hotel, on return from Mexico City he had his secretary/mistress meet me at the airport in a stretch limo, gave me the best suite in the golf section with a glass door that opened on to the first tee, alongside the blue Atlantic, which many top golfers have described as the most beautiful fairway in the world – and woke me in the morning with a gallon, repeat gallon (4.5 litres), of Bloody Mary.

Four years later the flights to an Olympics, this time the 1972 Winter Games in Sapporo, Japan, were memorable. I flew out with the party from Germany's main sports agency *Sport Information Dienst,* with whom I had started working as a freelance London correspondent prior to the 1966 World Cup in London and continued for 30 years.

I joined the Condor flight at Frankfurt with snow thick on the ground and have already chronicled how fur-clad chief reporter Ulrich Kaiser was whisked away at our Bangkok overnight stop after being mistaken as the Soviet ambassador.

He finally caught up with us at the hotel bar when I was deep in conversation with a photographer who had been a Luftwaffe pilot in World War II. As an Englishman accustomed to hearing Battle of Britain pilots plastering their planes with Messerschmitt numbers they had shot down, it was odd hearing him tell how he had done the same with Spitfires.

He incidentally had gained the nickname "double, double vodka" at the 1966 World Cup. Based with Germany in Birmingham he was horrified when his customary vodka and tonic tipple came in such a short measure. Hence "give me a double, double vodka, bitte".

Memories of the War also cropped up as I was driving from the airport into Moscow for the 1980 Olympics. As we passed the large memorial to where the advancing German army was finally halted in 1941, another German friend whispered: "This is as far as I got last time."

The last leg of the flight from Tokyo to Sapporo had me sitting next to an aged Japanese couple. As I was attempting to catch up on badly needed sleep, a voice asked: "You go Sapporo ice festival?" No, the Olympics.

"Oh Olympics. You American?" No, English. And then the conversation became bizarre.

"Oh English. How Tottenham Hotspur doing?" This cannot be true, I pondered, as an Arsenal supporter replying not very well.

"Oh, Jimmy Hill. I love Match of the Day."

WORLD CUP START

It was natural that my career as Fleet Street's Chief Rotter should start in earnest in 1966, with the World Cup and England's glorious victory. I was then on the old broadsheet *Sun*. Till then I had attempted, with little success, to whip up some semblance of enthusiasm among my immediate news desk executives and other heads of departments for the news aspect of sport.

I had always argued that major sport was often worthy of the news pages, rather than been always confined to the back, In the case of the *Daily Mirror,* news at that time was on both the front and back, with sport inside.

Wimbledon was the only annual event where a news reporter's attendance was never questioned. Perhaps it was the fact that it was the one aspect of British sporting life that women followed closely? As a result, the price of strawberries and cream, fashion and Royal Box lists were more important than McEnroe outbursts and Billie Jean King mutterings.

I got off to a wonderful start in my first year, 1964, with the picture story of line judge Mrs Dorothy Cavis-Brown falling fast asleep during an outside court match. A woman!

We were still living in a period when the private lives of sports stars remained exactly that – totally private. And, of course, the era of football hooliganism had not yet dawned. My extensive travelling with these yobs had yet to start.

Drunken shenanigans and outlandish behaviour off the field on major overseas cricket/rugby/football/Olympic/Commonwealth Games, etc events remained unreported. Reporters accompanying these often-long tours regarded it more important to keep the athletes onside – "he/she is a good contact, old boy". They wrote about sport, and nothing off the field of play was their concern.

They quite honestly did not accept that boorish behaviour such as when British Lions rugby players ransacked a hotel with fire extinguishers, or the sighting of a pair of famous gold medal athletes, from two different nations, "bonking in the bushes", were newsworthy.

(The latter occurred at the 1962 Perth Commonwealth Games. When the chief security officer in the athletes' village was informed, in the middle of a heavy drinking session, of this sighting, his immediate response: "Jesus, mate, just put a notch on the tree.")

And how was it that not one of the country's leading football scribes bothered to grab pen and telephone when Bobby Moore, the captain of the then world champions, failed to board the plane taking his England team from Bogota, Colombia, to the 1970 World Cup finals in Mexico?

Those who later said they knew all along of the shattering news that Moore had been arrested for the alleged theft of a bracelet should have remained in Bogota with the story; while those who learned after take-off had the chance of disembarking and returning when the flight stopped for refuelling at Panama City. Not one member of the press corps did so.

This is not a total condemnation of the top sports journalists I respected, and later worked alongside for many years in most corners of the globe, for times were different. The public did not expect, as now, a non-stop daily barrage of tittle-tattle about everyone in the public eye.

Cricket aficionados were only interested in Ian Botham's brilliance with bat and ball, rather than the "Botham Breaks Bed Bonking Miss Barbados" headlines which came later in his career.

Another perfect example was the marriage of England's blond haired football captain to a glamorous member of an all-girl pop group.

In 1958 Billy Wright, Wolverhampton Wanderers stalwart and the first player to win 100 international caps, married Joy Beverley, the eldest of the three high-flying Beverley Sisters. Every paper carried a picture of the wedding, but from then on they were left alone.

Forty years later a similar scenario brought together Posh Spice and David Beckham – a pop star and the blond captain of

England. How times have changed – but, of course, they have always relished the limelight.

There was always a strict dividing line between the news and sports departments on every newspaper. My attempts to convince executives that much of sport was news fell on deaf ears, and my typed copy was usually despatched from the back bench (where the night editor sits in judgment on what goes where in each edition) to the nearest spike. On a good day it was relayed by copy boy to the sports production area, -- and a shinier spike.

Sports writers did not then welcome the interference of news hacks, asking questions, which they saw as unnecessarily embarrassing, while we newsmen saw them as pertinent. I would like to believe that in a small way I pioneered the news coverage of sport, but I had a strict rule about being unfair and going too far.

There have been times when I have been threatened with the sack unless I matched a story emblazoned across the pages of a rival paper. Some I knew to be totally inaccurate, as I had witnessed them myself at close range, while others I felt were unjust.

One splendid example came in 1986 when I was covering the England cricket tour of the West Indies. After a quiet dinner out in Port of Spain, Trinidad, I returned to the upside-down Hilton Hotel (it stands on the side of a hill with the reception at the top and all rooms below), where I was grabbed by Mark Austin, now with Sky but then a BBC sports correspondent, and told to hurry myself to a nearby suite where his cameraman Derek Collier was celebrating his 55th birthday. I followed the noise of revelry and was soon glass in hand among players and media colleagues.

Before I could offer Collier happy birthday cheers, I was grabbed by a certain Ian Terrence Botham who launched into a forceful, but friendly attack on something I had written earlier. A good exchange of views between a reporter and the great England star who had been hammered in print with more than usual dollops of sex, drugs and rock'n'roll.

While he had me pinned in the corner, I could spot over his

shoulder that a group of merry men were contemplating a bottle-throwing contest from the balcony. I learned later the plan was to see who had the strongest throwing arm (a reasonable subject of discussion at a cricket party!), to be determined by those who could clear the tennis courts below.

The complication came at around 7.30 a.m. when BBC commentator Christopher Martin Jenkins and former player Geoffrey Boycott walked out for their customary early game of tennis, to find themselves ankle deep in broken glass. They knew nothing of the cause and were unable to find anyone in the hotel who did.

Despite intensive investigation there was not one single person who could shed any light on how such a thing could have happened. Funny that!

That evening the transatlantic telephone lines started buzzing frantically when the first edition of the *Daily Star* landed on Fleet Street desks. The exclusive back page headline blasted: "Botham in Bottle Throwing Incident". Within minutes I was ordered to match the story, and given a mini rollicking for missing it.

I hit straight back with the first-hand knowledge that it was "all bollocks". I explained that Botham had nothing to do with the foolery as at the time he had me pinned against a wall, complaining about the sort of irresponsible journalism as typified by this *Star* story.

I was well aware the reporter responsible had not been in the room. I explained that it was mainly press people involved and I had no intention of starting a career of filing copy about how journalists behave on tour.

I held my ground, despite threats of "come home and collect your cards" from sports desk underlings, and retired to the bar to attempt to "find out" what had happened.

Honesty and a direct approach were my ways of playing things. In Jamaica on the same tour, I was ordered by my *Daily Mirror* news editor to "get close" to captain David Gower and wicket keeper Paul Downton so I would be in possession of the "full story" when the *News of the World* hit the streets with "the big one".

The rumoured rumour was that Gower was having an affair with Downtown's wife of just a few weeks. Having already spent a long time with the two men on tour, and enjoying a good relationship with Gower, I was 99 per cent sure the suggestion was total nonsense.

I decided the only answer was to confront the skipper direct and told my fellow scribes of this intention. This brought about fits of apoplexy for old timers such as John Woodcock of *The Times* (I'd love to hear the numerous tales he could recount after decades of accompanying England's cricketers, going back to the days when they travelled overseas by ocean liner), and Christopher Martin Jenkins.

There had been some concern when I, a news hack, had been assigned to the tour, but I assured them this was the best way. If looks could kill, my days would have ended in Kingston, but it cleared the air, the story was soon dismissed as total crap, and Gower was quick to admit: "You were a total bastard, but at least you were honest."

The episode helped me over the remaining few weeks, with England being totally "blackwashed" by Viv Richards and his gang on the field. Batsman Allan Lamb, not known to suffer fools or new faces gladly, would introduce me in that thick South African accent: "Thees is Jacko. He knows fuck all about cricket, but at least he's honest."

And the Gower/Downton rumour? The madness started from a picture of Gower kissing Mrs Downton at her wedding. Which was quite acceptable: he was the best man.

Another of these rumoured exclusives had me hiring a car at dawn during the 1972 Munich Olympics, three days before the massacre of Israeli athletes, after the *Sunday Mirror*'s splendid news editor Monty Court had instructed me to grab racing driver Graham Hill as he breakfasted at his "hideaway" Gasthof in the Tyrolean Alps. I missed him by seconds but managed to race ahead to the Salzburgring racetrack where he was competing later in the Austrian Grand Prix.

The suggestion was that Hill "was playing away from home", which was not the style of the renowned family man with a loving wife and children, one of whom was young son Damon, destined to be a world champion himself in later years.

After a few moments of unsuccessful tussle with a Nazi-type steward, the hills all around seemed to be filled with the sound of my pidgin German: "Bitte, I only speak to Herr Hill for eine moment." The dumb insolence of Fritz remained unchanged but from behind me came a familiar voice: "I'm here old boy, but nobody can do anything till you move your ruddy car."

I swung round gleefully to see Graham Hill standing by the door of his sports car – but everyone's eyes were on the stunning blonde in the passenger seat. Whoops, was I on to a correct rumour? He suggested I park, climb in the back of his car, so he could reverse on to the verge.

"Right, how can I help you?" he asked. I stammered that it might be better if we stepped outside, which he understood. When I told him the position his first reply was: "God, I must have upset someone recently for them to spread a rumour like that." He stressed it was all nonsense and asked that no one start knocking on the door of his house, as it would be unfair to saddle his wife with such crazy suggestions.

And the blonde? "Oh, it must look bad, but the honest truth is that she is the secretary of team owner Colin Chapman who asked me to drive her to the course."

As it was a Saturday in the mountains, I had to make inquiries in three villages before I found the "weekend" telephone. (Yes, these things did happen before mobile phones.) On a crackly line from a restaurant kitchen, with the banging flat of Wiener schnitzels combining with the clatter of saucepans and yells from waiting staff to make hearing almost impossible, I explained there was no story. "Okay, old boy, let's have a nice crisp few pars saying 'Graham Hill last night denied rumours that...'," said a news desk assistant.

Oh no, I refused to fall into that trap. That would have been very unfair. The blonde, incidentally, was exactly whom Hill said she was.

So, times changed – and how. After Geoff Hurst's three goals had shot England to World Cup victory over Germany, and from SPORT to front page splash position for every newspaper, we Rotters became a fact of life. For the sportswriters this was a welcome relief. After years of protecting contacts, they were being told in no uncertain terms that contacts were established for one purpose – to use.

So now the message to the newsmen was reversed. Instead of blanking all stories because "he/she is a good contact" it became: "I've got a great story here, Jacko. But I would rather you take it over as the informant is a good contact of mine." I didn't mind. This meant, of course, that every wild rumour to emerge from a dressing room or after match drink would be passed without question to the news desk – "I'll leave it with you, as it's too close to home for me."

At this juncture perhaps I should unravel the mystery of why the nicknames Rotters, Blunts and Smudgers figure prominently in sports reporting-speak. It all dates back to those legendary photographers, my *Mirror* buddy Monte Fresco and his uncle Monty Fresco of the *Daily Mail*.

Perhaps tired of being referred to as "monkeys" by their colleague scribes, they suddenly came up with Smudgers for the lensmen and Blunts for writers. One gathers the Cockney logic, for the sake of a better word, behind this was that writers had blunt pencils and snappers had been known to ruin the odd print. When I and my ilk came on the scene, asking the questions they dared not and approaching stories which had earlier been taboo, Rotters was a natural name.

One night, in a hotel room somewhere after facing yet another marathon whingeing session about the Rotters by football writers, I decided I should put words to the individual letters of each name. I was quite proud of my results.

A Blunt obviously stood for "Bloody lazy unfortunately

no talent"; Smudgers was "So many under-developed grainy exposures return soonest", while Rotters was "Reporters of tact tenacity ever ready". I took a remarkable amount of stick from tired and emotional Blunts when I announced these findings to the world at breakfast, but at least David Meek of the *Manchester Evening News* was impressed enough to make me his diary lead.

The Fresco family's other claim to fame, other than being top class professionals, was to be kings of the freebies. Stick with the Monts and you could treble your baggage weight.

On arrival at the Montreal Olympics in 1976, the *Mail* Monty invited his columnist Ian Wooldridge and me to attend a gala dinner being hosted by Nikon. The reason was nothing to do with any thought that we might like a free meal and night out, but Fresco knew the present was going to be a rather expensive piece of photographic equipment and wanted more than one. Sadly, after what seemed an eternity of Quebec folk dances and singing, Wooldridge and I had to excuse ourselves and return to work – missing the presentation.

Next morning, I called for my Monte in hired Flat Fresco and spotted around a dozen of the gifts on the mantelpiece. How on earth had they managed that many?

"Easy," explained *Mail* Monty. "These Japanese couldn't tell us apart. I went up first as Monty Fresco, *Daily Mail,* then kept joining the end of the queue as Mickey Mouse, *Stratford Express,* Charlie Farnsbarns, *Ilford Recorder,* until they ran out."

Back in Rotterdom, one afternoon I spotted our star football writer scurrying away from the news editor, who immediately beckoned me over. "Harry tells me that ___ ____ is the first footballer to contract AIDS."

I knew that the international involved had been on the injury list for several weeks, but in all cases involving people in the north my first call had to be to our Manchester office. News editor Leo White, as always, had the answer. "AIDS? The reason he has been off so long is that he was found in bed with a young lady, and her boyfriend reacted by sticking a knife in his thigh."

The build-up to the 1966 World Cup had been keenly followed, but still no semblance of interest emanated among the utterances of old *Sun* news editor Barrie Harding. A former reporter with a tough reputation, he appeared to have no time for any sport.

In the Army he had been a Commando instructor with a habit of punching soldiers to the ground, then shouting: "Get up, and do that to me." He quite openly told the story of the young Somerset farmhand who, with obvious delight, obeyed the instruction to the letter. Not only thumped him but removed most of Harding's teeth.

When a member of the *Daily Mirror's* formidable New York bureau, he had once tackled a fellow guest at a drinks party who had persisted in giving him verbal earache. Barrie simply grabbed him by the throat, lifted him off the ground, edged towards the window and gestured he was about to throw him out. As the party was in the penthouse suite of a skyscraper, there was certain concern.

I had to play it cannily, by not mentioning the World Cup too often. A heaven-sent opportunity arose when Harding was short of news desk personnel because of holidays and persisted in rostering reporters in the boring slot reading sheaves of incoming copy. No screens in those days; just mountains of paper.

I was often seconded, as was fellow scribe Harry Arnold. The big debate between us questioned how we could get ourselves "released" back to our desks and jobs out of the office. Harry Arnold was one of the best reporters I have ever worked with. His record as an ace newsman with the two *Suns* and *Daily Mirror,* topped during his stretch as the *Sun's* Royal correspondent, tells it all.

But he could be an aggravating artful dodger who perhaps was the original model for Flash Harry. He decided to work his ticket by whistling non-stop, and this drove Barrie Harding mad. One down, now my turn.

I decided to loudly send everyone on foreign assignments. A flash from the Reuters announcing such earthshattering front page news as "Five-legged mole discovered in Bratislava", would see me leap to my feet and shout: "Peter Batt, have some lunch then get yourself to Prague and drive south." It wasn't long before Harding suggested I should take myself off somewhere horrible, and quickly. I suggested I should get myself accredited for the World Cup as it was an important news event, to which came the reply: "I agree. Anything to get you away from here."

It would be fair to say my life changed from that moment.

I should mention that while Harry Arnold and I were masterminding our news desk dismissals, there was even more action attracting attention on the picture desk alongside. Photographers were finding themselves chair-bound like us, sitting opposite the picture editor Len Hickman, a quiet-spoken gentleman who had doubled ballet with boxing in his early life. I never did get to the bottom of that combination!

One of the photographers trying desperately to work his ticket was Tony Eyles, commonly known as "Silly" (after the Scilly Isles). His departure was rapid when Hickman took a call to say there was an armed robbery situation in Brighton. He instructed Eyles, in his usual whisper, to contact the local freelance agency: "Tony, call Robson of Brighton."

With that, Eyles swung round on his swivel chair, kicked open the huge windows which flew outwards, cupped his hands to his mouth and proceeded to yell across the rooftops of Covent Garden: "ROBSON OF BRIGHTON". It worked, although he did find himself on more doorsteps than normal for a time.

So I was off on the great World Cup adventure. With a bit of luck, the news side of sport would become an accepted part of Fleet Street life from that moment on. Yippee!!

Along with the football correspondents there were just five news reporters who turned up at the Main Press Centre, situated in the basement of Kensington's Royal Garden Hotel, which had been built especially for the World Cup. No massive horde of feature writers, agencies, freelances, radio reporters and TV crews as today. Just us five – Barry Stanley (*Daily Mirror*), George Hunter (*Daily Express*), Keith Harper (*Guardian*), John Spicer

(*Daily Mail*), and yours truly John Jackson (*Sun*).

And I'm the only one still alive to tell the tale.

The chief press officer (where on earth did they find him?) was called Harold Mayes, who worked for a paper somewhere in the Home Counties. (His performance, or lack of it, prompted an early exchange between rival football scribes. Clive Toye, *Daily Express*, was overheard commenting: "This bloke has got to be the fool of the year?" This prompted an outburst from Ulrich Kaiser: "Nein, he is ours. We have already made him fool of the year.")

It was obvious from the outset that Mayes was completely out of his depth. Hemel Hempstead Horse Show fine; THE soccer World Cup, forget it. His immediate response to us five hacks as we requested accreditation was: "Please go away and stop wasting my time. This is a sports event and has absolutely nothing to do with news and the front pages." He soon regretted this as I was able to produce a major ace to slap down his joker persona.

With the other four very angry and threatening to physically cut short the Mayes reign, I calmed them down, and said follow me, but don't say a word, as I knew someone who would help. When we reached the penthouse executive suite and I pressed the doorbell they thought I had lost my mind.

The person in question who opened the door was the boss of the whole shebang – namely Sir Stanley Rous, president of football's governing body, FIFA. With instant recognition and a smile he asked: "Dear boy, how's Barbara?"

Four years earlier Barbara and I had with masterly guile, got ourselves from boredom in Canada to Chile for the 1962 World Cup. I had wangled a job with Associated Press after bombarding Ted Smits, the sports editor in New York, with letters and phone calls suggesting I was the only person in North America who knew anything about soccer – and AP needed me.

During a sneaky call, hand over the mouthpiece, from a tiny side room in the Supreme Court at Hamilton, Ontario (long distance phone calls were complicated procedures, and taboo in many offices in those days), Smits agreed. "Get yourself to Santiago," was his decision, and music to my ears.

On arrival I was despatched to Vina del Mar on the coast, while Barbara hustled for work and was taken on in the Santiago office of rivals Reuters – but on a half-day basis only. This did not pay enough for the broom cupboard she had been allotted as a room in the smart Hotel Carrera, so extra cash had to be earned.

Vernon Morgan, the venerable sports editor of Reuters, who had started the two of us on our Olympic and World Cup careers in Rome 1960, stepped in and phoned his good friend Sir Stanley. Barbara became the FIFA president's half-day secretary for the duration of the World Cup.

So, when the knock came on his door in Kensington, I was welcomed and when the Mayes madness was outlined to him he simply shut his door and said: "Follow me. This will not take long."

Minutes later, Mayes had been ordered to accredit us, but he managed one last act of defiance. On the bottom of each identity card was scrawled in black ink: "This person must not be allowed near a telephone at Wembley Stadium." The man was crackers!

The World Cup itself was uneventful news-wise in the early stages, although on the second day we all enjoyed a trip into the world of James Bond and finished on the *You Only Live Twice* film set with Sean Connery.

It was an occasion which highlighted the old adage favoured by news executives when reminding staff about standards of dress – "You never know where you might be sent. Maybe Buck House." (During 30 years in Fleet Street, the vast majority on the *Daily Mirror,* I never dreamt of attending the office in anything other than a suit and tie. And this applied to all reporters and photographers. Oh dear, how times have changed.)

The opening match, England vs Uruguay in front of the Queen, was a dull 0-0 draw but the following morning manager Alf Ramsey agreed the players deserved a fun break rather than extra training. I was among a handful of scribes who accompanied the England squad on the tour of the set at Pinewood Studios.

My lunchtime table companion, Alan Ball, suddenly spotted singer Lulu entering the room. He leapt up and gave her a bear hug. On return he said proudly: "The Queen and Lulu within 24 hours. Not bad for a lad from the back streets of Bolton. Good job I was dressed right."

Sir Stanley Rous ensured the five news hacks missed out on nothing. Each time he set out on an official function he would pass on the address. One famous evening he wandered through the foyer, beckoned me and said: "Mexican Embassy, just off Belgrave Square."

Our taxi arrived shortly after his car, and a pleasant Mexican welcome prompted an immediate introduction to the señor in charge of the tequila, who of course handed out proper measures with the lime and salt extras. Sir Stanley held a brief press conference so we had a few paragraphs to file, with the aside: "I better tell you now before this stuff takes control."

How right he was. It was when we returned yet again with empty glasses that the troubled barman explained he had been told no one should have more than four – "but as you are press we thought it better to keep you happy. But this will be your ninth tequila."

With this George Hunter uttered a rather disturbing giggle, crashed on to the nearest seat and declared: "I cannae feel ma legs." After observing that "bloody Scots cannae take their drink" I did, however, feel it was time to bid adios to our hospitable Mexican hosts.

The Royal Garden Hotel had the most comfortable public phone booths I have ever encountered, with a couch-like bench and little table. I remember having the clearest of heads as I carefully dialled through to copy and started dictating. But I had to admit that, Hunter-like, I was losing contact with my legs, and this feeling of numbness was gradually working northwards. I was 20 minutes behind Hunter, who was now a cot case.

The copytaker reminded me for years afterwards of how I started lucidly but then slipped into total gibberish: "Sir Stanley Rous, president of World Cup organisers FIFA, last night blasted critics of grrrambihatohopeta...". The tequila had taken hold, and the only consolation was that the Press Centre in the basement had a 24-hour bar, which allowed us to drink ourselves sober. McEwans bitter did the trick.

Being legless was a memory years later when one long lunch left me speechless – literally, I just couldn't speak. It happened in the Groucho Club in 1989 when long time *Mirror* editor Mike Molloy and I were suddenly joined at the bar by legendary thirsty scribe Jeffrey Bernard (who was far from unwell!) and his drinking companion, actor John Hurt.

To our surprise their immediate request was for a TV set to be placed on the bar so they could watch the marvellous grey Desert Orchid win the Cheltenham Gold Cup. Then the call for drinks kept coming, and coming, and...

Mike finally called for his office car and as we drove our mouths worked quite normally, but no words came forth. Drink had made us speechless.

Good old Sir Stanley. I was honoured to interview him at his Notting Hill home on his 90th birthday. After clambering across newly-delivered crates of expensive wine he glanced back and said, with a twinkle in his eye: "Oh yes. If I knew I was going to live so long I would have looked after myself."

Alcoholic refreshment in our trade was an unthinking part of its culture. Yes, looking back we certainly imbibed too much. As eldest daughter Catherine said after reading an early draft of this tome: "Every encounter or job you were on seemed to end with having a drink in the pub."

Yes, and more than one I'm afraid.

Like all good men Sir Stanley was brutally ousted from the FIFA presidency by politics. I was present at the FIFA executive meeting in Frankfurt on the eve of the 1974 World Cup when the knife hit his back.

The thorny problem at that time was South Africa, and a move by FIFA to expel the regime of apartheid from world soccer. Sir Stanley was against that, having lobbied successfully for several years that the world should not stop playing games with the country, despite abhorring its monstrous racist rulers.

The agenda in Frankfurt was expertly handled by his opponents. Standing against him for the presidency was Joao Havelange, of Brazil; the fifth motion on the agenda was the expulsion of South Africa; item seven was the application for full membership by several emerging African nations which had recently gained independence.

Frenzied lobbying by the Havelange camp assured them their vote for him would bring about the downfall of the hated South Africa; on the day Sir Stanley could only appeal in vain against an immediate motion to bring item seven forward to item four; it was carried so that the by then new full members could vote against on item five, which ousted South Africa and Sir Stanley, and hailed the start of Joao Havelange's long presidential reign.

Those sporting days of the 1970s had been good for this British sports news specialist. The president of the International Olympic Committee was Lord Michael Killanin, a wonderful Irishman who in his early life had been a Fleet Street correspondent, and was always available for a chat, while his predecessor had been Avery Brundage, who was equally approachable. And two pukka Englishmen, the Marquess of Exeter (he never travelled without a difficult jigsaw as he hated formal occasions) and Sir Stanley Rous, were the presidents of the International Amateur Athletics Federation and FIFA respectively.

Back at the 1966 World Cup, hospitality was a key word, with many veteran sports writers grabbing the opportunity to reciprocate welcomes they had received in foreign parts. None more so than my famous *Daily Mirror* colleague Peter Wilson, the columnist billed as "The Man They Can't Gag". He also saw it as a chance to meet his many readers.

He later wrote: "I pointed out to my editor Lee Howard that I had travelled the five continents and that wherever I had gone I had been royally entertained by my colleagues of the pen."

For each of the nine matches in England's group at Wembley and White City (England never played outside London) he set up his drinks table, alongside his Humber Snipe car, under a shady tree halfway down the thronged Olympic Way. No security, no barriers, just a sportswriter with an instantly recognisable face, standing behind a camping table covered with sumptuous food and booze to suit every palate -- in glasses (real ones, no plastic cups). On hand as always was his devoted American wife, Sally.

This wonderful gesture, of course paid for in full by the *Daily Mirror,* when it was a real, caring newspaper, managed to entertain just over 300 sportswriters from 20 countries.

Wilson outlined later: "Sally was magnificent – a female Fortnum and Mason. None of your meals-on-wheels stuff. She insisted on three courses: hot soup if we got a typical English July day, or melon hollowed out and enriched with port, or perhaps a shrimp cocktail; cold turkey, salmon, cold beef or lamb or the occasional game pie with salads and various kickshaws; strawberries and cream, chocolate mousse liberally laced with brandy, peaches in champagne, fruit salad and kirsch.

"The liquid side was my responsibility. Pimm's No 1 was the greeting drink, or sherry for the more serious-minded. Cooled white wine, or red at 'car temperature'. Lager, of course, Scotch, vodka or gin, with the various mixes. Tubs and containers of ice.

"'Claret is the liquor for boys, port for men; but he who aspires to be a hero...must drink brandy.' I think Dr Johnson would have been proud of our multi-national heroes; and our heroes seemed to find the brandy, among other things, very much to their taste."

Foreign journalists had been invited in advance, while *Daily Mirror* readers would doff their caps and make no attempt to move near unless invited by Wilson. There was not one moment of nastiness, no attempt by tattooed yobs of years to come to spoil the party. It remains one of my great 1966 memories.

Over the years I developed a close bond with Wilson, starting in 1964 when he suggested to the British Olympic Association

that I should be the GB team's press liaison officer at that
summer's Tokyo Games. The idea then was rejected but I finally
made it 36 years later and enjoyed the post at the Sydney and
Athens Olympics.

Wilson's gesture came after we had become involved in the
riotous medal celebrations at Innsbruck for Britain's gold medal
bobsleighers Tony Nash and Robin Dixon. Most of the bobsleigh
team were serving RAF and Army personnel and had enjoyed a
day of drink before the ceremony in the ice rink that evening.

When they were barred entry because the place was full there
ensued a fist fight with police. Peter Wilson summed it up in the
Daily Mirror: "The police acted like little Hitlers, which is not
surprising as the chap got his start here."

One of the regular visitors to the Wembley soirees was Jim
Rodger, a remarkable man who had started his working life as a
coal miner in Shotts, east of Glasgow, then turned his thoughts
to sports journalism and became the holder of the largest, and
most sought-after contacts book in Britain. "Wee Jum" knew
everybody and was totally respected by leaders in many walks of
life, not just sport.

I witnessed on more than one occasion the then Prime
Minister Harold Wilson arrive at a railway station, and
momentarily bypass the welcoming committee to greet the
smiling, rotund gentleman on the fringe of the crowd: "Wee Jim,
it is great to see you again."

When there was a major transfer involving a top Scottish
player, Wee Jim would be consulted. He helped take Alan
Gilzean to Tottenham Hotspur; when all scribes were desperate
to know where Charlie Nicholas would end up, with Liverpool
favourites, I spotted Jim Rodger at a Wembley international.
When asked where Nicholas was going, Wee Jim simply pointed
in the direction of the seats behind the Royal Box and whispered:
"John, just see who Wee Jum has made sure he is sitting next to."

It was Terry Neill, the manager of Arsenal, and sure enough
it was Wee Jim who had helped write Nicholas' signature on a
contract with the Gunners.

I first encountered Jim Rodger at the Royal Garden Hotel in 1966, and was pleased to find he accepted me as a colleague worth confiding in. "Just stick with the Wee Jum" was his suggestion.

For nearly 30 years I did just that. On one of the last days in 1966, with England already in the final, I was passing those comfortable phone booths, when a door flew open and I was hauled inside by this podgy hand. Jim whispered, with the customary twinkle in his eye: "Just listen to the Wee Jum."

With that he proceeded to dictate to his Glasgow office the exclusive information that Jack Charlton's wife was expecting a baby at the same time as Big Jack would be doing his stuff for the country on the Wembley turf. He was dead right, and perhaps this story told more about Jim Rodger than any other. Jack Charlton had told few people.

At this point I am unable to reminisce about the glorious 4-2 victory over West Germany - Geoff Hurst's hat-trick, the controversial "was the ball over the line?" third goal, and all that. Sorry, but believe it or not, I wasn't there. I was several thousand miles away in Kingston, Jamaica.

In fact, I only attended one World Cup final. And that was the first in 1962, Brazil vs Czechoslovakia in Santiago's National Stadium, which was later converted into a notorious prison camp when Chile sank into years of violent political mayhem.

In later years, especially in West Germany '74, Argentina '78 and USA '94, when England did not qualify, it was not worth the hassle for a newsman from a non-participating nation to apply for a ticket.

Perhaps it was the joy at this final breakthrough in my hard-fought battle over the reporting of sports news that drove me to Heathrow Airport and the BOAC flight to Kingston, rather than another drink with Peter Wilson on the road to Wembley and a treasured press seat for England's great day?

Barbara and I had been asked by John Farrow, the hard drinking but brilliant-at-his-job London sports editor of AP, to join him at the then British Empire and Commonwealth Games.

We had impressed him in Chile and at the 1964 Innsbruck
and Tokyo Games. But it meant abandoning the World Cup
immediately after the semi-final win over Portugal.

Mind you, there was an initial barrage of hiccups. Our VC10
plane developed an engine fault on take-off and we had to wait
for a replacement part to be flown in from Hong Kong. We were
put up in a hotel for the night, but due to the bookings for the
World Cup the nearest available rooms were in Southampton.

The following day we were taken for a tour of the docks,
where the flight attendant in charge used the only means of
communication, a public phone box, to check whether it was
time for us to head back to London. She reversed the charge, and
her office refused to accept it. Another delay.

With us was my *Sun* and later *Daily Mirror* colleague Frank
Taylor, who was the only writer to survive the 1958 Munich air
crash, which killed most of Matt Busby's great Manchester United
team. Eight years on he had completed his book, *The Day A Team
Died*, and was only too keen to get you to read it.

Once we were strapped in for a second time in the plane which
had already lost an engine part, he hobbled back (the crash left
him with one leg shorter than the other, rectified by a big boot)
with a copy, which needless to say had its fair share of pictures
of wreckage on the Munich runway and great footballers and
sportswriters recovering or dying in hospital.

It was of a strange interest to my neighbour who was returning
to Jamaica for a family funeral, with his only carry-on hand
baggage being a wreath which he placed under his seat. A total
comfort, all round! Each time we hit turbulence, I could envisage
the intro: "A wreath floating across the waves was the only
evidence of... "

And worse was to come. On arrival in the middle of the night
we were driven to the Myrtle Bank Hotel in downtown Kingston
to be told: "Welcome, but there is a problem. Because of your
lateness we have given your rooms to somebody else."

A drive then to a small bed and breakfast in the outskirts was made bearable when the immensely large landlady, who initially showed resentment, lit the dawn with a sparkling smile as she spotted Frank Taylor struggling to release himself from the back seat of the car, a straw hat perched on his head. "Welcome Big Daddy," she exclaimed.

We didn't bother going to bed as we realised in the nick of time, that with the time difference they were about to kick off at Wembley. We huddled around a small radio and found that Radio Jamaica was relaying the BBC commentary. But no one had told the local technicians that there would be extra time if the score was level after 90 minutes.

So, with the score 2-2 at the final whistle, our radio returned to local music. It was several hours before we learned the wonderful result, and then, it would be fair to say, large amounts of rum managed to drive away all signs of tiredness.

From that day on, until his death in 2002, I only ever addressed Frank Taylor as Big Daddy. He was a very successful president of the International Sportswriter's Federation, AIPS, and we had many a good time around the globe. He never allowed his injuries to hamper his ambitions and was an inspiration to many young journalists. One funny incident stands out.

On the way to the 1964 Tokyo Olympics Frank stopped over in Hong Kong and made a point of ordering some cheap suits. He stressed the situation with his legs and was assured more than once there would be no problem, and everything would be awaiting his return flight.

As promised the suits were ready, but there had been a problem. Frank came out flapping one leg with the trouser a good inch or so too long, while the other had the bottom halfway up his shin. They had reversed the legs.

Jamaica was a resounding success for Associated Press, thanks to a Jackson. And I am delighted to say it was Barbara who unearthed the exclusive that enabled her to reveal to the world the details of the first ever sex test at a world sporting event.

It was a quiet day before the Games had begun and the

Farrow-Jackson team was scratching around for the usual preliminary feature stories to keep our New York office happy. We decided to spend a lunchtime in the athletes' village, with Barbara sent to nose around in the segregated women's section, while Farrow and I headed off to interview the two superstars of the moment – Australian runner Ron Clarke, and the long-distance Kenyan police inspector, Kipchoge Keino.

We immediately drew a blank in both camps, and as was always possible, finished up drinking too much Guinness (especially in the middle of a very hot Jamaican day) in the office of the Northern Ireland boxing manager.

Naughtily we forgot Barbara, probably surmising she would be partaking in girlie chat away from the heat and male antics. How wrong we were.

We found her standing at the main gates, both hot and bothered, and not too happy at either our lateness or non-sobriety. Once she had explained what she had witnessed, urgent work plans went into action.

When she had entered the village at around noon Barbara had found all the athletes standing in a long line – wearing only their nightdresses. Further investigation was greatly helped when she found an old friend, Britain's wonderfully glamorous and then reigning Olympic long jump champion, Mary Rand. She explained that each woman had been told to wear only a nightie and wait her turn under the blazing noon-day sun.

At the entrance to a large building, team managers were ready to escort them inside where they stood in front of a table, behind which sat three, stern faced doctors. Then followed the instruction to raise the nightie well above their head, and the doctors visually inspected the body. They judged whether the person was female by a simple look at the necessary parts.

Mary Rand, who never left any doubt that she was all woman from the top of her head to her little toe, explained: "I was met by team manager Marea Hartmann. I was led in, lifted my nightie and heard the panel mutter in unison 'Oooh'."

One young athlete was told she would be banned. The heartbreaking reason: "They said I had very little to show up top."

The first ever sex test. With great exclusives like this one needs a bit of luck. Ours arrived immediately with the appearance alongside us of Dr Joseph Blonstein, the long-time doctor with the British boxing authorities. He knew me well, and I knew he loved seeing his name in print. He not only stood up the story but launched into a long attack on this method of judging gender. Brilliant, we had the lot.

Our problem then was to keep the story from the opposition, mainly arch rivals Reuters. This was not easy as the large Press Centre had been partitioned off into small square offices, with conversation quite audible over each wall. Barbara dictated in a whisper to John Farrow at a typewriter, following which he arranged for a telex line to whisk the exclusive to New York. Heroine-grams quite rightly followed.

This sex test did not cause a major sensation, as within the British Commonwealth there was none of the hanky panky and medical manoeuvring commonplace in Eastern Europe, which had prompted such tests in the first place.

A few weeks later at the European Athletic Championships in Italy, the procedure was substituted by a vaginal inspection and, lo and behold, several of the top "female" champions from behind the Iron Curtain not only failed to turn up but were never heard of again. Strange that! (It was third time lucky for the medical experts, when they introduced the simple inner cheek swab test that we know today.)

Two notable absentees in Italy were the formidable Soviet "sisters", Tamara and Irina Press, who had dominated the field events and pentathlon in the 1960 and 1964 Olympics. They were frightening, but obviously sad sights.

At an international meeting at the White City, with the Queen sitting just a few feet away, I was forced to move as Tamara set off purposefully from the shot putt area toward an exit obviously closed off for security reasons.

A brave commissionaire stepped forward to attempt to point out to this Russian visitor the alternative route to the locker rooms. Tamara did not break stride. With the feeblest of flicks, her right hand hit him in the midriff, he left the ground and flew backwards to a landing among the banks of flowers around the Queen. The monster in red walked through the iron barrier as if it was paper.

Mary Rand told of a horrific incident at the Rome Olympics when, while taking a shower in the women's village, the curtain was suddenly ripped back by the two Press sisters, who appeared to slaver as they ogled her naked body.

Barbara's Jamaican exclusive was well deserved for a brilliant journalist who had led the way earlier for AP at Tokyo. Her by-line dominated the early features on the AP world wire, once again through her capacity to get into the women's village and find good stories.

Mind you, the star of that area turned out to be a fellow British journalist – and a man. Dear Desmond Hackett, the old rogue in the brown bowler who dominated the sports columns of the *Daily Express,* was always thinking. He arrived in Japan with a white smock and stethoscope in his luggage.

Accreditations in those days were a far cry from the bar coded, laminated, security tags that hang round necks today. It was a simple card announcing the holder as "D. Hackett, GBR". Hackett carefully added a small "r", donned his smock and stethoscope, and entered the women's section as Dr Hackett. The British girls went along with this as dear old Des was a real charmer.

He later penned one of the great lines to brighten up what can be routine copy before the Olympic action gets underway. He wrote: "These Japanese are so polite, even the pigeons flew upside down over the Emperor at the Opening Ceremony."

While on the subject of weird items carried in Hackett's luggage, I am reminded of his many long transatlantic flights to cover the great world championship fights involving all the greats from Joe Louis and Rocky Marciano, to Muhammad Ali and Joe Frazier.

In those early days of the late 1950/60s, several of the American States were dry - not only on the ground but in the air above also. So when flying between major cities there were regular announcements such as: "As we are now flying over Nebraska, a dry state, the bar will be closed until we cross the border into..."

With that, Hackett and his regular travelling companion Peter Wilson would reach into their overnight bags and pull out – toy fire engines. A steward was summoned and two glasses of water ordered. Into that was siphoned the whisky which filled the tanks of both engines. Neat, eh?

IMPORTANT PHONE CALLS

Sudden calls to newspaper offices can often be the start of
something big. Not ones where people are after payment, but
those that can be a cry for help, a straight gesture to provide
information, or a situation where a personal grievance is involved.
Adventures can follow, to typify my enjoyment of waking in the
morning wondering where I might finish up.

One rainy afternoon I answered a crackly call from a man
holed up in a large hotel in northern Majorca. At first there was
every indication it was yet another "horror holiday" outburst, the
type that complained about package accommodation, no full-
length mirrors, noisy discos, and beaches considerably further
away than suggested in the brochure. Ho hum – but hang on a
moment.

He explained that he and his two children were locked in their
fifth-floor room because fellow holidaymakers were not allowing
them out. Why? Well, his wife had fallen over the balcony, was
lying dead by the pool, and other guests believed he had helped
her on her way.

They were saying he had murdered his wife? Yes, and he
couldn't get to the British or Spanish authorities to explain the
full story. Could I help? An instant trip to sunny Majorca on a
good story – of course I could.

Photographer Peter Stone and I flew into Palma in the dark,
hired a car to drive the full width of the island, and discovered
we did not have a clue when it came to turning on the lights.
Time was important so we had to keep going. The sound of
a police motorcycle siren soon pulled us over. We explained
our predicament, he peeled off his gloves and had a look, then
explained with sign language that he was equally clueless and led
us to a garage.

On arrival at the hotel, hunger and thirst had driven the baying
guests away from our man's door, but he was still confined. He
demonstrated every detail of his wife going over the edge, while
I managed to gain him access to British consulate personnel who

soon had the whole situation under control.

A drive back to Palma was necessary as films could not be wired with the ease of today. Departing passengers readily agreed, in those carefree days before strict security alerts, to carry the films for collection in London. And then Stoney attempted in vain to get me involved in some grab-a-granny contest. No thanks!

This finished as a quick two-nighter, a front page exclusive, and an acceptable conclusion for the poor man who had lost his wife. There was never any doubt that the whole horror scenario had been a complete accident.

There were lighter moments when you found celebrities on the other end of the line.

Spike Milligan, for instance, that comic genius/zany Goon. He phoned to say how he was looking forward to appearing in two separate West End shows that evening – "and don't forget to come and watch, folks, hum diddly dum".

As that was the complete message there was every inclination to dismiss it as Milligan after a good lunch. But that was not his style.

After only a couple of phone calls I discovered that a stage musical version of Alan Sillitoe's famous novel *Saturday Night and Sunday Morning* was about to be previewed at the Prince of Wales theatre. The director had a problem, however, as comedian Bill Maynard was otherwise engaged for the first few nights. This meant they urgently needed a stand-in comedian for the 15-minute bar scene which closed the first half.

Yes, no reward for guessing, Milligan "volunteered". He was appearing with great success in *Son of Oblomov* at the nearby Comedy Theatre and worked out that the interval in his show coincided to the second with the bar scene.

Photographer Ron Burton and I arrived at the stage door of the Comedy, explained to the doorman how we had been invited by Spike Milligan to witness his double act, and were promptly informed: "You know he's mad, don't you? When he comes off stage I won't bother to let him know you are here: waste of time. The other night Peter Sellers popped in to see his old Goon chum and Milligan shouted, 'Never heard of him,'and left through the front entrance."

As we spoke, Milligan was on stage, lying in a bed, as he did throughout the show, wearing a nightgown and a Wee Willie Winkie hat with tassel. As the curtain came down on the first half, he leapt out of the bed, brushed past Burton and me, and started wandering up the centre of Oxendon Street as if he was sleep walking.

To complete the lunacy, he was followed by the Australian comedian Bill Kerr ("I've only got four minutes" was his famous catchphrase) in the costume of a Russian serf. A bemused policeman who stopped to stare, was greeted with "What the hell am I doing here, folks?" from Milligan.

Into the foyer of the Prince of Wales he strode – and it then became patently clear Milligan had not informed anyone of his intention. He stripped off his nightgown and Wee Willie Winkie hat, to reveal a cowboy shirt and jeans. With that he strode through the wings and straight on to the stage.

There was then this wonderful collection of bemused stares from both sides of the footlights. The *Saturday Night and Sunday Morning* cast, with a brave "the show must go on" attitude, wondered what the hell he was doing, well aware that nothing was impossible; the audience couldn't decide whether it was all part of the play.

Milligan, with Bill Kerr still in tow, ignored all. He grabbed the central microphone and sang: "I once met a man named Maria/Oh what a funny name/It'll never be the same again." With that he fell flat on his back as if dead. The curtain was brought down hurriedly.

Spike Milligan suggested the cast "had no right in my room", then pulled on his nightgown and hat, sauntered with his Russian serf back to the smaller theatre – and clambered back in bed for the second half of his show. Milligan was certainly a one off.

A totally different aspect of comedy was set in place when
I took a call from a man who introduced himself as Romark.
Full name Ronald Markham, member of the Magic Circle and
little-known hypnotist on the music hall and working men's club
circuit.

I was mentally flicking through all the different ways of
curtailing the call when he explained that he would like
me to know he was about to put a curse on Crystal Palace
Football Club. The year was 1976 and the club's manager was
the flamboyant Malcolm Allison, he of big cigars, constant
champagne and a favourite of Playboy Bunnies.

Big Mal had guided the then Third Division club to the semi-
final of the FA Cup to meet Southampton, and at the same time
was battling hard to gain promotion for the south Londoners into
Division Two. But why was this hypnotist, certainly unknown to
me, so uptight about the situation?

Romark had been around for years, latterly in South Africa,
where he had mastered an end-of-show technique which involved
hanging himself, as in execution, on stage. He told me he had
suffered a stroke, which came as no surprise when you have been
hanged nightly, twice on Wednesdays and Saturdays.

He had recovered almost completely but had been left with
a rather unfortunate facial twitch which he appeared unable to
control, especially at times of stress. And, wow, did we have some
stressful times ahead.

It transpired Romark had contacted Crystal Palace by both
letter and phone to offer to hypnotise the players into winning the
FA Cup at Wembley, and then gaining promotion. But his letters
remained unanswered, his phone calls were never transferred to
anyone of importance – so he well and truly got the hump.

And phoned me, having noticed I wrote sports news stories.
He alleged he had earlier hypnotised the Millwall team and
"helped" them into Division Two.

My *Mirror* stories of this man who had put a curse on a football
team he was trying to help prompted our rivals at the *Sun* to try

to sabotage the situation. But, at least then, Romark would have nothing to do with it.

However, Southampton beat Crystal Palace, and went on to win the Cup, and a defeat away to Chester scuppered the last chance for Crystal Palace and Malcolm Allison to end the season with any glory.

Now was the time to strike. I had to bring Romark and Allison face to face. Hang on to your hats. I confirmed that Allison, his team and the national football writers had overnighted in Chester and were returning by train at around noon that day.

Romark, photographer Albert Foster and I were on the platform at Euston as the train pulled in. It was not hard to spot Allison, customary champagne glass and cigar aloft as he held court with his then assistant manager, Terry Venables, and a bevy of Fleet Street scribes.

First off the train was my colleague Nigel Clarke, who asked "Is that Romark?", and when I indicated in the affirmative with a nod of my head, muttered: "Oh, fuck", and hurriedly headed off up the platform as if he was returning to Chester.

Malcolm Allison, expensive coat draped as usual around his shoulders and fedora on his head, stepped from the train to be greeted by me: "Malcolm, I would like to introduce Romark."

Now this was a major moment of stress and Romark's twitch was in overdrive as he made the first move: "I am here as a friend. I want to lift the curse."

With station porters and passengers gathering with stunned expressions, the conversation continued:

An incredibly angry Allison: "You are nothing but a toad. You c…. You 'orrible c…. How can you help me?"

A twitching Romark, stepping backwards under the onslaught: "If you had shown some courtesy by answering my letters and speaking to me on the phone, I could have controlled your destiny."

Allison, whose fist was rising and would have no doubt struck a major blow of satisfaction if Foster's camera had not been flashing away on motor drive: "Control my destiny, you c.... You can't even control your own fucking face."

With that the twitch prompted a moment of silence, but Romark hit back: "I was successful with Millwall, but now I know you are going to be axed from Palace."

Allison was whisked away by Venables and his entourage, and a breathless Romark suggested: "I think I won."

It was a great story for me, but I did feel genuinely sorry for Malcolm Allison. Nigel Clarke told me later they had all fallen into the nearest pub where Allison broke down in tears and asked: "Why should I have to be humiliated by such people?" I could understand that.

That I thought would be it with Romark, but oh no. Allison and Crystal Palace were only the hors d'oeuvres; he had his sights now on plonking a curse on the biggest sporting fish of all – Muhammad Ali.

"I have proved my powers with Malcolm Allison. Now I am going to show my genius with Muhammad Ali-son," he declared with a triumphant twitch. This could be fun.

Ali was then at his height as the greatest heavyweight boxing champion ever to rule the world and was disposing of opponents with ease in different parts of the globe. The British champion at the time, when perhaps it would not be unkind to suggest there was a certain lack of talent around, was an affable Yorkshireman called Richard Dunn. Ali accepted the former paratrooper as a challenger for his crown, and a bout was set for Munich.

Fresh from his success with Crystal Palace, Romark phoned to ask if I could arrange a meeting with Dunn so he could hypnotise him. This would ensure Dunn defeated The Greatest, "probably in eight rounds", and return to the Yorkshire Moors in triumph as the king of the world's heavyweight boxers. Oh dear, but what a good story.

When this revelation reached the public domain the *Sun* tried everything again to discredit my man. They published a suggestion that Romark was an arch phoney and boasted totally false qualifications from Harley Street. I advised Romark to ignore this, but when *Sun* reporter Hilary Bonner managed to contact him by phone, his twitch went berserk again and he gave a quote which had to make a page lead. "I hope you get cancer," he told her.

I was forced to tell him he was a prat to have done that, especially as Bonner was then, and still is, a great pal of mine. Now a very successful author, I certainly list her as one of the great ladies of Fleet Street.

We were news rivals at the 1980 Moscow Olympics where, when not beating us all with vivid descriptions of the action on the nightly "Love Train" between Moscow and Leningrad (now St Petersburg), she was our social secretary who arranged evenings in top restaurants, even the famous Bolshoi Theatre.

The train was given the love tag as, in those hard days of Communism, with large families confined to tiny apartments, young couples could only "get at it" by seeking the freedom of a train compartment. A natural story for our Hils!

She is also credited with one of the greatest put-down lines in journalistic history. Bonner, a near 6ft tall woman with a heavy tread, especially when on a mission to bash the ear of an editor or executive, was approached by her *Sun* colleague Harry Arnold, he of small stature and four wives.

In what is now a treasured item of Fleet Street folklore, he allegedly said: "Hils, I'd love to fuck you." To which Bonner, gazing down on the shortest of the Royal rat pack, replied: "Harry, if you do, and I get to know about it, I will be very cross."

But back to Romark. Richard Dunn was duly contacted and I arranged to introduce Romark to him at his training camp in Leicester. Again, with Albert "Old Sport" Foster as snapper, we drove to the compact upstairs gymnasium, situated down a short side street opposite a small supermarket.

Romark commenced his "therapy" by placing Dunn in a

trance and proceeded to apparently pull a needle right through his rather thick wrist. Oh dear, what had I got myself into now?

Dunn came back to life, shook his head and appeared to have no effects. Romark then said he would require a young female to assist him. Now, boxing training camps, especially down Leicester back streets, are not a normal gathering point for young women.

I glanced out of the window and spotted two young assistants standing outside their supermarket, obviously trying to discover what was happening. The memory of what came next can bring a shudder down my spine. But anything for a good story.

I wandered out and asked slightly built 20-year-old Gail Loughran whether she would like to meet Britain's champion heavyweight boxer. And I added that if she was willing to assist us get some special pictures of him, she would be rewarded with £5. She readily agreed, although like me she was totally unaware what lay (literally!) ahead.

Romark explained he wanted to hypnotise her into believing she was an iron bar, so he could lay her rigid body across between the tops of two chairs, back of head on one and heels on the other, to make a bench for Richard Dunn to sit on. Fingers crossed here!

Romark placed the girl's arms by her side, muttered some mumbo jumbo, and declared: "You are an iron bar." She was out, totally under his spell. Gail weighed eight-stones. We lifted her carefully into position like a wooden plank, and the 15-stone frame of Dunn promptly sat on her, his feet dangling freely above the ground.

I had visions of this poor girl breaking in two, but fortunately everything went according to plan, and seconds later more mumbo jumbo brought her back to us and she was smiling happily. Then came the killer punch.

"Sorry about this, old sport. My flash didn't work. Have to be done again," said Foster. Before I could say "You must be jo...", Romark had repeated his iron bar command, the girl was back across the chairs, Dunn had taken another seat and it was all over. Never has £5 been so deserved.

The scene then moved to fight day in Munich. As with Malcolm Allison, I had to introduce Romark to Muhammad Ali. The best opportunity arose at the joint press conference given together by the two boxers, when all the international boxing writers could understand every word of Ali's southern drawl, but heads were scratched and an interpreter requested to translate Dunn's broad Yorkshire accent.

I kept Romark well at the back of the hall, firstly to stop him saying something unprompted and stupid so ruining our exclusive, and secondly to prevent opposition scribes, especially my long-time buddy Colin Hart from the *Sun* ("Jacko, my old son, what skulduggery are you up to now?" I could hear him shouting) spotting him and wanting their own story.

Luck was with me, as Dunn left the hall immediately followed by the British contingent, while Ali stayed behind to participate in a live link with a TV station in Las Vegas.

While the feed was being secured Ali continued with his limbering up exercises, determined to keep his body in shape for the fight in a few hours. With his hands on hips, he gently pushed his body from side to side. I watched with fascination, going over in my mind the best time to make my move with Romark.

Suddenly all thoughts were off, and panic set in. Unknown to me Romark had edged forward and in the most amazing way had become entangled with the world's best boxer, sending alarm bells ringing around his battalion of minders.

Romark had obviously intended to speak to Ali, but somehow managed to get his head through the triangle formed by his arm and hip exercise.

Ali had glanced down, spotted this strange twitching face under his armpit, and immediately grabbed him in a headlock. Fortunately, he instantly realised there was no danger and released him as I leapt forward to declare: "Muhammad, please meet the man who is going to hypnotise Dunn to take away your title."

Before even the Louisville Lip could utter, a by now very shaken Romark, his face drained of all colour and twitching away, shouted: "I put a curse on you." As Ali gave every intention of saying something, Romark appeared to go mad and raged: "This is not a man; this is a god."

With this Ali, fortunately, recognised a harmless nutter, raised his hands above his head and advanced like a ghost, whispering in an eerie tone: "Yeah, a black God."

My immediate escape plans were rendered unnecessary when someone shouted the TV link was up and running, and more than one American voice ordered: "Get him out o' here." I led a shambling Romark back to the hotel and told him to have a good lie down before we went off to the stadium for the fight.

While I enjoyed necessary refreshment to recover from this encounter, the bar was suddenly filled by the massive frame of Ali's great friend and minder, Dandini Brown. He asked: "Where's the goddam witch doctor? He's casting his spells." I assured him there was no problem as the person in question was sleeping, but of course I was eager to know the reason for his interest.

It transpired that from the interviews the boxers had proceeded to the official weigh-in. All was going well until Ali and his entourage stepped into the ring, and the whole thing collapsed under them. Fortunately, no one was injured.

Romark's response on hearing this was: "I told him so. I put a curse on him." And I finished with a wonderful *Daily Mirror* front page, showing the collapsing party under the headline "Ali-Oops". Brilliant! Needless to say, Richard Dunn was disposed of by an early knockout.

This, I thought, would be the end of Romark. It had been fun while it lasted, and we had benefited with excellent copy. How wrong I was. He obviously wished to keep up this free, fun publicity.

He phoned one morning to ask me to meet him, so he could put himself in a trance, take his body and mind back to the

Pharaoh times – and tell me exclusively where police could find the Yorkshire Ripper. This was the time of the massive hunt for the serial killer.

It just happened that a TV crew was in our office at that time, wanting to film an offbeat story for a series on newspapers. Romark was thrilled to know his expertise would be on camera – and off he went to be reunited with his Pharaoh chums.

He muttered some gibberish about walking down a country lane near Heckmondwike, but was so unconvincing he made neither screen nor paper. That surely must be it?

Oh no. In October 1977, after several months of no contact, Romark phoned to say he would demonstrate his new powers by driving blindfold down a main street in Ilford, Essex.

Photographer Charlie Ley and I found him in Cranbrook Road, with representatives from the local paper. It was immediately obvious he had not informed the police or local authorities of this publicity venture.

He told the rapidly growing band of shoppers that I was the only the person he would trust to ensure he was "blind". He placed a 10p piece over each eye, plastered on a large slice of dough to wedge the coins in place, then had me tie a black band tightly round his eyes. It was obvious he couldn't see as I guided him to the driving door of his small rental car.

While he arranged himself in the seat, groped for the ignition key and gears, a police Black Maria pulled up in front of him. Out stepped an inspector, sergeant and dog handler, interested in discovering what had drawn such a crowd.

Before they could utter "Hello, hello..." Romark was in gear and off. It took literally seconds, but he played a blinder.

He only travelled a matter of several feet, but in those few seconds managed to miss by a whisker an elderly woman halfway across a zebra crossing – and then smashed straight into the rear of the police vehicle. The coppers covered their faces and muttered: "Oh no".

Then they were on Romark like a flash. I must say that he had proved he could not drive a car blindfold, and his curses had not proved successful – but his magician's sleight of hand was up to scratch.

When the fuss had died down (it cost Romark a summons for reckless driving plus £200 damage to his car) and I reached into my pocket for my own car keys, I came out with two lumps of dough, with 10p coins embedded in them. He had ripped them off before the police reached his car, but how they got in my pocket I will never know.

Romark incidentally told the police, to no avail: "That van was parked in a place that logic told me it wouldn't be. I'm told by a qualified driving instructor that you broke the law on three counts – parking at a bus stop, on a double yellow line and six feet from road works."

That really was the end, as things went from bad to worse for Romark. He was jailed for three years for plundering his dying mother's fortune, then died in October 1982, four weeks after leaving prison. As for the pair he cursed – Malcolm Allison hit hard times before dying a lonely death, and Muhammad Ali succumbed in the end to Parkinson's Disease.

Sunday mornings were often the time, and may remain so, when a productive phone tip was best received. Sunday was always the leanest news day, with many hold-able stories filed away earlier as a "good Sunday for Monday". Canny public relations firms will use a Sunday for a major announcement as they realise they have more chance of making the newspapers.

So there was hope, rather than the usual dread of having to talk to another possibly discontented reader, when the news desk transferred a call early one Sunday morning in November 1981.

The angry comment from the other end of the line attracted immediate interest (especially for a lifelong Arsenal fan like me): "I'm a Spurs supporter, and well and truly pissed off."

This was the weekend when a new move in professional football was tried for the first time. All top club fixtures, held only on Saturdays then, were called off so England manager Ron

Greenwood could gather his international squad in one place to ensure they were fit and well for a World Cup qualifying fixture against Hungary at Wembley on Wednesday. This sort of move is automatic now.

But I could understand the frustration of the caller: "I live for my football every Saturday afternoon, and I travel the country with Tottenham. But when Greenwood said he wanted the lads to relax together for fitness I knew it was right.

"So what do I think when I continue drowning my sorrows at a club near our White Hart Lane ground and early on Sunday morning I am joined by Clemence, Hoddle, Shilton and Sansom, surrounded by booze and birds? Hoddle, my idol, is well gone and dancing with everything in a skirt. When I said to him that he should be training, he replied 'I am training.'"

So here were England's two best goalkeepers, Ray Clemence and Peter Shilton, and London players Glenn Hoddle and Kenny Sansom, obviously out on the town when they should have been tucked up at the team's hotel out in the Hertfordshire countryside.

I caught up with the squad the following morning after a training session, and these four players stepped from their coach with no apparent sign of fatigue. But none of them had the energy to say anything when I approached and asked why they had been drinking and dancing the night away in Tottenham. Clemence and Hoddle fled in horror when they realised their secret was out.

Ron Greenwood was totally puzzled as he had been assured they were in bed when checked at midnight. After investigating he sought me out to explain that they had been "very silly boys". Records will show that three days later only one of the night owls made the starting line-up – Shilton.

Other than when travelling to England's away matches, I had little contact with Clemence and Sansom after that. But Hoddle obviously bore a grudge against me. Tottenham Hotspur were riding high in the early 1980s and six months after our encounter Hoddle and his team won through to a second successive FA Cup Final at Wembley.

The *Mirror* wanted a profile piece on what this success (Spurs won the Cup on both occasions) meant to a top player, listing all the money and perks that would come his way.

Hoddle was the obvious candidate, and there was no one better in the world to arrange this than my colleague photographer Monte Fresco. Not only was he a fanatical Spurs fan, but everyone in the sports world who knew him, trusted him.

Fresco duly did all the arranging and we were to meet Hoddle at his home. Unknown to me Hoddle had not been told the name of the reporter accompanying Fresco. As we were leaving the office Monte said it would be a good move to phone and mention we were on the way. I heard him say: "Jacko and I are leaving the office..." and then a look of shock took over.

Hoddle it appeared had shown his total lack of humour and man management skills, borne out later by his failures as manager of England and his beloved Spurs. I gather his comment was short and to the point: "If it's that c..., everything's off."

So, the news editor decided a woman's touch might help, and sent Jill Palmer instead. Her female charm counteracted her earlier hobby of writing the programme notes for her favourite team, Leyton Orient.

Peter Shilton was a completely different animal. His love of gambling and the opposite sex brought him a fair share of headlines, but he was a character who accepted this came with the territory for an international soccer star, the best goalkeeper in the world who played 125 times for his country (what would the figure have been if there had not been the spell when he rotated appearances with Ray Clemence?).

There aren't many famous people who have crashed their Jaguar into a lamppost when their passenger was a married woman and they were being chased by her husband.

I have a soft spot for Shilton, not only because he was always approachable but because my last story in the *Daily Mirror* was an exclusive centre-page spread on his latest catastrophe, and it appeared on March 17, 1993 – the day I was fired. Once again it came about as a result of a phone call.

An employee of a building society in Derby said he could supply documents to show Shilton was in dire financial straits with his mortgage and was about to lose one of the four luxury homes he owned. He was six months in arrears, owed £15,000 and the Abbey National wanted £9,600 immediately or he could be evicted from the large home at Chilworth, near Southampton.

Shilton was then player-manager of Plymouth Argyle, earning a reported £3,000 a week. When I knocked on the door of the large house he was renting with his wife and two sons near Yelverton, Devon, there was every indication there was no one at home. But Shilton suddenly appeared at the back door to brush aside questions about his private life.

I returned to London to clear up the loose ends of the story. There was no immediate urgency as I had the story to myself and the Abbey National end had to be further explored.

I adjourned to Vagabonds, the *Mirror*'s drinking den, where a familiar visiting face belonged to old chum Hugh McIlvanney, top sportswriter with the *Observer* and then *Sunday Times*.

"How did you find Shilton?" he asked as we shook hands. Now I knew he was a terrific writer, but had he taken up clairvoyance? As I spluttered some sort of reply in the what-nonsense-are-you-talking-but how-did-you find-out vein he explained he had lunched at the Savoy with Jon Holmes, Shilton's agent. Their enjoyment was spoiled by a hurried call from Shilton to report "Jackson's sniffing around".

Another Sunday, another transferred call, and another chase after a "bad boy". This time it was early in 1991, and the first word from the informant confirmed it was worthwhile. "Gazza..." – and I was all ears.

It was a somewhat similar situation to the four footballers 10 years earlier. Paul Gascoigne was allegedly recovering from a groin strain and high temperature, so Terry Venables, his manager at Tottenham Hotspur, rested him from the Saturday home club game, told him to put his feet up indoors, to ensure he would be fit for an England match against Cameroon on Wednesday.

Over the telephone came the news that "sick" Gazza had decided to play away with a mystery blonde at the fashionable and expensive Chicken Rib Shack, off London's Knightsbridge.

He guzzled Long Island Iced Tea (mind-blowing cocktail of tequila, vodka, rum, whisky, Cointreau and Coke – not recommended as halftime refreshment), threatened to smash "through your fucking face" the camera of a fellow diner and Spurs fan who had asked politely if he could take a quick snap, sang loudly along with the piped music, grunted ape-like noises and continually stuck out his tongue (that is when he was not leaning across the table to thrust it down the young blonde's throat), and fed his companion chicken pieces from the end of a fork. All in all, he was a thorough nuisance and labelled a "total yob" by my informant.

Off to the Chicken Rib Shack I had to go, with photographer Bill Kennedy. For research purposes we had to sample Long Island Tea. I think it fair to say that after two I could certainly play for England.

The story made a good page lead, and next day I had to field the calls from readers eager to identify the blonde. There were several names given, but the general consensus, which turned out to be correct, was that we had just witnessed the first real outing between Gazza and his future wife, Sheryl.

On Wednesday evening I was at Wembley early to keep my usual hooligan watch. About to cross the road near the stadium I was suddenly conscious that the car nearest to the zebra crossing appeared to have accelerated. I stopped, to see my mate Gazza roar past, mouthing: "I'll get you, you bastard."

Later I was able to grab a quick word when he volunteered that his blonde companion had been his sister. "Oh, so you are into incest now. That's an even better story," I joked. He walked away with a puzzled expression – baffled, I am sure, by the word incest.

All was forgotten when I discovered him with his trousers down in the kitchens at the Savoy Hotel. Nothing sinister, he was simply trying to smarten his appearance for a meeting with Princess Diana. He had been ordered to watch his step, and for once in his life he did.

A few days before he had grabbed headlines by putting his arm around then Prime Minister Margaret Thatcher, but there was no way he was going to be allowed to make any bodily contact with this most famous Royal. Very simple, the event organisers just kept them apart.

The phone calls with more horror holidays banter keep coming. Be calm, listen carefully, as there is always the chance of a good story somewhere along the line – such as the case with the dead wife in Majorca.

This was certainly the case one Sunday morning in the early 1980s when a very cultured voice at the other end complained he had been delayed when returning by British Airways from an important business meeting in Washington, DC, "because the pilot refused to start the engines until a drunken Lester Piggott was removed from the plane".

Now we're talking. But who would have guessed my follow-up enquiries and resulting front page story might prompt "new evidence" in the trial that later sent this country's greatest jockey to jail for three years?

It appeared Piggott, who was approaching the end of a glittering career which had brought many a smile to battalions of punters over the years, had proved rather noisy when boarding the flight. He had won a major race the day before and, quite naturally, had enjoyed the odd glass of celebration.

After making the necessary checks with British Airways and received confirmation that he was now safely aboard the next flight and would touch down at Heathrow Airport only a few hours later than planned, I plucked up the courage to phone Mrs Piggott – the former Susan Armstrong.

Now Lester was never known to be the most cooperative of souls, but compared with his wife he was a regular Deep Throat.

Although I have never held any interest whatsoever in horse racing, I always enjoyed covering Royal Ascot and the Derby, in those good old days when it was held on a Wednesday and was the most colourful and enjoyable "working man's day out" of the year. Many a grandmother was "buried" on Derby Day!

The *Mirror* played a part in helping the event take its place at the very top of the world sporting calendar. The race immediately before the Derby at one time was the Andy Capp Handicap, sponsored by my paper and named after the great strip cartoon character brought to life everyday by the genius of Reg Smythe.

Needless to say, I kept an eye on the race for news stories and was never better rewarded than when the winning trainer was the legendary Sir Gordon Richards, the little man who rode the Derby winner in 1953, Coronation Year, when he was nearing the end of his career and heading for the title of "greatest jockey to never win the Derby".

The Andy Capp Handicap trophy was presented by Sandy Molloy, wife of *Mirror* editor Mike Molloy, who was thrilled to find herself congratulating the great Gordon. As she left the winner's circle she whispered to me, with a smile: "Look at his shoes."

Sir Gordon was immaculate in morning dress, complete with tails and top hat, which almost doubled his height. A quick glance at his footwear and I could see why Sandy was amused – he had one black shoe, and one brown.

When I confronted him for an explanation he had no hesitation in declaring: "It's all down to that bloody rabbit." It appeared he had been waiting for days to trap a rabbit which was causing a nuisance in his garden, close to the back door.

That very morning he heard a rustling: "I thought I've got you now, you little ba... bunny. I pulled the door open, let fly with my right foot, totally missed the brute, and kicked the step. My big toe was badly bruised, and in the hurry to get to Epsom I realised that only a brown shoe would allow me to walk."

But back to Lester Piggott, who, incidentally, as a 19-year-old won his first Derby in 1954, the year after old man Sir Gordon Richards.

As the newsman covering Derby Day, I always needed the first quote from the winning jockey, so made a habit of hovering near the finishing post, then haring down the course with stable lads to meet the horses cantering back.

This also meant I was always spotted on television, causing my Uncle Geoffrey in Leeds to report annually: "I know you're still alive, lad, as I saw you again with the Derby winner." Back in the office they had proof I was working rather than enjoying all that hospitality available.

To win the Derby is the highlight of their career for most jockeys, so there were always wonderful, off the cuff comments on the track, before the more formal, technical press conference with the racing hacks. Willie Carson, Walter Swinburn and their ilk were a delight, always lit up with a natural smile and busting to reveal their immediate pleasure.

But not old Stoneface. I spoke to Piggott as he returned to the winner's enclosure on six of his nine Derby winners (Sir Ivor, Nijinsky, Roberto, Empery, The Minstrel and finally, and magnificently, Teenoso, when he was two years away from his 50th birthday) but received nothing more than a cheerless "Fuck off", incomprehensible for many because, of course, Piggott has always suffered with a speech impediment. He seemed to have no perception that he and I were born in the same year.

So, it was with some trepidation that Sunday morning that I phoned the Piggott home at Newmarket. When I outlined what I knew about the delay, his removal and forced change to the later flight, the reply came back: "You have it totally wrong. My husband had no intention of returning home immediately. He has flown to the Bahamas on business."

"But Mrs Piggott, British Airways have confirmed everything, and I can assure you...".

"What did you say your name was?" came the curt cut-off question.

"John Jackson."

"John Jackson, you are a c…," and slam went the phone.

Needless to say, the opinion of my news desk was that her comment was spot on. Piggott arrived at Heathrow and said, believe it or not, nothing. Story over.

It made a good tale for the pub but was old hat a year or so later in October 1987, when the Fleet Street circus journeyed to Ipswich Town Hall for the moment when the great flat jockey was heading for the high jump. Lester Piggott was on his way to prison for tax evasion.

The Ipswich authorities had done their homework and devised a splendid system to cater for the expected media scrum and possible bun fight for seats. Ipswich Town Hall had been designated as the Crown Court for the occasion, and as reporters arrived they were treated like a cloakroom item – handed one ticket and told to occupy the seat on which had been placed the identical half.

As I was in the queue early, with colleague Peter Kane, I was well situated on the normal press benches, while others were in the not so convenient public gallery.

The first time I managed to glance around the court, with the benches full and necessary notebooks and pens at the ready, I was stunned by the icy glare from a woman directly opposite. Susan Piggott was indicating early her contempt, and intention of saying nothing.

The prosecution evidence was a lengthy catalogue of offshore accounts, earnings, bank statements, tax fraud, VAT evasion – and the figures were all in the multi-million pound bracket. We are talking massive money.

Heads were down, note taking reached a frenzy, with most hacks baffled by all the noughts which had to be added to amounts mentioned. There was total silence in court. Lester Piggott gazed into space from what was the dock.

Then suddenly the judge, Mr Justice Farquharson, was taken totally by surprise when smirking and giggling from the Press areas caused the prosecuting counsel to temporarily halt listing the sums, and glance inquiringly over his shoulder.

This was prompted when he outlined how, after all the main millions had been vetted and Piggott questioned at length, two further accounts were suddenly discovered in London and Newmarket – in the names of Armstrong, Susan's maiden name, and, would you believe it, John Jackson.

Had my phone call so stuck with the Piggotts that when they were looking for a throwaway name to help stash away more loot, JJ was the one?

Mutterings of "How much d'you know, Jacko?" and "They must trust you?" became audible as fingers were pointed from the balcony, and the judge had to ask for quiet.

In his defence, Piggott's QC played on the jockey's loved persona and treasured position in British sporting history, stressing these achievements had been accomplished despite him having been born with hearing and speech problems.

The judge listened intently and queried: "Will your client be able to hear what I am about to say?" When told in the affirmative, he declared: "Good. Mr Piggott, you will go to prison for three years."

Having a common name like John Jackson has caused problems before. Mind you, while travelling the world I have now left behind those boring moments when trying to transmit the correct spelling of your name to hotel receptionists/car hire clerks/ restaurant reservations/airline reconfirmations.

Whether it was Buenos Aires, Berlin, Benghazi, Bangkok or Baghdad, the answer always worked: "Jackson, like Michael Jackson."

On a very cold Saturday morning one February, I answered the phone at home: "Is that John Jackson?" And then: "Jacko, it's Big Ken here." Now there was only one Big Ken – Ken Montgomery, the chief football writer on the *Sunday Mirror*.

It was one of those rare weekends when the country was blanketed with snow and shivering, and only a handful of football matches were going to kick off. Big Ken apologised: "I'm sorry, but I've drawn the short straw. I have to ring around and ask people what they are doing on a Saturday when there is no football."

I answered honestly: "What a timely call. I am sitting down at this very moment with my youngest son, Tom. We are trying to work out the science set he received for Christmas, and I fear there is every chance we may blow the house up."

"Brilliant JJ, you're a darlin'," said Ken.

I returned to assembling the "explosives" with Tom, without a second thought. But later my mind started asking questions: why ring me, a newspaper colleague? Then it hit me.

I telephoned the *Sunday Mirror,* asked for Ken and was informed by the sports department's permanent Mr Reliable, Dave Ellis: "You should know better than asking a question like that at this time of the day. He's at the Press Club."

Dave would know the answer to my theory: "Has Ken done a story about what footballers are doing today, and got the Leyton Orient goalkeeper, John Jackson, blowing up his house?"

"Yeah, it's a brilliant lead as no one else was doing anything interesting," said Dave. As a result, Big Ken's endeavours were spiked, but he enjoyed the Press Club. In later years I was privileged to introduce this Montgomery to Rommel.

At one point in my career, I was forced to change my name, and that is why some former colleagues still refer to me as Charlton. It came about when I joined the *Manchester Evening News* and found there was a John Jackson well ensconced on the reporting staff. He obviously kept his by-line, and the news desk's dilemma as to what I should be called was solved in an instant when I revealed my full name was John Charlton Jackson.

So, Charlton Jackson was born, and at times John Charlton has made an appearance in publications. In Manchester it was a useful name, as Bobby Charlton was at the height of his career as the country's favourite Busby Babe (the term for youngsters discovered and guided to greatness by the legendary Manchester

United manager, Sir Matt Busby) and the biggest name in Hollywood then was Charlton Heston.

In South America, where the tradition is to take your middle name as all important, I was often asked if I was Jack Charlton.

The other JJ was John Henry Jackson, and we followed each other from Manchester through newspapers at Odhams to the *Daily Mirror*. Problems with our name continued, highlighted when I returned from abroad and phoned the Odhams switchboard in Covent Garden and asked to speak to John Jackson on *The People*.

The conversation went like this, when a friendly voice answered "Jackson":

"Hello John Henry, this is John Charlton here. How are you, you old bastard?" Total silence, then query:

"What is your name?"

"John Jackson."

"And to whom do you wish to speak?

"John Jackson."

"Which John Jackson?"

"John Jackson of *The People*."

"Sorry, you've got John Jackson of *The Eagle*."

The Jacksons cannot claim this problem as their own. There were two Peter Wilsons at the *Daily Mirror* causing a James Wilson by-line, while at the *Daily Express* young reporter John Clarke had some of the thrill of making the Fleet Street big time interrupted when told he must, like me, resort to his middle name – which for him meant the by-line Hardy Clarke.

The reason for this stemmed from the *Evening Standard*'s prominent cricket writer John Clarke, who complained his expenses were often confused with the new arrival (the papers were then owned by the same group) and when travelling the world he was not used to the paltry sum submitted by a junior reporter.

At the *Manchester Evening News* we had a double whammy. As

I doubled the John Jacksons, a second Bill Greaves arrived. He had a splendid middle name, Marshal – and I'm pleased to say that Marshal and Charlton reminisced over many years in those Fleet Street hostelries.

Middle names did not always suffice. George Pascoe Watson, later the *Sun's* political editor, arrived as a straight hack in the days of Kelvin MacKenzie's editorship. His name was greeted with a typical Kelvin comment: "Fucking stupid name. Too long for a single column." So George was chopped, and Pascoe Watson became a regular by-line.

WIMBLEDON MEMORIES

Needless to say, over 50 years covering the tennis at Wimbledon has brought an abundance of stories. In those days before agents, managers, and ultra-officious All England Club minders, players and press mingled happily.

There were many days when the players didn't matter as all cameras were trained on the Royal Box capturing the antics of Princess Diana and Fergie, Duchess of York. The latter won the title Duchess of Pork for the number of sweets she devoured there.

Billie Jean King (always ensured the ball boys, and later ball girls, were well supplied with sweets), Evonne Goolagong, Steffi Graf, Chris Evert, Martina Navratilova (cycled back one evening with a huge bunch of flowers when she heard the Duchess of Kent was not feeling well), Ann Jones, were a delight, always ready to stop and have a word.

Only a young Virginia Wade, who adopted the two-word Lester Piggott brush off, was hard to get close to. But her wonderful 1977 Silver Jubilee championship win in front the Queen brought an end to that.

On the male side life was never dull. Ilie Nastase was page lead fodder each time he raised a racquet or stuffed balls between an umpire's thighs and shouted "Call me mister"; Bjorn Borg just kept quietly winning; Jimmy Connors got more aggressive when young as his mother shouted "Come on, Jimbo baby" from below the Royal Box; permanently bad tempered Bob Hewitt (later convicted of rape) invariably shouted angrily at his wife to "get out of here" from her courtside seat: Boris Becker described his later nickname: "I know nothing about bonking, only vinning"; and there were such greats as Pancho Gonzales, Rod Laver, Stan Smith, Ken Rosewall, Roy Emerson, and John Newcombe.

Newcombe's first title win in 1967 brought a most memorable aside at his post victory press conference, in the tiny broom cupboard sized interview room under the Royal Box. He was celebrating a three-set thrashing of German Wilhelm Bungert.

Newly married to Angelika Pfannenburg from Hamburg, Newcombe fielded all the tennis questions, and then I asked: "What are you going to do tonight, John?"

Before he could answer, the *Daily Mirror's* Peter Wilson uttered the loudest stage whisper: "Another German is going to get fucked." Newcombe still laughs at the memory.

And, of course, there was John McEnroe!

Of all the encounters with McEnroe in his Superbrat phase the one that stands out prompted a punch-up in the interview room in 1981 that was beamed live around the world. The story started weeks earlier when he was bad tempered and beaten in the semi-final at Queen's Club. He even shouted at the umpire to stop a dog barking in the distance.

At the post match press conference I suggested his one achievement was to "stop that dog barking on Hammersmith Broadway". He angrily said he refused to talk to me and stormed out.

At Wimbledon he was luckier and won his semi-final (and went on to win the championship). The interview room was packed, and for the first time a TV crew, from HBO, was allowed in. After the tennis questions I was keen to know why his then girlfriend Stacey Margolin had suddenly flown home to Los Angeles.

My enquiry received a quick reply: "I've already said I'm not talking to you." More tennis questions then newsman Tony Snow from the *Sun* asked: "John, can you tell us why Stacey has left, especially as you are now in the final?" Superbrat just stood up and left.

And mayhem ensued! A New York radio man wondered whether this was a press conference or a circus – and my *Daily Mirror* colleague Nigel Clarke thumped him. The two were rolling around the floor, with HBO's live cameras zooming in on the *Daily Star's* James Whitaker and me for comments for the watching audience across the Atlantic.

(James Whitaker was soon a *Mirror* colleague and the doyen of the Royal correspondents – Princess Diana dubbed him the Big Red Tomato after his appearance on the ski slopes of Klosters – after he and wife Iwona were introduced to Richard Stott, and he swiftly signed up, at one of our Twickenham dinner parties.)

As a result of the interview room fracas I was court martialled by the All England Club. Peter Wilson offered to be my defence counsel, and I was given expert advice by the *Guardian*'s Frank Keating. He faced a similar situation years earlier for some obscure offence such as smoking his beloved pipe within smelling distance of the Centre Court.

"They told me they were going to suspend my accreditation for three days. I immediately appealed and asked if it could be for life."

My hearing was all very friendly and it was decided that for the last three days of the tournament I would be the only news reporter allowed to attend press conferences. I successfully suggested that the Press Association should be with me to feed all other papers. The strict ruling was that all questions had to be tennis related.

The next conference was with eventual winner Chris Evert, then married to Britain's John Lloyd and rumoured to be pregnant. I wanted to ask if this was correct. I thought hard and decided I could phrase it in tennis terms as previous winner Evonne Goolagong had just given birth.

"Chrissie, is it true that you are about to take an Evonne-type baby break?" Total apoplexy from All England Club minder and tennis journalists. As she was being ushered out, Chrissie shouted above the heads: "John, I'm told I can't answer but I'll just say I'm not pregnant yet." Good girl!

John McEnroe, however, is always first on my list when asked that old favourite about whom I would choose for the ideal dinner party. I know he would be great company – as proved later at that just mentioned Queen's Club fall out.

My newsdesk was not interested in his latest grumpy outbursts because "a woman has just come into the office with her young son who was christened John Patrick McEnroe. They're on the way to you and we would like pics of the two J.P.M.s together."

Great timing, I was muttering as McEnroe walked out of the dressing room toward me. Nothing ventured nothing gained, I approached, explained the situation and he replied "Sure. Five minutes, will that be okay?" We chatted like old buddies as we walked to the rendezvous. A true star.

Bonking Boris, Super Steffi, Naughty Nastase were all alliterations which helped light up a tabloid headline. But nothing could compare with when I decided to write a feature about the balls used at Wimbledon, which I learned had to be hand bounced individually to "complete Centre Court classification" – thousands of them.

Wimbledon veteran John Barrett, then promotional head of Slazengers, arranged for me to visit the test site in Barnsley. And there I met the two women who had the tedious task of day after day bouncing each ball to ensure they rose above the Wimbledon level.

Both their names began with B, and I am sure they were Beryl and Betty. So I had *Barnsley ball bouncers Beryl and Betty*. Even *Barrett's Barnsley ball bouncers Beryl and Betty*.

As a result of their splendid assistance I invited them to spend a day at Wimbledon.

And what was the one thing they wanted above everything else? – to meet Bjorn Borg.

Easy writing – *Bjorn Borg Beguiles Barnsley Ball Bouncers Beryl and Betty*.

Slazenger have supplied the Wimbledon balls since 1902, but there are no more Barnsley Beryls and Bettys. In 2002 the bouncing moved with the factory to the Philippines.

One further memory of that fun story. I feel I am still checking my knuckles after shaking hands with Bjorn Borg. His grip was crunching – in fact, for him, *crunching consecutive championships!!*

Early on at Wimbledon, when I was still on the old broadsheet *Sun,* I enjoyed an exclusive which prompted many awkward

questions – this time to the Home Secretary in the House
of Commons.

In the late 1960s the door to the small press room
overlooking the main gate was gently guarded by well retired
commissionaires. When I say that one of them had been personal
bodyguard to Queen Mary, our present Queen's grandmother,
you can see they were well on in years. Another gentleman, in
every sense, was George, a retired Metropolitan policeman.

One evening I spotted a shining new Rolls Royce, flanked by
two police motorcycle outriders with engines running, waiting at
the entrance to the Royal Box. What VIP had we here?

An All England Club official opened the rear door and the VIP
settled on the back seat – George!

What on earth? - as he drove off alone with his traffic stopping
escort.

He brushed aside my obvious question next day with "Sorry,
you are not supposed to know," but my colleague photographer
George Phillips and I made sure we were well out of sight to
capture the repeat event next evening. Our paper filled half the
back page with the picture story.

George was simply the messenger taking the next day's order
of play to the Queen, patron of the All England Club, and its then
president, Princess Marina, Duchess of Kent.

But MPs were not happy and Home Secretary Roy Jenkins
faced a barrage of complaints. Firstly, police motorcycle outriders
were not allowed on private property, and why was police time
and money being used to take order of play to the Queen, who
had no interest in tennis.

The Queen has visited Wimbledon twice during my 56
years covering it – for her Silver Jubilee in 1977 when Virginia
Wade obliged by winning the Championship, and in 2010 for
a walkabout and lunch with Roger Federer and others. She
was patron for 64 years before handing over to the tennis mad
Duchess of Cambridge but attended on only four occasions.

So, as a result of my scoop, police outriders now wait outside the gate on the public road, the Queen stopped receiving her early programme – but sadly we never saw George again.

Now a story for those tennis writers always unable to get near Wimbledon finalists, away from the stage managed press conferences, for a quote before their big moment on Centre Court.

On the second Thursday of my first Wimbledon in 1964 (the men's final was always on Friday in those days) I was at the tiny press bar when there was a tap on my shoulder and an Australian accent enquired: "G'day mate. I suppose you'd like a quick quote before we head into town for dinner?"

I turned to face Roy Emerson and Fred Stolle who in less than 24 hours would meet each other across the net in the final. Of course, I replied, with Emerson continuing: "Well, let's go down on the lawn and have a couple of lagers."

This could never happen now. And two further thoughts: Emerson beat Stolle easily in three straight sets both then and in 1965, with the prize being a silver cup (prize money of £2,000 for the men and £750 for women started in 1968. Both 2019 singles champions received £2.25 million each); and the lawns have been concreted over to make way for champagne ahead of lager.

HOOLIGAN HORRORS

Football hooligans en masse can only be described as vermin, but without them my job of promoting the news side of sport would have been a steeper uphill struggle. They were always a front-page story, so I had to be with them.

As a result I have received whispers warning I was soon to be stabbed in Stockholm; bombarded in a Krakow restaurant with plates and flower vases full of stagnant water; spat at, with painful accuracy, in Thessaloniki; come within a whisker of losing my manhood to a German police dog in Dusseldorf; been cracked over the skull in Cagliari; acted as an interpreter for a stab victim in a Paris intensive care unit; been pulled out of a crowd by my hair in Madrid; stranded in a collapsing beer tent in Malmo, and found myself in the thick of it in Vienna, Bruges, Oslo, Copenhagen and other cities. And that is without mentioning the Heysel Stadium disaster in Brussels.

I should point out at this juncture that this kind of football violence, as gauged from my first-hand experience, is an English disease. Okay, Germany, Holland and the old Yugoslavia suffered awful disturbances at domestic football matches, but hardly ever abroad.

England, and I mean England, as Scottish and Irish supporters appreciate there is more to travel than being total yobs, was the only country during my time to export this disgraceful behaviour. The culprits may be the minority, but they are the ones that are remembered.

The World Cups without England were a delight. Scotland in Germany and Argentina, and the Irish in America, typified how fans could enjoy themselves on each occasion after disappointing results.

The initial difference between the groups is immediately obvious. The Scots and the Irish, whatever the weather, like to dress up in their tartan and green. They are proud to wear national dress and the strips of their heroes on the field. The majority of the English simply undress, again whatever the temperature, to pollute bars and city centres with grotesquely flabby, tattooed, shaven headed bodies.

The Celts like to drink and sing their national songs; the English are keen only to chant abuse at all around. The Scots do like a fight, but usually among themselves after spats fuelled by the often stronger-than-normal local brew ("I dinna tak that from yoo, Jimmy"), rather than involving innocent locals; the Irish just sing and guzzle, preferring to enjoy themselves.

In those halcyon days of the Home Internationals, with Wembley a sea of tartan every other year as at least 70,000 Scots moved south to London, there was plenty of often annoying over exuberance, but never any real violence. It was a shame that the fixtures were ended, with the excuse that "unruly" Scots brought mayhem to the capital.

When too many bevvies meant a call of nature in Trafalgar Square, I often witnessed groups of Jocks forming discreet circles so the lassies could sit astride the waste bins. I am certain Nelson, even with only one eye, had seen far worse and, after all, there was no serious harm being caused.

One year London Underground staff voted to stop work on the day of the match because of the problems packing so much unruliness in trains to Wembley Park. So for those who could not afford, or find, a taxi, the only alternative was shanks pony.

My news desk came up with a brilliant idea – I should walk from Kings Cross Station to Wembley Stadium to list amenities and points of interest en route.

I covered the 12 miles without problem, although the tam-o'-shanter and Scottish flag I bought for the occasion prompted an early shout from a Baker Street newsvendor: "Oi mate, you're too bloody old for the Bay City Rollers."

My guide was given a great show in both the *Daily Mirror* and sister paper *Daily Record,* but the latter, based in Scotland, did point out that John Jackson was an Englishman. As if I would write anything to lead them astray!

After one famous Scottish victory, two happy chappies in

kilts staggered down Wembley's Olympic Way toward the
Underground station, only to find a police horse barring the way
and a voice from the saddle advising them that the queue could be
joined 100 yards back.

There was no instant release of foul four-letter expletives, or
"death to the pigs" cries from elsewhere, but one Jock gently
looked the horse between the eyes, spread wide his arms and
belted out his adapted rendition of the theme song from the
musical *Gigi*: "Gee gee, am I a fool or...?". Laughter and applause
all round, especially from the mounted constable.

Scotland's participation in the 1982 World Cup awarded an
earnings bonanza to the barkeepers of southern Spain. But it all
came to an end in Malaga with the Scotland vs Soviet Union 2-2
draw (billed beforehand as Alcoholism vs Communism – and
don't ask Alan Hansen and Willie Millar about their collision).
The tartan fiesta flowed without problems, so it was somewhat
surprising when police announced a Scot had been arrested for
raising his kilt in front of women.

The humour of the occasion was not tainted, however. After
the match the police revealed the culprit had watched the match
with the police on the touchline, and then released without
charge "as he convinced us he was simply performing the Can-
Can at the time".

There were occasions when my chronicling slightly offended
the Scottish nation. At the 1974 World Cup in Germany (the first
of two consecutive World Cups where England failed to qualify)
there was some drunken misbehaviour by fans in the centre of
Frankfurt.

I filed a light piece suggesting that the jocular Jocks had turned
momentarily into tartan terrors. Little did I expect that my expert
alliteration and following copy would lead the schedule at that
evening's *Daily Mirror* editorial conference.

Editor Mike Christiansen, who tended towards the eccentric
most of the time, thought it was wonderful. I received a call
while enjoying the best beer in the world and asked for more
description to go with a front page emblazoned "Jocular Jocks

Turn Tartan Terrors".

There was everything – frontline Frankfurt, World Cup warriors, blaring bagpipes, kilts ahoy.

North of the border was not amused, and the following day the Mayor of Glasgow flew to Frankfurt to apologise to the local burghers. The only people who took no notice were the Scottish players who, led by captain Billy Bremner, were having a running feud with manager Willie Ormond over payment for press pictures.

For this correspondent it was hard hat time for several days, and the most expensive I can recall. Each time when socialising with Scottish journo chums there would be an enquiry from an angry man in tartan: "Where's yon bastard from the *Daily Mirror?*"

Such great mates as Hugh McIlvanney, Alex Cameron and John Rafferty would take it in turns to say "He's away home, Jimmy" and then in my direction: "And I'm sure it's your round Fred, Alan, Charlie…" Great days!

Four years later in Argentina we had Ally MacLeod and his team failing miserably. They were boarding their early flight home just as hundreds of supporters were arriving for the quarter finals onwards as MacLeod had assured them Scotland would win the World Cup.

He had told everyone earlier that when he returned with the World Cup he would start his celebratory press conferences in Southampton and work slowly north. An obviously psychic Hughie Taylor, of the *Glasgow Herald*, advised him from the outset: "If I was you, Ally I would start in Inverness."

Many of the fans had travelled overland for days through North and South America and I celebrated their arrival in Buenos Aires with another light piece – headlined BO meets BA.

There were no complaints from fans but years later this and other Jackson reportage prompted a full-page feature in *Punch* magazine, headlined "Wacko Jacko and the Hack Pack". It was written by Patrick Collins, master columnist on the *Mail on*

Sunday. I don't know how we have remained such good friends for over 40 years!

The old adage really. It's much better to have such a piss taking piece about you than being ignored altogether.

An expert passed that on during one of my final jobs on the *Daily Mirror,* which was to read through all the Government documents released under the 30-year rule. Each late December journalists are allowed access to the Records Office at Kew to sift through files that affected history.

It was 1992 and the main mountain of paper related to the Cuban missile crisis in 1962 and the tense face-off between US President John F. Kennedy and Soviet Nikita Khrushchev.

But I discovered a short handwritten memo from then Prime Minister Harold Macmillan to his Postmaster General Reginald Bevins. (Ironically, as I read it I was sitting alongside Bevin's son Tony, a Fleet Street political correspondent.)

It referred to a recent episode of the popular BBC TV programme *That Was The Week That Was,* fronted by David Frost. One of the sketches had Willie Rushton ridiculing Macmillan for a large fur hat he wore on a visit to Moscow. It was rather rude and viewers complained.

Macmillan's memo ordered: "Do not, repeat do not, take any action against the BBC and *That Was The Week That Was.* Better they acknowledge us rather than ignore us altogether."

What is it that makes decent men, many of them respectable husbands and fathers, take on this animal persona once they travel abroad with the England football team? Why do they get carried away and follow the full-time yobs like sheep?

When England were billeted near Bilbao for the start of the 1982 World Cup, most of the "fans" camped in a tented village in the hills above San Sebastian. They were never any trouble, although they suffered from the international image which preceded them and prompted a totally uncalled for mass arrest late one night, after a donkey had been freed from its hobble and proceeded to wander into a bar where its owner was drinking.

Las hooligans were bound to get the blame.

At the campsite later I chatted with two men, draped in Union Jacks and their faces painted with the red and white cross of St George. One was a police sergeant and the other a gynaecologist at a top hospital in the Midlands. There was no indication either could be termed a hooligan, but they agreed that being with the "mob" was all part of the buzz that accompanied the travels with their England heroes.

Six years later in Stuttgart I encountered the other side of this "buzz". England and the Republic of Ireland were drawn together in the opening group of the European Championship, and the Irish celebrated after a 1-0 victory over Bobby Robson's men.

In the centre of Stuttgart, I was attracted into a popular Gasthof by the sound of merriment. Inside were the locals, sitting in their normal seats at the bar or around the customary *Stammtisch* table for regulars, and all enjoying the singing and banter from a sea of green clustered in a corner.

They may not have understood a word uttered but they were genuinely pleased to witness this free Irish entertainment, offered by visitors decently dressed and obviously enjoying being there.

Suddenly, all smiles were wiped; the English had arrived. Through the door came a handful, around a dozen, of loud-mouthed youths. All were bare to the waist, a dreadful sight which complimented the looks of hate and loathing that contorted their faces. Their contribution to the evening was predictable for me, but sent waves of shock and total disbelief through the bar.

Up went the Nazi salute and chants of "Sieg heil, sieg heil" were aimed at the Germans. They sat stunned. For the Irish it was "No surrender, no surrender" and "Death to the IRA". The few Irish who did bother to change their positions to glance at this sudden intrusion into the fun, raised their glasses and offered the odd "Oh, be Jasus" and "Cheers".

My observations from the bar were suddenly interrupted by one of the uncouth visitors, who elbowed his way forward and addressed the barman with: "Hey, Kraut". Fortunately, his accent and command of English were almost impossible for me to understand so none of the locals were prompted to react.

He was in his late teens and gave me one of those "we're untouchable" stares when I queried: "Why do you bring shame on English people like me, by behaving with such ignorance and total hatred?"

Needless to say, it took what seemed an eternity for what passed as his brain to comprehend what had been asked of him, before he spat back: "Listen you c..., my grandfather fought a war to get rid of bastards like this."

"Oh no he didn't," I assured him instantly. "He fought a dreadful war to rid the world of people like you and all your mates."

Another silence for his pathetic thought process to click into gear, and then came the snarl: "You'll be lucky to get out of 'ere without being cut, c.... Sieg heil." Oh, it did make you proud to be English.

It was hard to believe at that moment that six years earlier I had actually gone to the assistance of a bunch of these hateful thugs and assisted Greek police as they sheltered the little dears from rampaging locals.

Greece and Turkey are two countries where the reputation of English football hooligans is gleefully seen as a challenge and brings about a determination by local idiots to prove they are just as obnoxious.

I travelled by train from London to Thessaloniki in northern Greece for the European Championship qualifying match. This had been switched at the last moment from Athens, ironically for the protection of English fans, following violence around the preceding Under-21 encounter.

There was no trouble on the overnight journey, although, arriving at Venice, I narrowly missed falling victim to robbers who squirt gas through sleeper compartment keyholes, and when the occupants become drowsy use stolen keys to enter and rob.

But that's another story.

At the Salonika ground the small English contingent was herded into a segregated area surrounded by a high fence. But the police had appeared to ignore the spitting techniques of Greek fans, which can be as deadly as blowpipes. When the visitors were not clearing their eye and faces of spittle, they were dodging missiles thrown from all directions.

As the England players walked out, to an equally violent saliva welcome, the police ushered our bunch of great unwashed away to safety. And where did they deposit them? – in the box alongside the press, where they mingled with the England Under-21 players just two rows behind the VIPs and FA hierarchy from both countries. Somehow, they managed to behave.

I have to admit it made my job easier as my story had moved across the vast stadium to me. At the final whistle the police ringed our area and told the English supporters to remain seated. The other news reporter present, Paul Henderson of the *Daily Star*, and I were asked by the police if we could assist with their evacuation plans.

Everything went swimmingly. Not one English person was allowed to move until the stadium had been emptied, and all locals with intentions of confronting the visiting enemy had been driven a safe distance away. Two buses pulled up, the English boarded with police minders, and a motorcycle escort guided us along a safe route to an off-the-beaten-track hotel.

Many of the policemen spoke reasonable English, allowing them to joke with the fans and express hope that they might get to Wembley for the return fixture several weeks hence. Henderson and I agreed to keep the group confined to the hotel bar for a period to allow all opposition to disperse around the vast city.

We bought each a couple of beers, chatted about football and other laddish topics, and took turns to file our copy from the hotel foyer. With everyone apparently happy and talking about returning home to England, Hendo and I left for the downtown team hotel where we were staying.

It wasn't long before we were forced to update our stories. Shortly after we left, the thuggery returned when the chummies, now with a few more beers down them, discovered two motorcycle cops keeping watch outside. They battered them with pickaxe handles and bicycle chains.

Next morning, we were in court to see two of them despatched without ceremony to the tough prison nearby for two years. Will they ever learn?

In fact, one of them telephoned me on his release to say it had been an extremely hard learning experience inside the jail. He had many scars to prove it. But was he now convinced that football hooliganism was a mug's game? Was it worth it?

"I'm a Chelsea fan and always will be. For two years I have thought about nothing else but getting back among the lads. I'll be there on Saturday, and we'll see how it goes. But one thing is certain. I ain't ever going back to fucking Greece."

Well, I suppose that is something positive!

The Jekyll and Hyde aspect of this English disease was never better illustrated than when I tracked down a man who had been involved in one of the first outbreaks of violence when football hooliganism was in its infancy. It occurred at what became known as the Battle of Basle.

The full story was told by one picture which virtually filled the front page of the *Daily Mirror*. It showed a Swiss supporter, anguish written all over his face, as, it appeared, a knife was being thrust in his back, while at the same time another English attired spectator was roughly yanking his expensive watch from his wrist. Fortunately, the knife glanced off his thick belt so the only injuries were the scratches to his watch-less arm.

Once again it was an anonymous phone call to our office that took the story further. I was given the name and Bristol address of the person stealing the watch. After making the usual preliminary checks, my old buddy Syd Young, who ended his working days as the *Daily Mirror*'s West Country district man after sterling work in the Manchester, Belfast and New York offices, knocked on his door.

It was answered by a woman who was only too happy to tell us nice Mr X lived in his bachelor flat on the top floor and should be home as usual from the bank at... The bank? Oh yes, she informed us, he was a deputy bank manager.

Sure enough he arrived dead on the time mentioned, appropriately dressed in smart suit and tie, with briefcase. He invited us in and had no hesitation in admitting that he was the man in the picture. To further prove it he produced the watch from a drawer.

This man, aged around 30, went on to stress he was not proud of his actions, and had attempted to find the man to return the watch. But this is the crucial clue to a lot of what I have witnessed over the years:

"Once I pull on my replica England regalia I am a totally different person. I just get carried away and have done crazy things I would never dream of normally. It is very odd, but I am so passionate about following the England football team I seem to have no control over my actions."

He posed for pictures in both sets of dress and Syd and I thought we had a cracker. In London, the executives of the day, and probably a careful night lawyer, thought differently and all our copy was spiked. Shame, for I think a lot of people would have been interested to read our anatomy of a thug.

Other mishaps were all run-of-the-mill hazards when travelling with the hoolies. The Krakow vase throwing came as a result of me being recognised late at night by one of the regular nutters. England had just played Poland in Katowice and I had returned from this hellhole of an industrial city to my hotel amid the charm of Krakow.

With Fleet Street colleagues I was enjoying a nightcap or seven when our chatter was suddenly interrupted by a cry of "there's that c... from the *Daily Mirror*", followed by a hail of plates and vases. We dodged the objects quite skilfully but were unable to avoid the stagnant liquid they spewed everywhere.

Rescue was soon at hand, for the remains of the *Sun*'s Neil

Syson glanced through the crowd of ducking diners, spotted the ringleader, and announced: "I know him. He's a Man City fan."

This knowledge had been learned during the 1986 World Cup in Monterey, Mexico, when I and other colleagues were newsmen inside our hotel, while young Syson, a fanatical Nottingham Forest supporter, was following England from the pavement outside – and a fellow dosser was the prat bombarding me with crockery. Peace soon returned as reminiscences of Mexican street siestas accompanied a bottle of whisky to Syson's room.

In Malmo the Swedish police, as only they could, decided the way to keep English football fans attending the 1992 European Championships happy was to give them what they wanted, namely as much free beer as they could handle.

Beer tents shot up in main squares and everything went well, until the loons got pissed and promptly wrecked the tents and generally ran wild. I was quite happily drinking in one when the roof fell in, mainly because English oiks had climbed the guy ropes.

It was during all this mayhem that I enjoyed a most satisfying moment at the expense of a supercilious David Mellor. The Tory MP was then into his very short period as Minister for Sport and had flown to Sweden after crowd violence.

After a press conference in the stadium I approached him alone as he walked down the stairs. When I introduced myself as *Daily Mirror* he flashed one of those "please crawl back under your stone" expressions, and apparently waited for what he thought would be a typical banal tabloid question.

I ignored this and enquired: "Did you enjoy the Richter concert at the Festival Hall the other evening?" The man who prides himself on his vast knowledge of music could not prevent his mouth opening ever wider.

"Surely you weren't there?" he said, obviously feeling tabloid people never progressed further than Chas and Dave and would certainly know nothing about this classical pianist.

"I certainly was, sitting in the seat directly behind you." I

mentioned his movements during the interval and at last I think
he believed me. A satisfying moment, and an escape, if only
momentarily, from hooligan horror.

Back in Stuttgart I had enjoyed a very memorable interlude
away from the boorish behaviour of my countrymen. The
occasion was a civil reception thrown by the Mayor of Stuttgart
for the travelling English media.

Now the mayor just happened to be Manfred Rommel, son of
the famous World War II Field Marshal Erwin Rommel, who led
his troops so valiantly in the North African desert campaign that
he gained tremendous respect from his enemy, the British Eighth
Army "Desert Rats", commanded in victory by Field Marshal
Bernard Montgomery. Rommel was among those who showed
opposition to Hitler and in 1944 was forced to commit suicide, an
event witnessed by his son.

In 1965, friends working for Germany's main sports agency,
Sport Informations Dienst, whom I had met at events around the
world, hired me as their freelance London correspondent for the
run-up to the World Cup here. I was obviously successful for I
continued with this often hectic, but always enjoyable work for 30
years, and became a well-known by-line in Germany.

(When a call from Dusseldorf was taken in the *Mirror* office
by a colleague, it often prompted the shout "Gairmany calling,
Gairmany calling" from those who knew of Lord Haw Haw's
famous wartime broadcasts).)

It was only natural, therefore, that I was asked at the media
get-together if I would do the honours and introduce the
chairman of the English Football Writers' Association to Mayor
Rommel. I realised this was going to be an introduction with a
difference but was confident the task would be a great deal easier
as I knew from earlier meetings that Rommel not only spoke
immaculate English but had a splendid sense of humour.

So the conversation went like this: "Herr Rommel, could
I please introduce the FWA chairman, Herr Montgomery?"
gesturing to the large rotund figure of the *Sunday Mirror*'s Ken
Montgomery.

"Oh, not another one," laughed Mayor Rommel. At this moment I heard a cough above my shoulder and received a gentle nudge.

"Ah yes. Herr Rommel, please meet the deputy chairman, Herr Montgomery." The Mayor looked reasonably stunned as a hand was thrust forward by Alex Montgomery of the *Sun*.

Rommel then commenced to tell us how he and David Montgomery, the other Field Marshal's son, had maintained a friendly relationship, with frequent letters and visits to each other's homes.

Rommel and the Montgomerys were thoroughly enjoying their chat when there was a sudden interruption from one of the photographers: "Jacko, you might as well introduce me as I was the one who did all the damage."

So, I was off again: "Herr Rommel, could I also introduce Herr Lancaster?" and with that Reg Lancaster of the *Daily Express* brought resounding laughter from all parties. Rommel admitted that the RAF's Lancaster bombers had indeed played an important role in the defeat of Nazi Germany.

A meeting with another mayor brought about further laughter, but on a totally different subject. It was in Bilbao, shortly after the draw had placed England in that city for the first part of the 1982 World Cup, and I flew out to discover how the local burghers were facing up to an invasion of English "buggers".

Also, there was Leon Symons, *Daily Express,* who earned the nickname of Pocket Rabbi, as he was not only small and extremely proud of being Jewish but had a hairstyle and perfectly placed bald patch which gave every impression he was wearing his yarmulke.

The mayor expressed horror at the suggestion that there could be violence in his city, with the rather naive observation: "Manchester United played here in 1948 and it was a very pleasant occasion enjoyed by all." Yes señor, but sadly the world had changed in 34 years.

As he willingly posed for photographers on the steps of City

Hall, draped in a Union Jack, he explained: "We will treat the England fans with the same wishes we send before a bullfight. When the toreador enters the ring we pray 'May Jesus Christ go with you.'"

Little Leon promptly quipped: "That'll do me a lot of good, won't it?" We didn't translate for the mayor.

When all the action did start our hooligans ignored all such offers of divine guidance, and trashed bars and city centre areas as per usual. Frank Clough described Bilbao in the *Sun* as "The city of hate."

Peter Corrigan arrived for the *Observer* some days later, enjoyed the wonderful fish restaurants on offer, then observed in his first piece: "I have yet to find any hate, but I can assure you that Bilbao is a city of hake."

On an earlier visit, Bilbao and its Basque language brought difficulties for one hard drinking Scottish member of the Fleet Street football hacks, after he had wandered from bar to bar throughout one night.

I found him staggering along the main street around 10 a.m., and hauled him into the nearest coffee bar. He eyed the tapas on the counter and pointed a podgy finger at a newly arrived Spanish omelette. When the barman started to cut a standard slice he was greeted with: "No, no, no. I'll eat the lot." And he did.

While doing so he accepted an offer from the oldest shoeshine man in the world with instructions to "clean ma shoes, Scotia". With the omelette demolished, and shoes beginning to gleam, our red-faced scribe made a gesture with a pumping right arm to the alarmed shoe cleaning specialist and declared: "When you're finished my son, you find me a woman."

As if auditioning for the part of Manuel in *Fawlty Towers,* the poor bemused man rocked back in horror with: "Qué, qué?" The explanation involved further pumping of the arm, a pointed finger in his direction and: "When you're through, you me go rumpy pumpy."

It was obvious that this poor chap thought he was about to

embark on a bedtime romp with this massive customer, rather than procuring the required female company. Further fright: "No, no, no. Porqué, porqué?" This brought about an instant change in beer and omelette stuffed visitor.

"Did you say porky? Course I'm bloody porky, I'm 19 stone." Panic over and, as was the usual custom with this particular Scotsman, Señor Shoe Shine went away smiling with a mighty tip.

The news side of sport was always my specialty. I love all sport and was always on hand to suggest I should be involved in whatever sporty story emerged. But principally, I was always a news hack – and I certainly carried no mementoes to show I had shone somewhere in the sporting arena when growing up.

I played in those fun Journalists vs Pop Stars football matches, and in South Africa I made a short appearance in a Press vs Referees warm-up encounter before the main 1963 Cup Final, in front of 20,000 spectators, in Johannesburg.

And I mean short! I was playing right back, marking the referee who had competed for South Africa in the sprint events at the Olympics. My only action involved tripping him up, conceding a penalty, then scoring an own goal with my hand. I was probably the reason for one of the quickest substitutions on record.

My proudest sporting moment was as a 16-year-old when I was called up for the First XI at my school, Tollington Secondary Grammar School for Boys, Muswell Hill. I was named as the right half, number 4 in those days, with the responsibility of marking, and hopefully containing, the number 10 inside left of the opposition, our bitter rivals Edmonton Latymer.

As a staunch Arsenal fan, I set out to be as hard and impressive as their then right halves, Scotsmen Archie Macaulay and Alex Forbes. All I will report is that we lost 13-1, and their inside left scored seven.

His name was Johnny Haynes. He went on to play for Fulham and become the first ever £100 a week footballer, and played 56 times for England, with 22 of them as captain.

Our next meeting was at the 1962 World Cup in Chile when he arrived with his England team to play Brazil. I have a picture from the front page of the local *El Mercurio* newspaper, showing me chatting to Haynes, Jimmy Greaves and Bobby Robson. I saw more of him during that short discussion than I did on the playing field back in 1951!

At cricket, however, I did prompt an extremely unique scorecard. I was caught at silly mid-off by an Italian while mishitting a beamer from a Romanian.

This innings took place in the 1960s when the middle Sunday of Wimbledon was marked with a charity cricket match, Press vs Players. It was organized by BBC commentator Max Robertson and showbiz names with cricket talent (comic actor Sir Brian Rix was a splendid opening bat) helped boost the collection for the chosen charity.

On the occasion in question I was batting with Northern Irish actor James Ellis, renowned then from the long running BBC police drama *Z Cars,* and had successfully dispatched for four balls from Australian Tony Roche, a Wimbledon finalist, and British No. 1 Mike Sangster.

I was in a confident mood when a bowling change brought on Romanian Ion Tiriac. He may never have seen a cricket match but he certainly seemed aware of baseball, for he ran up and promptly threw the ball at me.

In an attempt, I must admit, to avoid serious injury I prodded at the ball, which simply rose skywards and plopped with ease into the hands of Nicky Pietrangeli. There is no mention in Wisden of Jackson J.C. c Pietrangeli, b Tirac 8!

Another regular feature in those happier days, impossible now because of security, agents, etc, was the garden party gathering by all involved at the Hurlingham Club on the Sunday before Wimbledon started.

Our four children loved seeing the stars and on one occasion a cry of "Hey kid, I need your help" saw youngest son Tom acting as caddy for John McEnroe on the pitch and putt course.

There was also the annual Horse of the Year show at Wembley Arena, which was a must for then horse-mad youngest daughter Stella. One memorable highlight was the tumultuous welcome given Sefton, the British Army horse which survived horrendous injuries during the deadly IRA attack on the Horse Guards in Hyde Park in 1982, which killed four soldiers and seven horses.

Believe it or not, I did play in an ice hockey match on one occasion while working in Orillia, Ontario. And I scored a goal – which was promptly disallowed on three counts:

My stick work was more like a golf shot and illegally went above my shoulder; I completely missed the puck, fell and kicked it into the net; and in doing so slid in with it, completely demolishing the goal and upending the goal tender.

There were reporters who had no interest whatsoever in sport and sought my help when lumbered with sports-related stories. One was *Daily Telegraph* stalwart Brian Silk.

When in Dubai in 1977 covering a Lufthansa hijacking by a Palestinian group, I noticed disgraced England football manager Don Revie sitting in our hotel foyer. Approaches by me, ITN's Gerald Seymour, and the *Daily Mail*'s John Edwards were rebuffed without any conversation by the man who had fled after the *Daily Mirror* alleged he tried to bribe players to lose against his club Leeds United

The newly arrived Silk was the man for the job, we thought, as Revie would not recognize him. Except "who's Don Revie?" did not inspire confidence. Needless to say, he failed also.

Three years later the setting was Plumpton Racecourse with Prince Charles making his debut as a jockey in a charity race. As he was walking to the saddling enclosure in the company of the *Daily Telegraph's* racing correspondent John Oaksey, a breathless Silk arrived.

"Thank God you're here. I haven't a clue what's happening." To which I replied: "Don't worry, Prince Charles is with your man." Of course, Silk wanted to know who I was referring to –

"your racing correspondent, John Oaksey".

Silk's reply was magic: "Ah Jacko, at last I realise you don't know everything. My desk told me to look out for a Mr Hotspur." (Hotspur was the name used by the paper's tipster.)

Another racecourse memory brought one of the truly great ripostes. While in Los Angeles for the 1984 Olympics, Sunday columnists Hugh McIlvanney, Ken Jones and others enjoyed a day at the Santa Anita track.

On arrival with VIP tickets McIlvanney said he would take care of tipping the valet parking attendant. As his smallest note was $50, he apologized and asked if the man had change.

He was stunned by the instant reply: "Around here, sir, that is change."

COURT REPORTS

On the news beat I always enjoyed court work. None more so than at the High Court when the colourful George Carman QC was in action. During many libel cases (I spent one day being kicked by an agitated Sonia Sutcliffe, wife of the Yorkshire Ripper, as the witness box adjoined my press seat) Carman would often ask for an adjournment (he was desperate for a smoke), give me a nod, and outside would enquire whether we reporters had enough copy.

When we often admitted that we were already overloaded with "good leads" he promised to hold back other newsworthy evidence till the next day.

In the first ever libel case to award a complainant a six-figure sum I had a personal involvement. It happened when the Leeds United and Scottish captain Billy Bremner sued the *Sunday People* over allegations he had tried to bribe Wolverhampton Wanderers players into fixing a match which would allow his Leeds United to win the 1972 Double.

This was a somewhat hasty follow-up by the Sunday paper after our *Daily Mirror* team, led by Richard Stott, had spent a week outlining the Don Revie allegations.

Having beaten Arsenal 1-0 to win the FA Cup Final on the Saturday, Leeds needed just one point against Wolves away on Monday to pip Derby County to the First Division Championship. They lost 2-1.

A succession of international footballers including Jack Charlton, Allan Clarke and Johnny Giles gave evidence for their Leeds teammate, but when the defence called Frank Munro, Wolves defender and fellow Scot, Bremner approached me during a short court adjournment.

Before the case opened the *Sunday People* had offered him £20,000 as an out-of-court settlement. He refused so a date was set for the High Court. Munro's arrival from Australia obviously changed matters in his mind and Bremner asked me to tell my

Mirror Group bosses that he would accept the £20,000 and walk away.

This was refused with the comment that a vast amount of money had been spent getting Munro into the witness box. The case continued and the jury awarded a white-faced Bremner £100,000 and costs, estimated at £65,000.

I witnessed one death sentence being passed at the Old Bailey, with the black hood placed on the judge's wig and the prisoner told he would be taken away and hanged. But the severity of the sentence brought no gasps as it was recognized then that all death sentences would be later commuted to life imprisonment.

During my first stint on the *Auckland Star,* however, the death sentence still prevailed. And by law one journalist had to witness the execution. The paper's aged crime reporter had fulfilled this task often, but when a convicted man had a connection with a story I had covered in Birkenhead, he wondered if I would like to attend.

I promptly refused. As someone who hates bullfighting and closes my eyes when the poor animal nears death, I would have been an embarrassment.

There were odd moments in court when I was taken totally by surprise. At the High Court Mr Justice Drake once ordered the usher to lock all doors "as I will not have my court used like a station waiting room" when colleague Chris Boffey and I arrived back slightly late from lunch.

But the most notable was when Streatham brothel keeper Cynthia Payne was facing the full force of the law and I needed a pee. To exit one had to pass in front of the dock so was forced to bend double while walking as quietly as possible, ensuring you did not block her view.

My awkward manoeuvre was met by accused Cynthia leaning from the dock with the whisper: "You're from the *Daily Mirror.* I like your face." Honestly, I never visited her well known establishment!!

George Carman was a character who made a reporter's life

easy. And in Canada I enjoyed his equivalent in the Hamilton Supreme Court, where I was the full-time reporter during my short spell on the *Hamilton Spectator.*

Judge Latchford liked to get through the day's schedule quickly. And heaven help a sometimes-new barrister who droned on. Latchford would slowly lean back in his chair until the counsel was left to present his case to the worn soles of two feet.

On one occasion he leapt from his chair, shouting "Court adjourned" and as he was escorted out by two attendants gestured with his head he wished to see me in his chambers. He threw off his robe and said the accused (facing an armed robbery charge) was blatantly guilty and wondered what sentence he should pass.

As I hesitated, he said: "I was going to give him 10 years but if that counsel bores me much longer it'll be 12, maybe more."

When an Italian pool club owner was having some language problems explaining his civil case, Judge Latchford swivelled in his chair and roared along the length of the bench like a train on rails, leaned on the witness box and said: "Giuseppe (not his name), for Christ's sake get on with it."

Away from the court he had the road near his house closed at weekends so he could mow his lawn in his pyjamas.

In Kingston, Jamaica, in 1962 where I covered courts for the *Daily Gleaner,* the world was different. A class system was most noticeable then in 1962 with lighter-skinned people lording it over their very black compatriots. They had an annual beauty parade to choose Miss Ebony, Miss Ivory, Miss Mahogany, etc.

It was noticeable in the courts, with the fans whirring and people sleeping peacefully in the public gallery. One morning a young black man who simply rode round in a circle for a few seconds on a bicycle he found leaning on a wall, before placing it back in position, was given 18 months.

Immediately, a lighter coloured police sergeant who during a row in his bedroom grabbed a full bedpan and clubbed his girlfriend unconscious received a conditional discharge.

But the most memorable was a simple shoplifting case.

The evidence was that the charged woman was spotted in a supermarket filling her basket with several small, cheap items before stopping in front of the freezer compartment, glancing around, then lifting her skirt and stuffing a complete chicken into her knickers. She was apprehended on leaving.

Her defence case had been taken by one of the rum-soaked lawyers who offered their services to the poorer accused for the price of their next drink.

He rose to his feet, and with a rather slurred tone asked the policewoman who had arrested the accused: "What was the sex of the chicken?" Before she could recover from her bafflement he continued: "I submit it must be male as no woman would have stuffed it in her knickers unless it was a cock."

This brought an instant rebuke from the magistrate: "That will be enough, counsel." I realised he had to pick his words carefully, as the solicitor's name was Cox. As a result, the poor woman was treated leniently.

Away from the courts I spent several interesting days with the then Prime Minister Alexander Bustamante. He suddenly adopted me when I was following up a story at his headquarters. "Come into my office for a drink, and help me out," was his greeting.

With Jamaica about to celebrate its independence he was receiving a procession of ambassadors presenting best wishes from their governments. He obviously found this tedious and needed the rum and me.

When the Australian High Commissioner was ushered in, his "On behalf of Prime Minister Robert Menzies and the people of…" was rudely interrupted with "Never mind that, how's your creaky cricket team now?"

The Independence Day celebrations were enjoyable, and very important for that part of the world. US Vice President Lyndon B. Johnson flew in and Princess Margaret represented the Queen. Her arrival was described by the *Miami Herald:* "The Princess was wearing a fashionable yellow dress and among her accessories were matching shoes, hat, gloves, and Anthony Armstrong Jones."

There must be few reporters who covered a libel case in the
High Court, and were then ordered to write a book about it.
But this was my task after Robert Maxwell had successfully sued
Private Eye in 1986.

Throughout the case Maxwell told me daily to "take every
word". When he didn't like a ruling, he ordered his QC to go to
the Appeal Court. On one occasion he had flown to New York
and told me to instantly phone his private number, whatever the
hour, with the outcome.

This meant wandering out in the snow and speaking to him
from his Range Rover's phone. When I explained that, without a
thorough legal knowledge, I felt he won some, lost some, he asked
to speak to the *Mirror* office lawyer who was standing shivering
alongside my window.

He took the phone, said "Good morning, publisher" and
received a two-word reply: "You're fired."

Maxwell was awarded £50,000 damages and gloated. On my
return to the office, I was summoned with political editor Joe
Haines, feature writer Peter Donnelly and secretary Gloria Sharp
to the presence on the 11th floor. The Mirror Group's three editors
were also present.

Maxwell told us we were going to make publishing history
by producing a book in 10 days which would be called *Malice
In Wonderland*. He stressed it would be sensational so not a word
must be uttered outside "these four walls".

As he spoke his secretary said that his weekly call to Radio
Oxford (his home territory where his family lived in Headington
Hall, a luxurious council house) was ready. He knelt down, and
bellowed down the phone to this handful of listeners: "Today I
have taken £50,000 from that scurrilous magazine *Private Eye*,
and now I'm arranging to publish a book…"

So much for keeping everything within said four walls!

We did complete the book. He paid a vast amount to have the
full transcripts from every day of the case. I edited these while Joe
Haines had the more difficult task of writing a full summary. As

I worked, Maxwell would sit at my feet, surrounded by pictures, suggesting: "Here's me with Gorbachev, we must have that" and "Here's me with…"

When Maxwell decided in 1984 that the *Mirror* would be the first to have a £1 million bingo winner and that he would present the cheque at the Labour Party conference in Blackpool, I was part of the team sent to collect winner Maudie Barrett from her home in Dovercourt, near Harwich.

The problem was she demanded that most of her large family come with her, including Thumper, her cocker spaniel. All I need to say is it was a roller coaster week getting them to Blackpool while hiding Maudie from rival newspapers, starting with colleague Paul Callan treading on Thumper's paw and muggins given the responsibility of taking him to a vet for splint treatment.

There were many interesting interludes in the years when a very active Robert Maxwell owned the Mirror Group. But little did I dream that five years later I would be escorting his widow into a cramped room in the Canaries to identify his body.

On November 5, 1991, I was enjoying a champagne lunch at a wine bar in Holborn, not celebrating Guy Fawkes but fulfilling a bet I had with news editor Steve Lynas on the rugby world cup. I had lost, so the drink was on me.

Mid sip a phone call from editor Richard Stott summoned me to return immediately to the office – and I, with photographer Ken Lennox, was off to join Betty and Philip on the helicopter.

Before landing in the Gulfstream jet at Las Palmas, Betty suddenly sat down beside me. She whispered: "I must tell you one thing. Bob will not have killed himself. Despite his many problems, suicide is totally out of the question." And then the air-sea rescue pilot told us he did not drown due to the absence of water in his lungs.

These two observations have stuck with me over the years when theories of murder, suicide and natural causes have been bandied about by "experts". After all I witnessed, I have reached only one conclusion.

Robert Maxwell died of natural causes.

Events for me started at around 4 a.m. when a sick and worried Maxwell (he knew he had major financial problems) phoned the bridge to complain about the temperature in his cabin. On a rough night he wandered naked out on to the deck for a pee (a habit of all male yachties, I am told). He edged alongside a tender where a single chain replaces the vessel's protective side barrier.

As the yacht rocked on a windy night, he either suffered a heart attack, grabbed the chain, couldn't hold on, and was dead by the time he hit the rolling sea, or he stumbled, grabbed the chain, but with his weight was unable to hold on, and the cold water prompted a fatal heart attack.

My theory was strengthened when I escorted Betty and Philip into the room and saw he was lying like a baby, with his arms bent upwards and his hands folded as if gripping something.

With the 2020 arrest of Ghislaine Maxwell for her association with convicted sex offender Jeffrey Epstein, the life and death of Robert Maxwell have become hot topics again. So, 30 years on I have been recounting memories, as above, for biographers, podcasts, and Netflix and BBC TV series.

When often asked about the biggest stories, with worldwide interest, that I have covered, the Maxwell death saga rates alongside Nelson Mandela's release from prison, the Munich Olympic massacre, and the death of Sir Winston Churchill.

YOU HAVE TO LAUGH

Without a sense of humour, it must be very difficult to enjoy life as a tabloid hack. Unless you can laugh at the requests, but at the same time relish the thought of fulfilling the latest whims of news executives, then it might be better to pack up and seek a new fun job – say, traffic warden.

I certainly had my fair share of what must appear to ordinary members of the public, cuckoo assignments, plus countless predicaments other jobs forced me into. But I loved every moment.

Other than laugh, what else could I do when asked to fry an egg on the pavement during a very hot spell; ghost a first "bird" piece with a female eagle; have dreadful problems with the Queen's personal loo when desperate for a pee; search for a Chinaman my loopy editor had said was seen eating grass; test the newest craze to cure baldness; help the coffers of a world champion boxer by getting him married; stand on the terraces at a football match in a dragon outfit; spend a week existing on food costing a total of 5p a day in order to report how Africans survived; ask elderly women about contraceptives outside a supermarket; face an over from the world's best fast bowler at full pace... and many more?

Oh, and how about the day I was told to book into a posh London hotel and cause a punch-up between Clint Eastwood, James Bond, Starsky and Hutch, and Kojak?

Then there was the odd request for items to be brought back from assignments abroad. A master of this was P.J. Wilson who was a superb reporter before he became news editor. To say he bordered on the eccentric at times would not risk accusations of unfairness.

P.J. was also accident prone. How could one forget the day he arrived late at the office, giving a masterful impression of a waxwork dummy? Had the real P.J. stayed on at Madame Tussauds while the dummy had been released to an astonished world, asked a gaggle of reporters, convulsed with laughter?

As his suit appeared to crack with every syllable, he explained that on the way to work he had popped into a carwash, which halfway through the cycle suddenly stopped. P.J. decided to climb out to investigate and had managed to step from the driving seat just as the expensive hot wax finish programme re-started. Hence one very waxed Wilson.

This, really, was nothing new. We were still reminiscing of the morning a late P.J. hastily hitched a ride on the pillion of a friend's motorbike. On arrival he was forced to tiptoe, hopefully unobserved (no chance), to his desk in stocking feet – as the crepe soles of his then very fashionable brothel creepers had fused to the bike's exhaust pipes.

P.J. and I were scribbling frantically at a very important air crash inquiry when the proceedings were brought to a sudden halt, at the most crucial point, with a message about P.J.'s roof tiles. The investigation was into the tragic crash in the centre of Stockport in 1967, when an airliner approaching Manchester Airport appeared to run out of fuel. No one died on impact, but then fire roared through the cabin with horrendous results.

The most important witness was the surviving pilot, who was actually walking past the press bench to give evidence when he was overtaken by a breathless usher with an urgent message for the chairman.

The pilot was momentarily halted in his tracks, with the chairman asking: "Is there a P.J. Wilson in the room? If so, will he please leave to investigate reports that a strong wind is causing tiles from the roof of his property in Ramsgate to cascade down on frightened passers-by." As my mate Richard Littlejohn would say: "You couldn't make it up."

After assigning me to follow English football hooligans yet again, this time to Vienna, P.J. added: "Off you go, old man. And don't come back without some *Sachertorte*." This is the most famous of Viennese cakes.

Everything went well in Vienna, but when I phoned in to say I would start heading back to London, P.J. came on to order: "Get straight to Frankfurt, old man. Some chap has been found dead in the toilet on a British Airways flight. He spent the night in a small village outside Frankfurt. Suss it out."

Needless to say, I thought quickly on my feet: "But that means there will be no *Sachertorte*." Quick as a flash came the reply: "Where are you going? Frankfurt? Well make it Black Forest gateau."

When P.J. was off, there were always others to maintain the merriment which made the *Mirror* such a delightful office to be part of. Barry Wigmore, for instance. His sense of direction was so dreadful that his long-suffering wife, Pauline, bought him a special car compass so he would find it easier to exit the underground office car park.

Well aware that after one half-pint of beer, Wiggers was well on his way to being a cot case, she produced a marvellous neck label which pleaded with fellow train passengers to "please put this man off at Reading".

When we all received those then revolutionary bleepers for the first time, it was Wigmore who volunteered the information that he would never give the number to his wife. Oh, no! Virtually, at the very moment he passed on this secret, there was a loud beep, beep – and he blushed slightly at the message, which read: "Don't forget the potatoes on the way home."

You have to be slightly bonkers to be a good journalist, and P.J. and Wigmore were top rung.

With those already mentioned I was extremely lucky to work with, or against, many members of the splendid Fleet Street family, with friendships forged and occasional social gatherings now bringing back all those memories:

Colin Mackenzie, Mary Riddell, Scotsmen Ramsay Smith, Gordon Hay, Ian McKerron and Colin Adamson, Hugh Whittow, Bill and Liz Hagerty, Geoff Sutton, Simon Hughes, Jim Davies, Phil Dampier, Bob and Christine Chesshyre, David Williams, John Blake, Frank Thorne, Matthew Engel, Vic Chapple, Geoff and Alison Webster...

And allies throughout those crazy days were the brilliant

promotions team at the *Mirror* who helped boost circulation, headed by the other JJ, the late and sadly missed John Jenkinson, and Peter Moeller, now helping organise the annual Mirror Old Farts Christmas get-together.

Immediate heads of departments such as news editors and sports editors can be expected to conjure up zany ideas and gimmicks, as they have to answer to the editor when the call comes for new ideas. But when the editor goes nuts then everyone suffers.

This was often the case on the old *Sun* with Dick Dinsdale, a bluff Yorkshireman who had earned his editor's stripes as a top back bench executive on the *Daily Mirror,* with its 5 million circulation per day, who knew just one way of addressing people, whoever they were – "cock". He was the only person on the staff to be banned from one of the office pubs in Covent Garden because of his language.

A splendid example of Dinsdale's thought process came at an evening editor's conference when news editor Ken James said he would be staffing the Albert Hall for the first concert by "the young singer Bob Dylan".

"Dylan," cried Dinsdale. "I thought that fooking Welsh poet was dead, cock?"

When he was stopped for speeding in his office Jaguar more than once on the same stretch of road, teams of reporters had to conduct an in-depth investigation into the Surrey Police traffic department. In the end some executive was brave enough to advise him to slow down when driving – "fook them, cock".

Then the editorial staff became experts on Bognor Regis sewage problems when "I had a funny smell this morning, cock."

But without doubt, the most bizarre incident unfolded when Dinsdale, always early in the office, shouted at the news editor: "I've just seen a Chinaman eating fooking grass, cock. Let's have a word with him."

Now it appears Dinsdale had spotted said person in St James's Park while being chauffeured down The Mall. For days the early reporter and photographer (I was dispatched on two occasions) found themselves on this weird hunt. We all came back with possible explanations but none was accepted until Harry Arnold found a Japanese ballet dancer performing some strange Oriental exercises and, to everyone's relief, there was an: "Okay, it must be him, cock."

Mind you, Dinsdale did have a motley crew on his editorial staff, the behaviour of whom might have driven him to speed rapidly away from the office and have visions of grass-chewing Chinamen. There were often unscheduled visits to the cells of nearby Bow Street police station.

Bob Adam was a quiet spoken Glaswegian who would indicate that your life might be in danger when he grabbed your wrist and snarled: "Don't start". When writing copy in a Glasgow milk bar he had taken exception to the music from a jukebox, and when no one responded to his "turn it fucking doon", he simply ripped the machine from the wall and threw it through, not out of, the window.

On another assignment during the journalistic turf wars in Glasgow, Adam, then on the *Scottish Daily Express*, took exception to the arrival of a reporter from main rival *Daily Mail* – so grabbed the ignition keys from his car and threw them over a cliff. On return to his office, Adam was severely reprimanded by his news editor for "not pushing his fucking car over yon cliff".

His removal to Bow Street was via the painful route after he had driven, full of a good liquid lunch, into a car park shared by many companies (it was an old World War II bomb crater), squared up to a man whom he thought was in a *Sun* bay, and when this driver claimed he was a police inspector simply knocked him down with one punch.

The man was speaking the truth, and his colleagues decided that it would be fun to drag Adam across the cinders of the temporary parking area and along the pavement to Bow Street. His knees took some time to heal.

Bob Adam left the *Sun* shortly afterwards – to become the fine arts correspondent of the *Daily Telegraph*.

Sitting alongside Bob Adam was Peter Batt. Now his antics could fill a book, and did - his autobiography *"Batty, The Life and Wild Times of the Guvnor of Fleet Street"*.

Here was one of Fleet Street's greatest characters, progressing from news reporter to the massively read sports columnist on the Murdoch *Sun,* before, as he explains so vividly in his book, he was brought down with a massive bang by the dreaded drink.

Perhaps he is best remembered for his first foreign assignment in 1963. A plane carrying British holidaymakers crashed into the side of a French mountain killing all aboard, and Batt, then of the *Daily Herald,* was one of the first to arrive at nearby Perpignan.

The next morning, after enjoying more than the usual French delights, he overslept, then disorientated and dishevelled attempted to conquer a blizzard and climb to the crash site. It was not long before he was apprehended by a group of locals, who, horrified at his "state of distress", excitedly leapt into emergency rescue mode and led him to a nearby hamlet where he was put in the care of some nuns.

The news spread like wildfire – there was one survivor from the crash. Fleet Street hacks came tumbling excitedly down the mountain, only to find a very hung over, and totally bamboozled Batty enjoying the comfort of a hospital bed

Sir Winston Churchill, one of the world's greatest statesmen, died in his sleep in January 1965, unaware that the final peacefulness of his passing had been initiated by Peter Batt.

The impending death of the 90-year-old war leader naturally attracted a massive media circus to encamp outside his Hyde Park Gate home. Nothing to compare with "doorsteps" these days but it did prompt scaffolding for TV cameras and noisy comings and goings from public telephones. Not the ideal sounds for a dying man.

It was the first occasion when the few radio reporters felt they were superior because they had microphones which did not distort comments. But we scribblers soon put paid to that!

The answer came when Sir Winston's son, Randolph

Churchill, who had a major drink problem, came lurching from the house and wandered up the road. The radio chaps felt they should have him to themselves, but we discovered that by clicking the tops of our pens (probably fountain pens in those days) we totally buggered their recordings. Problem solved.

The nearby Kensington Palace Hotel quite sensibly took the decision that Christmas had been extended and decided to keep an all-night bar for residents. Each national newspaper booked a room, but the management turned a blind eye to the non-residents when drinks were being ordered at 4.30 a.m. Batty and I fell in the latter category as we were the night shift for most of the week.

Now Churchill's physician was the very elderly, very frail Lord Moran, who had to be assisted to and from the house, with a policeman placing a rug over his knees once inside the car. There was betting talk about which man might go first, with the thought that any moment Churchill could be wheeled out to announce that "Lord Moran passed away at..."

It was after another round had been ordered in the early hours, and Batty was going strong in a card school, that the news flashed round the bar that Lord Moran had suddenly turned up at the house. At that hour, it had to be serious news. *Daily Express* reporter Keith Graves, later to become a star BBC and Sky correspondent, tried to sneak out for an exclusive, but was spotted – and the mayhem began.

We reached the top of Hyde Park Gate as Lord Moran, chauffeured as usual in his small Hillman Minx by a woman soldier, was heading for the main road. The car was forced to stop, and the aged doctor suddenly found himself eyeball to eyeball with a head that had taken advantage of his open window.

Lord Moran had at the best of times what could be described as the shakes, with his head permanently nodding. The sight of the Batt visage at nose rubbing distance made the nodding more pronounced, continuing as Batty asked: "Is he at his lowest ebb, Yer Lordship?"

When the nodding failed to stop Batty took the answer as

affirmative and released himself from the car to tell the world Sir
Winston Churchill was at his lowest ebb. The headlines next day
so infuriated Lady Churchill, she ordered the police to remove all
the press from Hyde Park Gate. Sir Winston lived another four
days, during which he heard nothing. And for the record, Lord
Moran died not too long afterwards.

On the morning of his death, we were all despatched to
churches and Churchill "interest areas". There was only one
story on the schedule that day. My assignment was St. Margaret's
Church, Westminster, the traditional place of worship for
everyone connected with the Houses of Parliament.

In attendance was former Conservative Prime Minister, Sir
Alec Douglas Home. As he strolled from the church – there was
no such thing as bodyguards and gun toting security in those
simple days – I tagged alongside him and asked him for a short
tribute to Sir Winston.

Sir Alec politely told me he had sent a personal message to
Lady Churchill, but he would prefer to wait until he addressed
the full House of Commons to make his full statement. I thanked
him and pulled away.

As I did so Sir Alec was forced to stop in his tracks and smile
for an elderly man who stepped out to take his picture. It was
pretty obvious from his appearance that he was American, and
this became patently clear when he offered his "Thanks, sir",
then turned to me and said: "That is one of my great ambitions
achieved. I have always longed to meet and photograph the Duke
of Windsor."

It was the Los Angeles Olympics 19 years later which brought
the curtain down on Peter Batt's Fleet Street career. He was
then a sports columnist on the *Daily Star,* and from where I was
positioned throughout those memorable Games, he did a splendid
job. With the killing nine-hour time difference, and the demand
from London for updated pieces each edition, Batty found himself
working into the early hours.

This meant drink was taken, mostly in the bar of the dreadful
Mayflower Hotel in downtown LA, where he was aided and

abetted by a barman who resembled the great boxer, Marvin Hagler. It was true that there were cockroaches in our rooms (demolition of the complete hotel complex commenced the day after the British Press left for home) but when Batty started complaining to reception that his were pink, the danger signals were hoisted.

At the Opening Ceremony the president of the International Olympic Committee, Juan Antonio Samaranch, brought total silence to the massive stadium as he launched into the traditional announcement before asking President Ronald Reagan to officially open the 23rd Olympiad.

As, in French and English, he started: "We are gathered here to...", the silence was broken by Batty, sitting directly behind me in the press box. He leapt to his feet and belted out one of his favourite pub songs: "'Ere we are again, 'appy as can be, all good pals and jolly good company".

For an encore at the Closing Ceremony, he managed to send a desktop TV set crashing to the ground.

It is sad to say that some of his colleagues grassed on him to the management in London and were conspicuous by their absence when he needed help to prevent the sack.

Singing in pubs had almost brought about Batty's downfall before. One evening Dick Dinsdale walked into the *Daily Herald/ Sun's* office pub known as the Radio Arms, as that was where the public radio had been situated during the Second World War Blitz, to find Batty having a knees-up with several of the old ladies from Covent Garden's Peabody Buildings.

Dinsdale suggested to news editor Ken James that he should tell Batty to shut up, or sack him. James quite rightly said he had every right to sing in a pub, especially as he was on a night off. Next morning Dinsdale was followed up the stairs by a still singing Batty: "Christ, not you again, cock! You're like a bloody walking jukebox."

That evening Dinsdale was a co-sponsor with Hugh Cudlipp and other *Mirror* top brass at the Snow Drop Ball at the Royal

Albert Hall. Batty and his great drinking companion Neville Hunter, a sub-editor on the *Daily Sketch,* were invited backstage by the *Mirror's* top show business writer, Don Short. Within minutes, as they would, they found themselves in the dressing room of the glamorous dancing troupe, the Tiller Girls.

As Batty told us all next day: "I am chatting up this bird when she and her mates start moving. I followed and fuck me I'm on stage at the Albert 'all." What made it worse, especially for Dick Dinsdale in his box, Frank Ifield was well into his hit "I Remember You", and an exuberant Batty joined in.

"Christ, cock, it's that walking bloody jukebox again," could be heard from afar.

The evening did not end there for Batty, Hunter and their two chosen Tiller Girls. The foursome boarded a taxi but the driver suspected from the slurred conversation that there might be a problem when it came to collecting the fare, so drove straight to the nearest police station.

Hunter then took over. A splendid piss artist who always sported horn-rimmed spectacles and pinstripe suit addressed the constable: "Good evening, hofficer. I am Neville Hunter of the *Daily Sketch,* this is my colleague Peter Batt of the *Daily Herald,* and these young ladies are Tiller Girls."

"Yeah, and I'm bleedin' Napoleon", brought an end to that romantic encounter.

They threw away the mould after Peter Batt decided to enter journalism. But how dull life would have been without him and his ilk. I feel privileged to have enjoyed his company as colleague and friend.

The singing at the Los Angeles Opening Ceremony also prompted another tale to tell about my *Mirror* colleague Frank McGhee. Frank, who took over the sports columnist role from Peter Wilson after the 1972 Munich Olympics, was a stubborn little chap, especially after his customary drinking sessions, which could take him through the complete card of spirits.

As the athletes of the world enjoyed themselves in the vast LA

Olympic Stadium the announcer blared out: "And noooooooow, ladies and gentlemen, the one and only Lionel Ritchie."

As this great singer of that time bounded into the arena, Frank turned to me, pushed his spectacles into position in order to focus on the rapturous reception, and asked: "Who's he?"

When I replied Lionel Ritchie, Frank hit back: "Don't be a prat all your life, Jacko. He plays for Sheffield Wednesday." There was indeed a professional footballer called Andy Ritchie, but he never topped the singing charts.

Frank's complete lack of showbiz knowledge had reached spectacular heights when in America to cover world championship fights. Several colleagues persuaded him to tag along with them when they were lucky enough to get seats for a club session by the great jazz pianist Oscar Peterson.

Needless to say, the performance brought a standing ovation, except for McGhee who remained seated. When the others queried his appreciation, he said in a rather loud stage whisper: "I've heard better pianists in my local pub." Hefty security guards decided it was time he departed.

His encore was even better. In Las Vegas he was handed a ticket for a Frank Sinatra concert. Perhaps the security guards had been tipped off but they were soon into action when our Frankie summed up the famous Frankie with a loud: "He can't sing."

On one occasion in Bilbao, McGhee lost more than his memory, and marbles. It was during the 1982 World Cup and the English media were enjoying a quiet night in the bar of the Ercilla Hotel. With former manager-cum-TV-frontman Lawrie McMenemy we all downed a few aperitivos before adjourning for a late (as ever in Spain) dinner.

Frank McGhee was there for the drinks but passed on the idea of food. So we left him, well seated at a convenient section of the bar. Many hours later, after a very jolly dining session we returned – and, yes, Frank hadn't moved.

The reason was simple – he was incapable of moving. Now all the English Press were resident at the hotel, except F. McGhee who always preferred to stay elsewhere away from the pack.

Long-time Madrid freelance Tim Brown made it quite clear
that he was not spending another late evening transporting the
man from the *Daily Mirror* to his bed – "I may be your stringer
but I have done my duty this week." So Kent Gavin and I moved
in to assist.

This entailed clutching him under each arm and literally
dragging/carrying the almost dead weight across the bar and
reception area out to a waiting taxi. Now this was not a simple
task, for the entrance to this particular hotel was underground
and the route from reception to pavement was up 20-odd steep
steps.

As we huffed and puffed to haul the remains of McGhee
upwards all we could hear were cries of: "Gavvers, Jacko – for
Christ's sake..." followed by a chorus of raucous laughter. We
couldn't stop, move our heads and reply: Frank was far too heavy.

Tim Brown had gone ahead and when we arrived breathless
on the kerb, we could see him gesturing towards this pitiful sight
from the nearby taxi rank. Several taxis cruised over, took a quick
look and, bafflingly, accelerated off without stopping. Gavvers
asked the unanswerable: "What's happening, Jacko?"

It was the seventh taxi driver, I believe, who happened to point
a finger at our problem, prompting us to look downwards.

Bloody hell, Frank's trousers had fallen down, were twisted
around his ankles, and the part they had left uncovered was not
a pretty sight. Gavvers and I had dragged this trouser-less sports
columnist all that way, totally unaware of his state.

The trouser situation was soon remedied, with me clutching
his belt while Gavvers persuaded a taxi driver that the comatose
McGhee would be no problem. He agreed to take him, with the
condition that we went with him.

At his hotel, Frank hung on to us but calamity hit again
when he attempted to salute the cheery "Buenos noches, Senor
McGhee" from the friendly doorman. His trousers promptly fell
to the floor again.

Gavvers and I lay Frank on his bed, checked he was still breathing and left. I telephoned early to ensure he was okay, to be greeted with the customary early morning McGhee: "Who do you think you are, calling at this hour? Fuck off."

The camaraderie among *Mirror* folk was underlined again in Los Angeles when McGhee fell into one of his periodic diabetic comas. I was in a room of the Mayflower Hotel a few doors away from Frank when I received a frantic phone call from sports news editor Tony Cornell in London.

Frank had been in the middle of dictating his Olympic boxing preliminary when there was a thud, and all the copytaker could hear was heavy breathing. I rushed to Frank's room, and receiving no reply, asked the chambermaid to open the door. But we were in the US of A: "No sir, I cannot open that door as you may be threatening violence, even worse."

Joined by the *Sunday Mirror's* columnist Ken Jones, we managed to convince the hotel manager of the true position, and in we went. As I attended to Frank, out cold on the floor, Ken picked up the dangling telephone which was uttering: "Hello, Frank. Are you still there, Frank?" and asked the copytaker how far he had reached.

Ken then carried on dictating, no doubt using much of the material he had reserved for his later *Sunday Mirror* piece. And was Frank grateful? When he came round, he looked at me, grabbed the phone from Ken, and shouted: "What are you doing in my room?"

As I was completing these memoirs news came of the death of dear chum Martin Johnson, sportswriter with the *Independent, Daily Telegraph* and *Sunday Times*. His wit upset many a superstar.

Of Mike Gatting's 1986 Ashes squad in Australia he reported there was only thing wrong: "They can't bat, they can't bowl, and they can't field."

After we had witnessed a failed performance by British slalom skier Emma Carrick-Anderson at the 1998 Nagano Winter Olympics he wrote: "Emma went one side of the poles, Carrick went the other, while Anderson went through the middle."

But perhaps the funniest experience came when Martin was sent at the very last moment to Las Vegas for a Lennox Lewis world championship fight. He arrived, checked into his hotel, then rushed to a taxi and asked to be taken to the weigh-in.

When the bemused cabbie ascertained which weigh-in he simply advised: "Just keep going east, buddy, until you see the sea, and then you'll find the weigh-in." The fight was taking place in New York City.

Martin belted back into the hotel, checked out, and as required dropped his card in the "have you forgotten to hand in your room card" box by the door. At the airport, when attempting to buy a ticket – calamity!

For payment he pulled out his hotel room card, having deposited his Visa card in the box at the door. He did make the fight.

One cold, miserable day just before Christmas 1965, my idea of a good job was not yet another marathon session in London's Regent's Park staring up at an escaped eagle called Goldie. I had endured enough hours gazing at this creature as day after day it played hide and seek and gave police, park keepers, media and interested onlookers nothing but the bird.

You can imagine my inner horror when news editor Ken James, with his customary formality when he knew he had a sticky assignment to hand out, shouted across the newsroom: "Mr Jackson, please pop along to Regent's Park and give us a nice ghosted interview with Goldie's wife." Ugh!!

I cannot recall which hostelry should have been credited with a dateline, or what sort of refreshment was needed to gain the confidence of this old bird, but the result was a large page lead headline in the broadsheet *Sun*: "My Selfish Husband – By Mrs Regina Goldie – in an interview with John Jackson".

"He needn't think he can come home to a warm nest and loving peck on the beak. As far as I am concerned the welcome perch outside the cage

can be removed and 'Goldie' struck off our joint plaque.

"I just cannot understand his attitude. He knows full well how I fretted and anxiously chirped the hours away when he flew off for 12 days freedom in March.

"He occasionally swooped then to give me an 'I'm okay' yelp, but shivers went through my feathers each time I thought of those humans with nets.

"Goldie and I have often squawked of one day getting away from the bars, damp weather and peering faces to return home to Finland. Being a male he has the wanderlust more than I — but I feel these cage escapes have been most selfish.

"I know I have hen-pecked him into flying up and down the bars in desperation. And, of course, I have failed in my duty by not giving him an eaglet he could treasure.

"But, I'm afraid eagles do not breed in captivity. This he understands, but from what I gather it was only hunger which brought him home last time.

"I don't think I can stand another dose of that. Goldie made a fool of himself flitting from tree to tree, and then there was that terrible business of him attacking the small dog and eating the muscovy duck.

"The Regent's Park Zoo authorities tried to help us patch up our wing-wide differences.

"We were happy for several months, but then those rumours of me 'expecting' (I think it was that evil old vulture next door who started them) caused the yelping and feather-raising again.

"At the moment all I can think is 'Never darken my roost again'. But like all wives I will probably relent when dawn comes and I hear his yelp echoing across the park".

If only half the well-known personalities I have interviewed during my time had been as forthcoming. She was a true Regina!

On the occasion I had the honour to meet yer actual Regina, Her Majesty, I finished up having a slight disagreement with Prince Philip. It was 1974 and I was covering the Royal Tour

of New Zealand following the Christchurch Commonwealth
Games.

At a reception on the Royal Yacht Britannia, berthed at
Lyttleton, I shook hands along the receiving line with the Queen,
Prince Philip, Prince Charles, Princess Anne and Captain Mark
Phillips, and then had a chat with Philip, standing alongside the
Queen.

We could not agree over the recent decision to drop the
word British and refer only to the Commonwealth Games. He
suddenly, without glancing in her direction, threw out an arm,
narrowly missed Her Majesty's left ear with his pointing finger,
causing a frightened expression and her handbag to quiver, and
declared: "The Queen is head of the Commonwealth."

My suggestion that British Commonwealth was more
appropriate brought an instant change of subject, but the
Queen smiled.

Then there was the lunchtime when a phone call from Ken
James interrupted a very good Guinness session in the Cross
Keys and I was ordered to get myself to Buckingham Palace
immediately. Singer Frankie Vaughan was about to arrive to
present a large cheque to a gathering of Duke of Edinburgh
Awards Scheme youngsters.

As ever in a suit I was appropriately dressed when I climbed the
stairs to the ballroom, with the musicians playing in the gallery
and flunkeys everywhere, but the Guinness had worked its way
downward. And that meant a pee – and urgently.

I outlined my predicament to a uniformed footman, who
was quick to point out that I was out of luck as the only way
to the public toilets was now blocked off by hordes of excited
youngsters heading up the stairs to a meeting with Prince Philip.
My expression was enough to convince anyone that an emergency
situation was at hand.

Without another thought he issued the relieving instructions,
stressing that he would only say them once so I needed to pay
careful attention: "Follow me as I walk around the back of Her

Majesty's throne. I will turn right, and then right again. When I turn the second time you must keep walking straight at the wall. You will activate the opening of a door which does not appear to be there."

Oh yeah! He turned immediately, without waiting for my response, and I set off on what I envisaged would be an embarrassing incident involving Man Full of Guinness Crashes Into Palace Wall. But, true to his prediction, I somehow tripped a device under the carpet and this wonderful hole appeared in the wall.

Inside I used the loo which was obviously reserved for a lady. The seat was firmly secured, and impossible to lift. (I presume Prince Philip has his own or has learnt not to splash.) I even enjoyed a short rest on the sofa, looking out over the Royal Gardens, wondering how often the Queen might use it as a bolthole to escape boring receptions. Who was impressed with meeting Frankie Vaughan after that experience?

Years later in 2000 when I was hovering around the same spot on the occasion of the reception for the triumphant British Olympic team, fresh from golden glory in Sydney, I wondered if I might uncover the floorboard from which I could cause the door to fly open again.

Fortunately, I decided to check my immediate surroundings, and to my horror found both the Queen and Princess Anne heading my way. I thought they might be needing a similar "Guinness break" so moved aside. In fact, they were being escorted to a chat with heavyweight boxer Audley Harrison.

A boxer who spent many an evening in the company of *Mirror* people was John Conteh, who became a very worthy world champion. He enjoyed chewing the fat in our pub.

Just as John Conteh was at home in the company of us *Mirror* hacks, the contact worked both ways. We always had a lead on any story away from the actual boxing ring, which, of course, in turn placed a few extra readies in his pocket. His greatest pal was snapper supreme Kent Gavin, a *Mirror* man to his bootstraps, who gave a splendid rundown of his career, including exploits in

Tramp and other night spots with the great names of sport and showbiz, in a racy autobiography appropriately entitled *Flash Bang Wallop*.

Gavvers is one of these people who obviously exited his mother's womb on the telephone. In this day and age he can have his mobile permanently plugged into his ear, but in days gone by he had to be as close as possible to a "dog and bone" at all times. When in the *Stab* its one phone would never stop ringing, and 99 per cent of the time it would lead to "Gavvers" being yelled from behind the bar.

Regular callers would be George Best, Joan Collins, Bobby Moore, most winners of the Miss World contest still under 40, Alan Ball, Linda Lusardi, the secretary of Arsenal FC – you name them, Gavvers knew them and, most importantly, they trusted him.

The liver specialist who managed to prolong George Best's life might be interested to hear that on the great man's 40th birthday he phoned Gavvers, and the *Mirror* had yet another exclusive.

George came to the office, Gavvers and I took him across the road to our favourite drinking hole, Vagabonds, where landlord John Mulally, a fellow Ulsterman, was ordered by George: "Mineral water, please. Life begins at 40. I'll never drink again."

By the time the *Mirror* hit the breakfast tables next morning, with our front page "Best will never drink again" exclusive, news was filtering through that George had "somehow" forgotten his pledge and had been involved in another Tramp incident.

So, it was no surprise on a cold lunchtime in January 1979, that the warmth of the bonhomie in the *Stab* was interrupted with a call for Gavvers. He returned from the phone on the end of the bar, downed his customary cold light ale, and declared: "Jacko, we're getting Conteh married for a grand." A visitor from Mars would have scratched his tentacles and left for saner climes.

But I appreciated that at that time of day we needed a quick scoot up the A1 to the Conteh home in Bushey, Herts. The situation was simple. Conteh had finally succumbed to pressure to tie the knot with his long-time companion, ex model Veronica Smith, and was canny enough to know the expense, and some, could be covered with a few quid from his mates at the *Mirror.* Why not?

On arrival, with the January light fading, Gavvers rushed in to grab the happy snap of the newly married couple and their children, Joanna, eight weeks, and James, 18 months (now a successful golf professional). Once completed, John Conteh turned to me and asked: "Okay, John, what would you like?"

I suggested that the ideal exclusive story line would be for Conteh to explain how, when awaking that morning, he had been told he was invited to a wedding and on arrival found it was his own. He went along with that and his "story" read extremely well:

"As I am in training for my next fight, I went out for a morning run at 6.30, then climbed back into bed when I got home.

"When I was woken and told I was going to a wedding, I felt in fine shape for a few glasses of champers while somebody else got lumbered. When I got to the register office I found I was the bridegroom."

Veronica told how she had finally decided to take matters into her own hands when Conteh had proved impossible to pin down. On the spur of the moment, she paid £25 for a special licence and told him the day had come.

Great story. The new Mr and Mrs John Conteh, were happy, my *Mirror* bosses were very pleased. So it was back to the *Stab* for a celebration drink, and more phone calls for Gavs.

The whole scenario almost blew up in my face a few days later, however, when, attracted I am sure by my story, John Conteh was invited to appear on the popular Eammon Andrews TV chat show. Everything went well with the primarily boxing chat, until Andrews turned to the wedding news.

"I gather congratulations are in order."

"Oh, thank you. Yeah, it was great," replied Conteh.

"And you knew nothing about it until you arrived at the register office," said Andrews, glancing at a copy of my cutting I could see stacked with papers near his elbow.

Then horror.

"No, it had been planned days...", muttered Conteh, prompting me to yell certain suggestions at the TV set, just as the boxer's seconds did when he was in the ring. Fortunately, Conteh remembered in time. Whether he spotted the cutting, or suddenly thought back to discussing the best storyline with me, he confirmed the story.

"Yeah, that's right. It was quite a surprise." Panic over.

Whatever the panic then, it could not compare to my reaction seven years later when asked by the *Mirror's* wonderfully enthusiastic sports editor, Keith Fisher (I refrain from using the more descriptive crackers, potty, crazy or even loopy, as Fish is a character) to pad up and face an over from the world's then top fast bowler, West Indian Malcolm Marshall.

I was in Jamaica and just happened to be watching closely through high powered binoculars when a beamer from Marshall splattered the nose of England's Mike Gatting. Fellow West Indian quickie Joel Garner found a piece of bone embedded in the ball.

Fisher thought it would be a great first-person piece for me to face Marshall at full pace on the same Sabina Park wicket and describe in detail what Gatting obviously went through. Well, I made enquiries (honest, I did!) but Marshall, photographer Graham Morris and I just could not find a time during the Test Match when all would be free for me to walk out to the middle and take guard. Phew!

It was this nasty injury which brought one of the great questions of all time. Gatting flew back to London for treatment, with bruised nose and black and blue eyes and cheeks giving him the appearance of a panda.

At Heathrow Airport he was met by the press posse, and found it hard to stifle a smile, causing pain across his battered visage, when a microphone appeared under his nose and an ITN reporter asked: "Where did the ball hit you?"

This was not the first of Keith Fisher's determination to get
a "different" Malcolm Marshall in the paper. Before I left on
this 1986 England tour, he shouted down the *Mirror* room:
"Get Malcolm Marshall dressed up as Mr T." (Mr T was then a
favourite, colourfully garbed character in an American TV series
which children, certainly my four, loved.)

When I dared query the reason for this he replied: "Cos I've
got the headline ready for your prelim piece – *The Killing Fields*".
When I pointed out that Mr T was a TV character and The
Killing Fields referred to atrocities in Cambodia, there was no
waning of enthusiasm from dear old Fish. Sadly, again Marshall
could not find time to help.

Keith Fisher, who unhappily fell on hard times after the
Maxwell *Mirror* bubble burst, was a constant source of fun, often
embarrassment, but always a laugh.

No better example than a performance in the hallowed
Wimbledon halls of the snooty All England Club on the occasion
of the annual, black tie Lawn Tennis Writer's Dinner just before
Christmas. Fisher arrived late, having inspected several hostelries
en route from Holborn Circus, and proceeded to tell all within
shouting distance of his passionate love for Arsenal Football Club.

Another reason for the obvious necessity to imbibe on the
journey was to mourn the death that day of Freddie Mercury,
sensational singer with top band Queen.

So here we were in the All England Club executive lounge,
a mere lob from the famous Centre Court, with Fisher about
to show anyone interested that he had an Arsenal tattoo on his
shoulder. His jacket had gone and his shirt was about to follow,
when the top table, obviously unaware of this sideshow at the
other end of the room, called for the loyal toast.

As the traditional call of "The Queen" amplified around
the room, a totally dishevelled Fisher leapt on to a chair and
responded to the name with a vociferous: "Freddie Mercury. God
bless him."

Not even John McEnroe on his bad days could bring such

looks of disdain.

Sitting at the top table was the All England Club chairman, R.E.H "Buzzer" Hadingham, with whom I had crossed swords a year earlier – over the said John Patrick McEnroe. The incident also prompted a certain four-letter barrage from Fleet Street's then most famous, and successful, editor.

This was a classic example of a story which, because of breaking news agenda, had to be chopped and changed from edition to edition, resulting in a shortened, and obviously for the person concerned, distorted final report.

John McEnroe, at the height of his Superbrat period and the Wimbledon champion the previous two years, was enjoying a relationship with film star Tatum O'Neal, whom he later married. It was well documented that his off-court tantrums up to then had come after he was photographed with girls or questioned about his love life. The previous year he had been on his own and Wimbledon enjoyed a quieter fortnight

So it was a valid question I put to Buzzer at the March All England Club press conference when the prize money and other details were announced for the 1985 tournament. (For the record, McEnroe would have earned £130,000 if he had won his third successive singles title. But he exited in the quarter-final and handed the glory to a red-headed German teenager named Boris Becker.)

"Mr Hadingham, do you feel it might be better in many respects if John McEnroe attended Wimbledon this year without his girlfriend Tatum O'Neal?"

Buzzer, then 69, agreed, and although he admitted he did not concern himself with the private affairs of players, said he would write to McEnroe and others about off-court behaviour.

At around 1.30 a.m. the following morning I was woken from a deep sleep by an agitated acting night news editor, Philip Belsham. He explained that Mr Hadingham had just phoned in a somewhat excited state, complained about the story, "called you a c..., called me a c..." and said he would take it up with the highest authority, before slamming the phone down.

At times like that it was always important to find out what exactly had appeared under my by-line, as once I had submitted the copy by whatever means, events would dictate any action taken by sub editors and their masters on the back bench.

No problems were apparent with the front-page single column, topped EXCLUSIVE and headlined "Don't Bring Tatum, Wimbledon chief's plea to McEnroe". My words had been, shall we say, "manoeuvred" into seven crisp paragraphs, but all the facts were intact.

Needless to say, I lay awake going over the events in my mind and it was not long before something in the brain indicated forcefully that the man who had phoned the news desk was not Buzzer Hadingham. He may have been alerted to the story at that late hour by other newspapers trying to catch up – but he would never use such language.

It did not take long next day to unravel the mystery. The call had been made from our drinking den, Vagabonds, by a certain Kelvin MacKenzie, then editor of the *Sun*.

Unhappy at missing the story, when shown our first edition, he decided to cause a bit of mischief with a phone call to the news desk, pretending to be Hadingham. These things happen. No harm was caused, although a totally innocent Belsham was not too happy at being described so harshly.

Buzzer may not have made the call, but he was soon putting pen to paper to outline his disquiet at the *Mirror* story. In an officially typed letter to my home he stressed he was "both amazed and not a little angry at the total inaccuracy of the report".

I replied by return, expressing sadness that he was upset but pointing out that the story had been cut hurriedly at the last moment following a football riot at a Luton Town match.

I added: "This is a fact of life in national newspaper journalism, which often brings problems for the reporter on the spot. I repeat, however, that I do not offer this as an excuse for at the end of the day I was the person to originate the copy."

This brought a handwritten note from Buzzer: "Thank you for your letter, and your handsome apology! I propose to forget the whole thing now and I do of course know how things can get distorted."

But Buzzer was soon to realise he did not know everything about the newspaper industry, so couldn't immediately forget his annoyance. He was obviously unaware that my story would be sent out worldwide by the news agencies such as Reuters and Associated Press, and possibly followed up in other countries.

So, the next communication from him a few days later enclosed a photostat of a short piece published in *USA Today* headlined: "Official hopes McEnroe stays with singles" At the top he had scrawled: "John Jackson. Now see what you've done!" then highlighted a sentence and written alongside: "More fabrication. Even you did not say this."

His final comment: "Who first thought of the expression POPULAR Press? Not with (sic) me! Buzzer H."

The pleasant end to this flurry of correspondence was prompted by my mentioning that our temporary fall-out had come in my 21st year covering Wimbledon. Buzzer wrote that when I reached 25 "I will look forward to standing you a drink – always assuming I am around at that time."

When he retired as chairman in 1989, I sent him a letter wishing him well, and received a delightful reply: "Dear John. I much appreciated your letter and the good wishes. I have had a flood from all over the place, but yours gave me considerable pleasure – thank you. Your wishes are reciprocated. Yours sincerely, Buzzer."

And when I reached my 40th Wimbledon, I am very pleased to say Buzzer Hadingham was still going strong as an All England Club vice president.

My tussle with Buzzer Hadingham was nothing to compare with the possible "aggro" I was instructed to stir up between all the great action men of film and TV screens. Can you imagine standing at a bar with Clint Eastwood, Sean Connery, Paul Michael Glaser, David Soul (Starsky and Hutch) and Telly Savalas (Kojak), and provoking a situation to prompt a rare old punch-up?

It happened on the occasion of the annual Bob Hope Classic Pro-Am Golf Tournament at Moor Park, which always attracted a host of show business names to join the top golf pros. The initial handout said all these five stars would be staying at the Mount Royal Hotel in Knightsbridge.

"Book in and get amongst the action when everything goes up in the bar," was the order from my news desk. The room was arranged, and Barbara arranged a babysitter. It was very rare that we had the chance to stay in a top London hotel.

Needless to say, we had a very quiet evening. Although Telly Savalas played in the tournament he did not stay at the hotel, while the others remained at home. The only celebrities we espied over dinner were former US President Gerald Ford, a golfing nut and regular in the Bob Hope Classic, and the man himself, Eltham-born Hope. Both were surrounded by battalions of large men having long conversations with their cufflinks – and neither went near the bar.

This was a far cry from my other encounter with Bob Hope. This took place on the night of the 1970 Miss World contest in the Royal Albert Hall. Hope was the cabaret hired to fill in the time between the international beauties changing from the bikini parade to the customary, and excruciatingly embarrassing, question and answer session.

I was always of the opinion that Bob Hope was not a very funny man. He was brilliant at situation comedy, and often prompted me to laugh during his stand-up comic routines, but it was obvious he was nothing without the scripts and jokes from a multitude of writers. He could not ad lib – and in front of the bevy of beauties on this occasion he proved it.

His act was totally shattered when flour bombs started raining down on him as militant Women's Lib supporters let vent their opposition to the annual Miss World "cattle market". A true comedian – Eric Morecambe, Jimmy Tarbuck, Bob Monkhouse spring to mind – could have carried it off with humour and cutting quips. Hope lost it and stumbled from the stage a sad figure.

My job on the night was to cover the outside happenings (yeah, I always got the big ones!) while colleague Kenelm Jenour was with the excitement and glamour inside. In my area the police immediately sprang into action, as further protestors attempted to break through cordons to confront the paying customers, in black tie and posh frocks, with such chants as "emancipation, emancipation" and "show us your Y-fronts, men".

One unhappy snapper that night was my colleague Kent Gavin. Now Gavvers had been very close to the Miss World contest from its inception, and he was always ready to suggest possible mates as judges.

But on the Bob Hope night everything went wrong. The winner was a total outsider – Miss Grenada – who had not featured in the Gavvers Guide. I might just add that the Prime Minister of this Caribbean island was one of the judges.

The Miss World contest was devised and run throughout by Mr and Mrs Morley – hard task master Eric, who first told the world "I will announce the result in reverse order", and Julia, who has acted as headmistress/chaperone/mother superior to generations of those, who in those far distant days, we still called "lovelies".

After one contest at the Lyceum, when the winner was a Miss United Kingdom with a history in the Portsmouth area that was bound to make front page headlines for several days, I was invited back to the Morley suite at the Waldorf Hotel.

With me was a great mate from the *Daily Express,* an old rascal called Frank Howitt (he was very proud of his son Peter who went on to star in the TV soap *Bread* and later wrote an award-winning film script).

Now Frank had enjoyed the Morley hospitality and made the mistake of rather rudely criticising the absent Eric as Julia was praising some new programme he had introduced that year.

An angry Julia stopped speaking but the rest of her body sprang into action immediately. With a right hand cross and a look that Mike Tyson would have paid for, she hit Howitt so hard that I was sure his head moved several inches away from his spinal column. "Apologise," she cried.

"Okay," said Howitt, but promptly repeated, from just above his right shoulder, his earlier comments.

The only consolation was that Julia this time chose a more vicious left cross, which bashed Howitt's head back into place. It would be fair to say we were asked to leave. Howitt phoned me next day to say Covent Garden was out of roses, as he had sent all available with apologies to Julia.

Members of Parliament are well known for often making unremarkable statements. But it's rare that they admit they don't know what they are talking about. One did to me.

It was 1969 and a press conference with the then Postmaster General, John Stonehouse. He is best remembered for trying to fake his own death, being named as a Czech spy, and eventually being jailed for fraud.

The conference was to announce that Government departments now had computers that would work away together at night after being fed material by humans. Now for a person who today still finds some new technology baffling this was, 50 years ago, science fiction. And Jimmy Lewthwaite from the *Sun,* sitting alongside me, agreed.

As he finished reading his prepared statement, I posed the first question: "Postmaster General, I am not the only one here who hasn't a clue what you are talking about." To which Stonehouse smiled and replied: "Thank goodness. Nor do I. I simply read the statement prepared by my staff."

The man who was at that time deputy leader of the governing Labour Party often failed to understand what he was doing, but that was down to the dreaded drink. He was George Brown, whose drunken escapades filled many a column inch.

The most famous came when he was on an official visit to Peru and was attending a dinner in his honour in Lima. When the music struck up he informed his party "I'm going to have a dance with the lady in red."

He was immediately rebuffed by his chosen dance partner: "I will not dance with you on three counts. One, this is not a dance tune as it is the Peruvian national anthem; two, I am not a woman I am a man; three, I am the Papal Nuncio to Peru."

There was a personal occasion when I discovered a very sober George Brown holding the hands of two of our children and pointing out the birds in St James's Park. Barbara and I had taken them up to London for a warm summer outing.

As we reached the park they ran ahead and the next thing we knew they were chatting with this small man. I said to Barbara that it looked very much like George Brown. It was and he explained that he was walking slowly to the House of Commons but so enjoyed seeing the large variety of birds.

I was on the night shift at the *Mirror* and casually suggested on the way home that it would be ironical if I was given another George Brown drunk story. Lo and behold, on entering the office I was sent straight to the Garrick Club where George had been blackballed for throwing bread rolls at famous columnist, broadcaster and theatre critic Bernard Levin.

I never dreamt that being a father of four would assist when one Sunday morning in 1974 I was despatched to Chelsea to question Health Secretary Sir Keith Joseph who had managed to outrage most of the nation again.

He had further encouraged his nickname of Mad Monk by suggesting that poor people should stop giving birth as their "low intelligence" produced problem children. After he explained he was quoting from a Child Poverty Action report written by a married couple, both doctors, I asked how many children he had.

"Four," he said. I said that I had four also.

Back at the office I set out to contact the doctors, found they were at a conference in Montreal and managed to get through to the wife. After she explained that their report only concerned the situation in Scotland and certainly produced no statistics to support Sir Keith's "horrible" comments, I asked how many children she had.

When she replied four, I said: "That's interesting. Sir Keith has four, you have four, and I have four."

"Ah yes," came from across the Atlantic: "but in our time we just pinned our ears back and got at it, didn't we?" I can't remember if I replied!

An observation at a press conference can cause one of many reactions. Humour was the order of the day at an announcement in the early 1970s by Cardinal Heenan, Archbishop of Westminster, outlining that the Catholic Church was to allow the laity to conduct all services for a week.

Sermons would be limited to 10 minutes, but I asked what would happen if a refugee from Hyde Park's Speakers' Corner refused to stop preaching?

Cardinal Heenan knew the answer: "You must always remember the words of St Augustine: 'The laying on of hands need not necessarily be gentle'."

Another occasion when a question of mine was used by a celebrity to emphasise his feelings came at the first wedding of Beatle drummer Ringo Starr in 1965. As their honeymoon started at a friend's house in Brighton, he and bride Maureen patiently spared a few moments for us hacks.

With the Beatles topping the world's pop charts I asked cheekily: "Your fame could have chosen any woman in the world, so why is Maureen the lucky one?" To this, dopey *Daily Sketch* reporter Mike Ward commented: "What a bloody stupid question."

Ringo hit straight back: "No it's not a stupid question. I love her, that's why." Ward got worse: "What a bloody stupid answer." Ringo smiled.

After telling us all that the story was a non-starter and he was off for a livener, Mike Ward received the mother of bollockings

from his office and chased the rest of us all evening to retrieve the
quotes he had failed to note.

And then there was comedian Max Wall who couldn't
remember any of his jokes. This happened in the early 1970s
when this talented entertainer made a comeback after a
turbulent marriage to a former Miss Great Britain, and a nervous
breakdown.

The *Mirror's* night editor Mike Taylor was a great Max Wall
fan and decided to brighten up a wet Sunday with a "welcome
back Max" story featuring ten of his best jokes. I was dispatched
to Richmond Theatre in south-west London to ask the funny
man his favourites.

As I clambered over crates of Guinness in his tiny dressing
room, with him made-up as his famous character Professor
Wallofski, Max took a swig of the black stuff and said: "Sitting
here, I can't remember any Max Wall jokes." He explained that
once he walked on the stage that evening, they would come
flooding back.

That would be too late so we had the hilarious situation where
Mike Taylor and others collated their favourite Max Wall jokes, I
relayed them to the man himself to which he kept saying: "Oh I
like that one." It does make you laugh!

There was one big showbiz story, trying for an explanation
from actor Richard Burton, when I and the press pack agreed to
keep quiet and leave the tricky query to the man from Reuters
who said: "I'm Welsh and I know him well from the old days."

We were waiting outside London's Dorchester Hotel for
Burton and his beautiful, equally superstar wife Elizabeth Taylor
(they married and divorced each other twice) to discover the
truth about rumours they had argued and he had given her a nasty
black eye.

The taxi pulled up and Burton leapt out, leaving a distressed
Taylor, wearing very large dark glasses still seated. As he stormed
into the hotel his "mate" from Reuters said: "Dick...".

Burton stopped momentarily, and with that marvellous

baritone voice which had graced many Shakespearean stage, replied: "My name is Richard" – and strode through the swing doors. It was a simple "Thanks, mate" to our Reuters colleague, but the pictures of Elizabeth Taylor stood up the story, and saved him.

On another occasion I wandered into a St Martin's Lane pub behind Burton, Taylor and fellow thespian Peter O'Toole. Without asking, Burton ordered three pints of bitter. The very hard drinking Burton and Irishman O'Toole downed them immediately, while Taylor, more accustomed to a glass of champagne, hovered.

Because of the growing interest in them the men decided to leave. Burton turned to his wife and shouted: "Drink it." She took a sip then raced after them.

An occasion when fame interrupted our reporting at an Olympics came at Montreal in 1976 when Scottish swimmer David Wilkie was going for gold. We arrived at the pool to be told we could not sit in the press box. I glanced down to see just two men enjoying our rows of seats and asked why.

"Because they want to be alone," said the official. They turned out to be Mick Jagger and Telly Savalas.

Fortunately, they escaped serious physical damage from certain Scottish scribes, as Wilkie stormed home and we all progressed to his press conference. Both Jagger and Savalas apologised later over celebratory refreshment.

Having breakfast with Hollywood greats was a regular occurrence when I was on the *Auckland Star*. It was the late 1950s when everyone travelled by ship and those who crossed the Pacific all called at Auckland. I would go out regularly at the crack of dawn on the customs launch, scale up a ladder and go in search of stories.

There were plenty from all areas but none better than a sumptuous breakfast with Hollywood stars Gregory Peck and Ernest Borgnine.

People who disembarked for a weekend found Auckland dead.

(Sir Clement Freud was one of many who claimed to be the first to announce: "I arrived in New Zealand on a Friday and found it closed.")

For night owls in Auckland, with pubs closing at 6 p.m. and restaurants limited, the answer was the Pie Cart, a splendid Café de Wheels hitched up to the fire hydrant in Shortland Street.

Customers in my time who enjoyed standing on the pavement with their pies included the American singing group The Platters, comedian Stan Freberg, and 1950s pop star Tommy Sands, then married to Frank Sinatra's daughter Nancy.

There were times when one had to "mind" stars so as to keep an exclusive from rivals. I momentarily lost Lena Zavaroni, the unfortunate Scottish singer who found fame aged 10 but anorexia nervosa and clinical depression brought a tragic death at 35. Having smuggled her away from her home I let her go shopping alone for a set time in Oxford Street, and panicked when she was late returning.

But I had no such problem with Hollywood great Natalie Wood. She was on crutches following a leg injury.

People in the public eye quite rightly complain when strangers rudely interrupt their enjoyment when dining out. It is rare that the roles are reversed. But it happened during my two pleasant years on the *Manchester Evening News.*

And the perpetrator was the famous Irish poet and playwright, who did enjoy a drink – Brendan Behan.

He had suddenly arrived in Manchester, announcing he wanted to renew his memory of Strangeways Prison, then meet the writer Shelagh Delaney who was being praised for her play *A Taste of Honey.* He described her as "the only flower left in this cultural desert".

After writing a diary piece about two former French Foreign Legionnaires opening a restaurant in Manchester's Moss Side, Barbara and I were invited to dinner along with *MEN* colleague Jack McNamara and his girlfriend Una.

Jack Mac, like Barbara, hailed from New Zealand's North

Island, and remained the newspaper's celebrated rugby league correspondent for 36 years.

The four of us were enjoying the new restaurant's cuisine when there was a sudden commotion in the kitchen. The door flew open and out fell the easily recognised Brendan Behan. Barbara has always said that on such occasions "John attracts them like flies", and sure enough the inebriated Irishman made a beeline for our table.

He grabbed a chair, pushed it between Jack and me, placed his arms round our necks and stared across the table at Barbara and Una.

"All right," he declared in his broad Dublin accent. "I know what you're thinking. We three drink too much, smoke too much and go out with too many other women. But I'll tell you one thing, we fooking love you."

With that he got up, strode over and hoisted the chef by the seat of his pants, shouted "three cheers for Monsieur le chef", dropped him, and disappeared out of the front door.

Probably the two words that are most hated by a news reporter are *vox pop*. Having to venture out into a busy shopping thoroughfare and accost people with the question your news desk had conjured up a few moments beforehand, is not a task logged under the heading bliss. Even for the hardest nuts, it can become embarrassing.

So allow me to divulge the odd secret. Next time you glance through your local paper and enjoy answers given by readers to a current question of the week, study the names and addresses. This, I should add, is when a vox pop does not include pictures of each individual.

You will no doubt discover the surnames are rather common, and they all live in the longest main roads or largest blocks of flats. And I can guarantee that if you were in the mood to contact them by phone to discuss their thoughts on whether a new sewer pipe should run through the local swimming pool, or the incoming mayor should be allowed to list his pet tortoise as his deputy, they will all be "not listed".

How do I know? There have been many occasions when I
have found a cosy corner in a nearby pub and "made contact"
with these readers. It is amazing the times they lived in Stockport
Road, Levenshulme, (*Manchester Evening News*), Borough Road,
Birkenhead (*Birkenhead Advertiser/News*), Old Kent Road and
Harrow Road (*Daily Mirror*) – and the majority were called
Smith, Hill, Jones, and, always a winner, Patel and Shah. And
what a variety of answers.

When accompanied by a photographer, there was no
alternative to fronting up genuine people. Mind you, many
love the thought of having their picture in the paper, so life was
somewhat easier.

One famous occasion, however, almost had me under arrest.
The old broadsheet *Sun* had recently launched and was using vox
pops in certain pinpointed areas as circulation boosters.

I was despatched to Bedford to approach shoppers leaving the
major supermarkets with our question of the day (we are talking
1964 so it was then controversial): "Will the slot machine sale of
contraceptives be an incitement to promiscuity?"

There were two problems. Firstly, the question was such a
mouthful that I needed to take a deep breath, make sure my
teeth were in working order, and think deeply in order to get
the question over clearly. Secondly, the accosted residents,
predominantly middle-aged women laden with bags of food,
either blushed with horror if they understood the question, or, the
majority, continued to stare at me as if I was totally off my trolley,
before replying: "What was that?" Another deep breath, and I
was off again, with many walking away without waiting for the
second rendition.

Matters were getting increasingly difficult when a tap on the
shoulder and a familiar "Now then, now then..." indicated a
gentleman of the law was wishing to ask *me* a question. In plain
clothes, and immediately admitting he was an off-duty sergeant
waiting to pick up his wife, he did not hide the fact that he felt
I was harassing shoppers, which might suggest a summons to his

colleagues at the nearby nick.

I identified myself and the photographer and explained how we were asking our question of the day. Of course, he wanted to know the question. Deep breath, teeth checked: "Will the slot machine sale of contraceptives be an incitement to promiscuity?"

Quite frankly, I did not know what to expect, but was not only shocked but thrilled with the reply: "Ah, I'm glad you asked me that. It is a very important question for family life today. I am the leader of the local youth club and feel this sort of thing is a dangerous, and backward step."

He not only posed for a picture, but also helped us approach people who would assist with our enquiries. If only other occasions had been so easy.

The vox pop prize, if there ever was such a thing, must however go to the marvellous freelance in York who was called during the early days of the present *Sun* and asked to conduct a ring-around among top religious leaders to put to them a special question of the moment.

The Anglican Archbishop of York was receptive, as were other top church men, but from the Roman Catholic diocese the hungry stringer, who I remember as Bernard, struck a consistent refusal at every attempt to get through to the bishop.

Now Bernard was himself a staunch Catholic, and this persistent act of non-cooperation over several days, prompted him into what many might describe as an over-the-top reaction. He wrote a letter of complaint to Rome.

It worked. A few days later he received a grovelling phone call from the bishop's secretary, was assured that no offence was intended, and could he make his way up to their office immediately? Bernard arrived, and was ushered straight through to the religious presence.

The bishop did, however, after another lengthy apology, point out that he thought a letter to His Holiness at the Vatican was a slight over reaction, and did not hide the obvious fact he had received something of a Papal bollocking.

"But let's put all that in the past," said the bishop. "What was it you wanted to ask me?"

"Right," said Bernard. "It is the *Sun* question of the day."

"Certainly, go ahead," replied the bishop.

"Okay, do you think the mini skirt is here to stay?"

The full reply has never been officially recorded.

Perhaps the one time I would have willingly volunteered to carry out a vox pop was when I was told to live for a week on food costing no more than 5p a day. It was during the early days of Oxfam in the 1960s and a report that starving people in Africa were being forced to survive on a diet costing one shilling (5p in today's money).

A rotund, extremely well fed old *Sun* deputy editor called Roger Wood decided I was the ideal candidate to lose a few pounds while testing the horrors of such a situation.

Barbara did sterling work in purchasing the food for my daily nosh (lentils and the like were available for a shilling), and I set about this near hunger strike assignment at our small flat in Barnes, south-west London, while the rest of the country continued to enjoy the Swinging Sixties down the Kings Road in nearby Chelsea and other spots.

We did have a TV and the then "rabbit ears" aerial, which had to be continually readjusted, but the reception virtually disappeared when traffic lights were erected outside our window. I was not the happiest of guinea pigs. Starving did not come naturally.

My reports attracted some prominence when towards the end I described how hourly brushing of my teeth with tasty toothpaste helped curb the hunger pangs. That was true. One Italian magazine devoted a complete page to my predicament, but I never dared obtain a full translation or peruse the wording carefully in case the word *stupido* was given prominence.

IS THERE MUCH MORE OF THIS?

Communicating with the office or, more importantly, getting your story over always provided a challenge. After all, you could be holding a notebook with the biggest scoop in the world, but what did it matter unless you were able to get it to the bosses who mattered?

The days of cables from far flung places were over by the time I hit the "big time", although I can remember cricket scores from Old Trafford being delivered to the *Manchester Evening News* offices by pigeon.

Copytakers at the end of a crackly telephone line and telex were my era, before the Tandy arrived to herald the start of the instant communications revolution we know today. Telex could be an absolute nightmare, especially when having to punch out the words "blind" on a live line to your office. Replies of: "Utter gibberish, find a phone and get on to copy" were often the reply to your valiant efforts.

For people who wonder what I am talking about, filing blind on telex was the equivalent of using a typewriter without paper, or a laptop without a screen. All you had was a keyboard, and absolutely nothing to show your progress. The slightest interruption to your deep concentration and the copy flow was blown.

You could be in the middle of a word and not know it, you may have failed to hit the line return (as on a typewriter) causing letter to pile upon letter, you realised you had made a mistake, or wished to go back to re-write something, but hadn't a clue where you were – now you can see why "gibberish" was often the only word from base.

The real experts, such as the foreign correspondents who faced the problem daily, learnt to read the punctured tape that was issued by the machine. This was very complicated, but once achieved, made life a lot easier as it became possible to read backwards over what you had already written.

Needless to say, there are humorous stories to linger over from the many frustrating hours spent bashing the telex keys. My first attempt came as an Associated Press correspondent deep in snow in Bad Gastein, Austria, covering a top women's ski championships. I lost all track of what the hell I was sending (the lengthy German and Austrian names which had to be studied letter by letter did not help) and old friend Eric Waha back at the Innsbruck office, broke in with the advice: "Copy so far resembles a recipe for strudel. Suggest you find telephone, or start yodelling results over mountains."

While in Bucharest reporting on an earthquake that had severely damaged the then still attractive Romanian capital, there was just one place where filing was possible. Phone calls, despite the customary bribes with cartons of cigarettes, could take hours to get through, so the two telex machines in the Inter-Continental Hotel were the answer. But, of course, every correspondent in the world was fighting to grab a moment with a keyboard.

When I managed to sneak on to a seat, with my concentration totally geared for the solitary keyboard and blind filing, I had forgotten the nearby presence of a great chum, but totally irrepressible rival, Guy Rais of the *Daily Telegraph*. It was always impossible to keep Guy (so named as he was born on November 5) quiet.

Everybody to Guy was a "silly old flabby dog". Earlier that day we had approached an area of Bucharest where a 12-storey building had collapsed to a pile of concrete probably no higher than 20 feet. All around was silent as those wonderful, specially trained dogs combed the rubble for any signs of life.

We were approached by a white-haired man in uniform, almost bent double in traditional Eastern European style due to the sheer weight of medals on his chest. Before he could utter, Guy accosted him: "Hey, you Communist flabby dog. I am from the *Daily Telegraph* and we hate you type of people, but what can you tell us." Without a flicker, the officer replied in most cultured English:

"If you could just wait for a moment until this search has reached completion, then I will be only too pleased to take you to the rescue headquarters and supply all information available."

On one occasion in London's Belgrave Square, when every Sunday afternoon saw a protest march of some kind, I was joined by Guy outside the Portuguese Embassy. We immediately spotted, standing alone, the newly appointed Commissioner of the Metropolitan Police, Sir Robert Mark.

As he kept a close eye on the noisy procession passing before us, we decided to try for a quote. Sir Robert courteously explained that as he was new to the job, he was simply observing, so all information must come from the commander in charge.

As we walked away, Guy said in a rather loud voice: "What's the name of the silly old flabby dog – Groucho, Harpo, Chico, Beppo?"

So here I was in Bucharest, typing each letter slowly and carefully in order to give my *Daily Mirror* office a graphic eyewitness account of the horrific damage caused by the earthquake, when there was a loud query in my ear:

"John, how does that Communist flabby dog spell his name? Is it Ceaupescu, Chowchesku, Ceausescu – what an old fool?" Concentration totally shattered, and Jackson was forced to off-load hundreds more cigarettes to get a telephone call through urgently.

Guy almost met an uncomfortable end during a rush interview at Heathrow Airport. At around the time Southern Rhodesia (later to become Zimbabwe) was about to declare independence (UDI), a Scottish padre flew home after witnessing the execution of two Africans, who were hanged back-to-back, naturally prompting world outrage.

Now it was clear to colleague Edward Laxton and me that it might take some coaxing, but the padre was ready to speak out. Guy was someone who had a habit of answering fellow reporter's questions, often letting the interviewee off the hook. Laxton asked yet again: "Padre, what were the last words of the two men?"

Back came Guy: "Silly old flabby dog, you've already asked that question and..."

Laxton, a former hooker with Wasps rugby team and a strong man with it, thrust out a long arm, grabbed Guy by the throat, and squeezed. Guy gurgled as the padre told in full the dramatic last words of the men seconds before they were hanged.

There was one occasion when Guy's immediate response did bring a smile to the eye, although it was not the comment expected from a galaxy of top military brass.

During World War II Guy had served with the RAF during the vital North African campaign, which ended with the decisive battles between Field Marshal Montgomery and his highly respected German foe, Field Marshal Rommel.

So come Montgomery's return to the scene of his greatest triumph for the 25th anniversary of the Battle of El Alamein in Egypt's western desert, the *Daily Telegraph* knew Guy was the man to send along with hundreds of Desert Rats.

As he stood on the sand addressing the massive attendance for such a memorable event, Montgomery asked how many people present had been there, under his command, in 1942. Guy raised his hand, and Montgomery pondered: "You must have been very proud?"

Guy came back with his response which caused many a medal to wobble: "I didn't share your confidence, sir."

Another reporter who brought a spluttering attack to a top army officer was my long-time *Daily Mirror* colleague, Ed Vale. I sat next to Ed for many years, and regularly spoke to him through the cloud of cigarette smoke caused by his habit of buying three packets of 20 each time he went to the pub. And that was often.

Ed Vale was an East End man through and through. He was always immaculately turned out (his ever-glistening black shoes, he assured us, were the result of spit and polish sessions every morning by his lovely wife Molly. But knowing Molly, I doubt it.) Permanently polite when in company, Ed was as hard as nails. He was often taken as a top police detective, and in turn he always earned great respect and trust from real policemen.

He was a perfect crime correspondent, who later, believe it or not, switched to the Royal reporting job. Among that circle his best contact was Princess Margaret, who like Ed thought hands were provided to constantly raise a cigarette with, whenever possible, a glass of something alcoholic.

Ed was, however, a softie when it came to one totally unexpected joy. Bagpipes! When drunk he was prone to raise a table chair, turn it upside down over his shoulder, with the four legs in the air to represent bagpipes, and parade around the bar/restaurant with a loud "Prrrummmprr".

This hailed back to a Scottish military background, started when his father was an officer in the Highland Light Infantry. Ed was very proud that a fellow officer, David Niven, who went on to become one of Hollywood's greatest stars, was best man at his parents' wedding.

With this connection, Ed left East London to complete his National Service with the HLI in Scotland. This meant he was a squaddie serving at times under his father.

Ed told the story of how one weekend, when he was leaving barracks for recreation in the nearby Scottish town, he committed the grave offence of cutting the corner of the parade square rather than walking all the way round.

This prompted a screech of "Soldier, come here" from the orderly officer. He marched to the officer, stood rigidly to attention, but was pleased to spot it was his father. As he was given the dressing down expected for breaking this strict regimental order and told he would be confined to barracks for the full weekend, he replied, without thinking: "Oh, come on, Dad".

The sound of orderly officer father telling private son what he thought of that request could have been heard in Northern Ireland. Ed was confined to barracks for two weekends.

This HLI experience brought the love of bagpipes, and hard nut Ed would shed the odd tear whenever the strains of pipes and drums reached his ears. He was probably the first to buy the record of "Amazing Grace", the runaway hit made by the band of the Argyll and Sutherland Highlanders.

One day I groped my way through the Vale Fog to be told by the news desk to cover the presentation of a Platinum Disc, or whatever you get for selling billions of records, to the Amazing Grace band. All the pipers, drummers, complete with Sgt Major soloist, would be at the ceremony at Chelsea Barracks.

Ed was green with envy when I told him, and he said he had to be there. A quick phone call, assurance to the news editor that he was meeting "contacts", and the pair of us took a taxi to Chelsea.

Now for such a special occasion, the commanding officer was present and was keen to speak to the press after the band had performed their phenomenally successful arrangement. Glancing at my tearful but beautifully groomed companion, he exclaimed: "I feel so proud of my regiment."

It was pretty obvious that this general, who had not the slightest trace of a Scottish accent, hadn't a clue what the fuss was all about.

So I made the first attack on the question front: "Sir, once you have achieved such success, your thoughts must turn to your follow-up record. What are you thinking of?"

He looked at me as if I was from another planet, and was stuttering into what could have been a reply, when Ed, his tears now gone, stood to attention and barked, probably as loudly as his father on that day on the parade ground:

"Sir, with respect, there is only one possible follow-up to Amazing Grace."

Somewhat relieved general: "Oh, and what may that be?"

"Fucking Amazing Grace."

End of interview.

Needless to say, Ed Vale also enjoyed a penchant for Scottish songs. One night, before the breathalyser, when any driver stopped had to walk a straight line, count a handful of threepenny bits, and with his eyes closed guide a finger to the tip of his nose,

Daily Mirror night news editor Dan Ferrari received a phone
call from a police station to say Ed had been arrested for
drink-driving.

Dan drove immediately to the station where he offered a stout
defence to the duty sergeant for the responsible Ed Vale he had
known for many years. It was when he observed the station was
very quiet, and then volunteered the information that Ed always
sang Scottish songs when drunk, the sergeant gently pushed back
the door to the cells, allowing a resounding rendition of "There
was a soldier, a Scottish soldier..." to boom forth.

Ed was charged but in those days you had the choice of going
before a judge and jury. He opted for this option, and duly
appeared at the Old Bailey. And to his delight he was found not
guilty.

Returning to the Stab in the Back he ordered probably five
packets of 20, then uttered his famous call: "Give 'em all a drink."
As we all toasted Ed's great success, he was approached by two
men in overalls, who asked quietly: "Two pints of light and mild,
please, Mr Vale."

Ed was quick to point out that he hadn't a clue who they were,
had never set eyes on them before, but as he was celebrating a
victory of true British justice, he would be delighted to buy them
a drink.

One said quietly: "We are inkies across the road at the *Mirror,*
Mr Vale, and earlier today we were both wearing suits, as we
were members of your jury."

Perhaps my favourite telex story concerns the receiving rather
than the difficulties of transmission. And it could qualify as one of
the great Irish stories.

The world's press descended on a small Irish village called
Monsterevin in 1975 when the IRA kidnap of a prominent Dutch
businessman started to unfold. For the *Daily Mirror,* Ireland had
always come under the control of the Manchester office, with
Dublin staff men filing and reporting direct to them. But the
importance of this story prompted London to ask that all copy be

sent straight there.

Oh, it's the big time, they thought. They obviously honed every syllable before finally pressing the button that sent their reams of copy – page after page after page of descriptive material – zinging over the Irish Sea.

Nothing was to be overlooked. They were determined to graphically describe the scene, but at the same time checking every word they wrote. After all, this was the big chance to impress the masters at head office.

They told how Monsterevin had seen nothing like it since famous singer John McCormack had held a concert in 1936. A football match with an adjoining hamlet had been postponed as battalions of journalists and TV crews set up camp.

And then, the main revelation, all typed perfectly, and very carefully so as not to cause offence, on the telex machine (Jasus, we've got to get this right):

"Many reporters knocked on doors to ask to use telephones and toilets. After a while villagers became annoyed, and one was heard to shout: 'F... off, you cunts."

Copy taking stories abound, with every journalist able to tell of those mutterings from the other end of the line: "Is there much more of this" or "I've just had all this from a freelance" or "I don't think this is worth much". But I have some memorable recollections, and one involves our same Dublin office.

It all happened in one of those moments of high tension in a newspaper office when something is demanded a few moments before deadline. In this case a story involved someone called MacNamara and the night editor decided the headline needed to incorporate the first verse of the famous song "MacNamara's Band". A frantic call to the library failed to unearth it, and then someone thought of the Irish staff.

The Manchester newsdesk was alerted, and in turn they made instant contact with a Dublin reporter at home. London waited anxiously as the seconds ticked away. The Dubliner said he knew the words but, and so many of us can empathise with him, only when he shut his eyes and sang them.

Fine, said Manchester, I'll put you straight on to copy. The copytaker answered immediately, and the newsdesk explained that he was about to be given the first verse of the song which London wanted, well two minutes ago. So no time could be wasted. But, oh no!

"Sorry," said the copytaker. "We have banned everyone from taking copy from that reporter in Dublin as he is always drunk."

"No problem," assured a frantic news desk executive. "He is on day off, sober as a judge, and watching TV with his children."

The copytaker was persuaded, agreed, and flicked the switch to receive the incoming copy. His customary welcome of "Copy" was met by an ear blasting burst of song, and an out of tune "Oh, my name is MacNamara, and I'm the leader of the band..."

The plug was pulled, the news desk informed that their man had obviously downed more hooch than normal, so no copy was taken. The London bosses were unimpressed.

North of the Irish border, the doyen of Northern Ireland sports reporters hit problems with a copytaker who was not impressed by a rare event – an away victory by the Northern Ireland football team.

Malcolm Brodie, MBE, who boasted the staggering record of covering all Northern Ireland international matches since 1942, as well as 13 World Cups, phoned excitedly from Buenos Aires to report a 1-0 victory over Argentina.

The copytaker who answered appeared to have no interest in football, was not a great fan of Brodie, and apparently watched the pennies on behalf of their employers at the *Belfast Telegraph*.

The conversation from one hemisphere to the other, went like this:

Copytaker: Good afternoon, copy.

Brodie: It's Malcolm Brodie in Buenos Aires. We've beaten the Argentine. Isn't that wonderful.

Copytaker: I am waiting for your copy.

Brodie: Okay, isn't it great. Right: "Dateline Buenos Aires. Scoreline, Argentina 0, Northern Ireland 1. Magnifico, magnifico, magnifico...

Copytaker: I heard you the first fucking time.

Copytakers were a very important part of the daily life of newspapers. They were the vital link between the reporters on the road and the office staff waiting to fill the paper with their copy. Often a news desk could ask a copytaker to contact a reporter, or make sure one needed urgently did not ring off.

A classic example came when news was flashed around the world in 1958 that American Marines had stormed ashore in Beirut and extensive battles were raging around the city. This was the start of the dreadful troubles to hit the Lebanese capital, one of the world's greatest cities.

The *Daily Mirror* news desk went into panic overdrive as the time did not allow anyone to reach the area in order to file for the next edition. The situation was rescued when a chap from the sports desk wandered down the room to say that Joe Humphreys would be landing at Beirut airport within the hour.

Now Joe Humphreys was a gentle, pipe-smoking northerner, who had spent most of his career covering rugby league. At that moment he was sitting aboard an airliner carrying the Great Britain rugby league squad to a tour of Australia and New Zealand, and in those days of frequent fuel stops Beirut was the next.

The copy room was alerted. Stand by for Joe Humphreys, and, whatever happens, do not let him go. Graphic eyewitness copy was needed. Every red light on the copy panel was watched eagerly.

And within minutes there was a gruff: "Joe Humphreys here with copy, which I hope you will pass on to Manchester urgently. It's a real belter of a story but the line is not the best and there's a lot of noise here."

Ready? News executives were alerted and raced to the copy room. The back bench spiked everything in sight to allow space

for this "*Mirror* man watches the horror" exclusive – and they
waited. The copytaker shouted to Joe that everything was ready,
and his fingers hovered over his solid stand-up typewriter.

This is what was shouted into his ears, causing what must
have been the highest mass reading of high blood pressure levels
imaginable:

"Wigan wonder winger Billy Boston will miss the first match
of the Great Britain tour due to a lingering leg injury. His
likely replacement will... hang on. What? Can you hear me? I
can't hear a bloody thing here as there are tanks, machine guns,
bloody soldiers running and shouting everywhere. Its bedlam, it's
ridiculous to try to continue, I'll ring you from Perth."

And with that, the *Mirror* man with a front seat for the first
invasion of Beirut, hung up.

Another example of sports reporter-does-not-recognise-news-
story-as-it-is-not-my-patch (a state of affairs readily accepted by
all sports editors then) came when the England football team was
playing in Poland. On the day it arrived there were massive bread
riots, following food shortage, throughout the then hardline
Communist country.

One football scribe was asked to delay his departure home
with the team so he could wander around the streets among the
hungry protesters and file a colour piece. He refused with the
simple excuse: "No need to. Totally untrue. There was bags of
bread available at breakfast in our hotel this morning."

At the *Daily Mirror* we had a copytaker who was brilliant at his
job, both fast and a clean typist – that is when, however, he could
fully understand the person dictating. He often found trouble
with accents, and on top of that he was terribly pedantic.

One person who often fell foul of this was Frank McGhee,
who did not suffer interruptions kindly when trying to file a
match report in the presence of 60,000 screaming football fans.

So there was the sight of an apoplectic McGhee one night in
Liverpool when he started into his intro: "Anfield rose to the
supreme brilliance of the Liverpool team last night... what, what?"

Copytaker: Oh no Mr McGhee. It cannot be "an field", it must be "a field".

The language from the press box could have turned Liverpool's strip blue.

Matters were even worse for blood pressure levels when I sat with Frank at the Wald Stadium in Frankfurt, as a valiant Scotland drew 0-0 with mighty Brazil at the 1974 World Cup. Ordered to file his first piece at 9 p.m. at the latest, he asked me at 8.58 to get through to copy as he finished scribbling.

Same copytaker answered, I told him to head the copy Frank McGhee, and passed the phone to Frank. Before it had been transferred to his ear he was in full flow: "Little Billy Bremner, the fiery redheaded Scottish captain... what, what?

Copytaker: How do you spell "leettle"?

As steam began emerging from McGhee's ears nearby VIPs, German Chancellor Willy Brandt and British Prime Minister Harold Wilson, glanced sideways to witness an early role model for Victor Meldrew, and obviously wondered why a match report should include: "I can't fucking believe this. Oh, for Christ's sake put me over to the sports desk."

Now this was a good move as the *Mirror* sports desk at that time was alongside the copy room, divided by a glass partition. Sports news editor Tony Cornell was asked by McGhee to watch for the moment the copytaker in question picked up the phone for another call, and then transfer him back. This happened almost instantaneously.

Next copytaker was a very jolly fellow, a regular at the bar in the Stab, and he gave Frank a friendly welcome. McGhee was straight into action again: "Little Billy Bremner, the fiery redheaded... what, what?"

Copytaker: I'm afraid you'll have to go more slowly Frank. I've just returned after suffering a stroke and can only use one arm for typing.

I honestly thought McGhee would die.

The problem of accents and difficulty in understanding over

dodgy telephone lines has always caused problems. During the 1964 Olympic Games in Tokyo I dictated all my boxing copy to either my wife Barbara (no hiccups), or a delightful colleague from the American Deep South called Dorothy. Every time I said "it", she would query: "How do you spell eeat?"

And then there were live links to US radio stations which would be thrown at you on occasions, especially when you were the early reporter, to talk to some middle of the night DJ on Radio SPQJ in Punk Falls, Iowa, desperate for something new to explore.

So one morning I went live in such a situation: "Oh, well good morning and hi all you early risers. Let's make Monday our fun day, and hello Jaahn Jackson on the Daily Mirroor in London. What's your paper telling its lovely readers today, Jaahn?"

I told this gathering of obviously yawning, shaving, coffee drinking, egg eating, possibly fornicating, listeners that we were highlighting the fact that Prince Charles, the heir to the throne, had fallen off his horse during a polo match and been taken to hospital with a fractured elbow.

This appeared to have little impact and chummy came back: "Great Jaahn, but does the *Daily Mirror* carry noos anymore?" A strange question but I flicked through the pages and said we had news from Vietnam, Germany, Japan, and many other countries as well as home news.

"What Jaahn, you have noos from many countries?" Of course, I replied, wondering what idiot was at the end of the line. That was it. With a swift "Thanks", not even another "Jaahn" and I was talking to a dial tone.

It took me some time to realise that the question which had been thrown at me across the Big Pond from the American Bible Belt was, if spoken properly: "Does the *Daily Mirror* carry nudes anymore."

Circulation would have rocketed if we could have distributed our edition packed with embonpoint from around the world in that neighbourhood.

Returning rather swiftly to Frankfurt, and my seat alongside the fuming Frank McGhee, my task, other than being his gofer at the crucial World Cup match, was to keep a close eye on Prime Minister Harold Wilson. The main reason for this was that the Rt Hon Gentleman had enjoyed the odd welcoming drink.

As a result, there was a regular call to the public loo in the bowels of the stadium which, of course, in his case involved the usual battalion of accompanying civil servants, security men, and inquisitive press men. Wilson's press officer was Joe Haines, with whom I had worked for many years when his by-line from the House of Commons was J.T.W.Haines.

Joe was quick to realise that we British hacks would appreciate a word with the Prime Minister so, using me as a familiar face and guide to the other scribes, said: "Prime Minister may I introduce John Jackson of the *Daily Mirror.*"

As Wilson held out a limp hand and stared with a glazed expression at this bunch of news hounds, I in turn introduced Andy Fyall (*Daily Express*), Iain Walker (*Sun*), Jimmy Grylls (*Daily Mail*), Gerald Seymour (ITN) and so on.

"What did you think of Scotland's performance, Prime Minister?" was the obvious question after he made his umpteenth loo visit at the final whistle. He thought for a moment and then slurred:

"As I said in a recent election address in Bradford, Leeds United are a very good team." This could have been a baffling statement until one realised that four of the Scottish XI that day played for Leeds United – goalkeeper David Harvey, captain Billy Bremner, Joe Jordan and Peter Lorimer.

With that, Haines reminded the Prime Minister he had a busy schedule and dragged him off to meet the team – and near disaster. Once inside the dressing room it was obvious to anyone that the visiting VIP was "pished" (a Scotsman can spot such a condition quicker than it takes to announce "It's your roond").

The Scottish players were in the communal bath, celebrating a formidable result against the mighty Brazilians, but standing on the side, his raincoat draped nonchalantly over his shoulders, was the great Denis Law. No one dared suggest then that this superlative footballer had played his 55th and last match for Scotland just four days earlier. The opposition was Zaire and many people blamed Law's almost "piss taking" performance for the disappointing 2-0 victory which eventually cost Scotland a place in the quarter finals.

Law, ever the joker, grabbed the Prime Minister in a bear hug, swung him round so that he had his back to the bath, and mouthed over the famous guest's shoulder to teammates: "Pished".

Ever alert photographer Ken Lennox was ready for the Prime Minister to enter the water in a spectacular unscheduled way as several players rose in their naked state to welcome Wilson with a dragging wet hand, but officials soon saw what was possibly planned and decorum was restored.

In all, it was one of my more memorable days and the Wilson visit helped build my reputation, and certainly produced one of my nicknames. Earlier I had travelled to the match with *Sunday Express* colleagues Danny Blanchflower (a former great footballer with Tottenham Hotspur) and Alan Hoby, and arrived at the Wald Stadium to discover unprecedented security the likes of which had not been witnessed before.

As Harold Wilson and his entourage arrived by helicopter the area was surrounded by police and armoury, which prompted me to write "Ring of Steel" in the *Mirror*.

To my knowledge this description had not been written before, and there are still old timers who greet me with "Ah, ring of steel Jacko". If I could have copyrighted the description, I would be very rich today. Needless to say, only two years after the Munich Olympics massacre, the Germans did not want another international disaster.

THE START

As the comedian Max Wall always observed: "I was born at an early age." In my case it was in a small nursing home in Wood Green, North London (a few years later to be blown out of existence by a World War II doodle bug bomb) that I emerged into this world on March 9, 1935

I was the firstborn to Harold and Kathleen Jackson (always known as Jimmy and Kitty) who lived in Alexandra Park Road, under the shadow of the famous Alexandra Palace as it became the birthplace of British television, in the rather more upmarket Bounds Green. A short time later we moved to a newly built home in nearby leafy Woodfield Way. Sister Gillian arrived when I was three.

Our father worked for Barclays Bank, at that time in the important West End branch in Regent Street.

During the 1939-45 conflict, with our father away in the Intelligence Corps and later returning from Italy as a wounded soldier, our mother was a magnificent lone parent (as were so many other women during those dark days of war) who overcame the many obstacles to give Gillian and me a perfect journey through early childhood.

My early memories consist mainly of me standing as a toddler at the top of the hill leading up Woodfield Way from Bounds Green tube station, awaiting my father's return from work on a Saturday lunchtime with bags of fruit.

When I was four, I gather the actions of a German chappie named Adolf Hitler made it sensible for us to move out of London. Gillian and I became evacuees, but with a very special difference from the norm – our mother came with us.

So there were none of the heartbreaking farewells at one of London's main railway stations, as tearful parents waved off their small children, weighed down with a suitcase, gas mask and large label giving full details, as they left for foster homes in safer parts of the country.

We packed our belongings, let the London house, and set off for an open-ended stay in the tiny Somerset village of Spaxton. The reason for this spot, between Bridgewater and Taunton, was that the local vicar was the Reverend Guy Graham, who had officiated at the wedding of my parents several years earlier in Bradford, Yorkshire. We were tenants in the sprawling vicarage, located in large grounds, for quite some time, before moving to a small cottage a mile or so away.

It was a marvellous, very healthy childhood, despite the restrictions imposed by war. We were in the country and I spent most of my spare time on the adjoining farm, helping Geoff Cook with all aspects of farm life, such as shoeing horses Robin and Jim.

I attended the local village school (this was a two-mile walk each way from our cottage, which sparked my lifelong opinion that walking is the finest exercise of all) where two women teachers provided a splendid junior education.

One "highlight" was when I fell from a tree in the woods surrounding the vicarage and badly gashed my leg on a rogue branch. The doctor had to be called from another village but as he had no stitches my deep cut was pulled together with clips. At school I was allowed to play with the girls only (embarrassing). Eighty years on I still have the scar, which I proudly display as my war wound.

The 1939-45 war was perfectly dated for me for I took my 11-plus in 1946, shortly before we moved back to Bounds Green, as education was slowly getting back to normal. I am proud to say that two people passed – Dennis Chidgey and me, the first boys to do so since 1936.

This resulted in an entrance exam and interview at Dr Morgan's Grammar School in Bridgewater, where I apparently impressed (although I feared the worst when blurting out "he had his head chopped off" when questioned about Charles I) and was recommended for Tollington Secondary Grammar School for Boys, Muswell Hill, North London.

This recommendation placed me in Class 1A, but I am afraid the country yokel in me wasn't able to compete with the clever North London boys and a year later I was relegated to 2B (much to the disappointment of my father), and remained in the B stream until I left aged 16 in December 1951.

I managed to gain five O Levels (it was the first year of O Levels, which replaced the old School Certificate) at the second attempt – English Lang, English Lit, French, History, Spanish. Maths was too baffling. I have always been good at arithmetic and passed that with flying colours, but a maths O Level was only possible if you gained at least 30% in both algebra and geometry as well. To this day I find geometry impossible. I think I received five marks, which I am sure were for spelling my name correctly and getting the date right.

This pretty poor overall performance prompted headmaster J. Westgate Smith to suggest an attempt at A Levels would be a total waste of time. When he enquired as to what profession I had in mind I simply followed all my classmates and said chartered accountant. A sudden cough preceded his reply: "Not with your maths."

I had always thought of journalism, primarily because I hoped to travel widely. I also enjoyed the thrill of writing a piece for publication and seeing my name in print. This came from my first attempt – a letter published in *The Star*, the London evening newspaper, in their series about "how fate changed my life". I told how in 1947, when on a school train trip to Switzerland (quite an adventure just two years after the end of war) we missed a connection, which crashed, killing many people on board.

I think I am correct in boasting that I am one of only two national journalists who started their careers in short pants. The other was one of the funniest men I have met, Tony Smith who became the well-respected sports editor of the *Sunday Mirror*.

(When mentioning earlier the long Fleet Street lunches, I should have heralded Tony Smith as champion. A late afternoon caller to the *Sunday Mirror* was told Smithie was still at lunch. When he declared his knowledge that he always went out at 1p.m., the reply took him aback: "That's right. He did. Yesterday.")

You might note a clue as to our beginnings when I say that each time we met we prompted odd glances as we bent our knees, crumpled our fingers into the Boy Scout salute and chanted: "Dib, dib, dib, dob, dob, dob".

So, in 1952, I took over from Tony the position of office-boy-cum-trainee-journalist on *The Scout,* the official organ of the Boy Scout Movement based at its headquarters in Buckingham Palace Road, opposite the Royal stables. We performed all office chores and wrote a round-up of gossip from Scout troops nationwide under the name of Jeep.

One of the conditions of the appointment was that you wore only Scout uniform in your working hours, which included travel to and from home. This meant a strapping 6-foot teenager in short pants venturing daily during the rush hour on London Underground's Piccadilly Line from Wood Green to Green Park and return.

As I was one of only a few people who can boast they were both a King's Scout and Queen's Scout (I had attained all the necessary badges shortly before King George VI died, but was not invested by the Chief Scout Lord Rowallan, at a special Mansion House ceremony, until our present Queen had succeeded to the throne), I cut quite a colourful figure with my shirt covered with badges, Bushman's Thong tucked under my arm, scarf, woggle, corduroy shorts, long socks and sheath knife on my belt. Needless to say, I rarely enjoyed a seat as I was expected to constantly display that Scouting spirit.

Tony and I often agreed that short pants could be somewhat uncomfortable in our particular office as the secretary was the most statuesque, Sophie Loren-like beauty. The third person with us was deputy editor Connie Booth, a formidable spinster whose stare could frighten the bravest of souls.

My daily commute involved walking through Green Park and round Buckingham Palace. In those days, just seven years after the end of the war, security around the Royal Family and top politicians was not unheard of, but certainly low key.

This allowed the guardsmen performing their ceremonial stints outside Buck House to be positioned in sentry boxes on the pavement in front of the main gates – four when the Queen was in residence and two when not. They were sadly moved inside with the advent of the IRA and other danger threats.

In 1952/53 they became accustomed to this lanky Boy Scout striding past each morning and evening. It was not uncommon for a voice to sneak from a sentry box on a cold, wet day: "What's the time, mate?" It was usually around 8.50 a.m. which brought the military response: "Thank God for that. I'm desperate for a slash."

On more than one occasion, with Her Maj indoors and the guards acting in pairs, one would tap his rifle butt on the ground, to signal they should come to attention, shoulder arms and march toward each other.

This was not necessarily because they were bored, or cold, but because they needed an excuse to have a "quiet word". As they approached each other, before performing the expected precision about-turn, I often witnessed a swinging hand offer a V-sign, accompanied by such exchanges as: "Who are you going to fuck tonight, big boy?" "You, unless you shut your trap." Not the sort of language for a Boy Scout!

One day I received a surprise call. It was the traditional Bob-A-Job Week when Scouts, in those innocent days, knocked on doors and were safely given a menial task for which they would be paid a "bob" (slang for one shilling, which became 5p), or hopefully more.

It was the height of the Cold War and the Associated Press wondered if I would agree to knock on the door of the Soviet Embassy in Kensington's Millionaires' Row, where I would offer to cut their hedge for a bob.

The Soviet Ambassador in those dark days was Andrei Gromyko, who went on from London to the United Nations and later became Foreign Secretary in Moscow. They agreed, perhaps surprisingly, so I was photographed doing the job, and was promptly rewarded with 2s.6d or half a crown (12.5p).

When the picture hit the Fleet Street desks, I was in demand. Every picture editor wanted their own shot, and reporters needed extra quotes. First around were the then three London evening papers – *Star, Evening News* and *Standard* – and I was photographed on the office roof and in Hyde Park (with a new set of shears).

My exciting day ended, or so I thought, when from work I went straight to the London Palladium. I loved music hall and made a habit of going to the first house every other Wednesday as, with the exception of Danny Kaye, Judy Garland and Betty Hutton, all the great stars stayed for just two weeks.

My Scout uniform was then a bonus, with the woman in the box office always able to see me arrive and ensure, however full, that I got in - either a seat or standing position (allowed then) in the stalls.

During the interval on this evening a message was passed along my row addressed to "Boy Scout Jackson". Could I pop outside? There I found a photographer from the *Daily Express* who breathlessly asked if I would be good enough to drive with him to Hyde Park. He told the sort of story I would hear endlessly over the next 45 years (although he had a politer turn of phrase than his present-day equivalents):

"The bloody news/picture desks have cocked it up again. We're late, it's almost dark, but Muggins has to come up with the goods. They'll know about this on my expenses."

In fact, it was dark and, of course we didn't have a pair of shears. So, I was photographed, with as much flash as possible, in a cutting pose by the nearest hedge - and the shears were painted in later by the Express artist.

In February 1952 King George VI died and I was seconded to St James's Palace to work as a messenger for the Earl Marshal, the Duke of Norfolk, as he organised the funeral. Among the official invitations I delivered were those for Princess Margaret and the

Archbishop of Canterbury.

On the day of the funeral I was given a privileged position on Marlborough Road at the front of the palace, and my abiding memory is spotting a curtain opposite pushed back to allow Queen Mary to peep down on the gun carriage bearing the coffin of her son.

Two writing assignments for Jeep involved participation in the annual St George's Day march by Queen's Scouts past the Queen at Windsor Castle, and the Ralph Reader Gang Show.

Reader, who nowadays might attract strong comment when let loose with his gathering of big boys in short shorts, had carried his Boy Scout shows over from World War II where his RAF Gang Shows had discovered such talent as Peter Sellers, Harry Secombe and other top stars.

The 1952 Gang Show was fun. I was part of the large cast, along with boyhood friends Tim Clark and Derek Nowell. It was nightly at Golders Green Hippodrome for two weeks. I can remember, of course, belting out the chorus of Ralph Reader's anthem "*We're riding along on the crest of a wave, And the sun is in the sky*", being dressed in a skimpy sarong for a sketch entitled "A pretty girl is like a melody", but the moments that stand out were the visit by Princess Margaret and her "friend" Peter Sellars, and the nights of London's killer smog which meant that from the stage we were lucky to see the orchestra pit.

During National Service, with nineteen enjoyable months spent in Germany as RAF Senior Aircraftsman 2588182, I used my Boy Scout past and a few tips gleaned from that brief insight into Fleet Street practices to get to my first major sporting event. Until then, a last-minute ticket for the 1950 FA Cup Final between my team Arsenal and Liverpool had been the highlight.

I managed to wangle a week on a Scout mountaineering course in Switzerland, where I learned the European Athletics Championships were being held in Berne within the next few days.

The big attractions for me were distance runners Roger

Bannister and Christopher Chataway, who earlier had joined
with my soon-to-be fellow journalist and great travelling buddy
Christopher Brasher in helping Bannister break the four-minute
barrier for the mile.

I wired a well composed telegram to my camp at RAF Wahn,
situated on land now adjacent to the Cologne/Bonn international
airport, explaining I was delayed by weather and travel problems.

I managed to talk my way into the stadium, which after
a splendid day of athletics, produced one solitary topic of
conversation. It concerned a small blond man in a red shirt who
no one had heard of, and who appeared to be heading for a
massive heart attack as he raced away with the 10,000 metres.
Vladimir Kuts had entered the world stage, and two years later
won the 5,000 and 10,000 metres at the Melbourne Olympics.

My successful telegram, which fooled the officers back at camp,
was never likely to be quoted in future years in any compilation
of famous messages sent by reporters in the field. But I was
pleased with it.

In 1946, as the world got slowly back to business after a nasty
World War, joining the Boy Scouts was quite an attraction for an
11-year-old boy. It was a way of enjoying a life which, to say the
least, was packed with interests and opportunities for fun. No one
had any money, and most things were rationed.

Sitting at home with families gathered round the radio for
comedy shows like *ITMA* (It's That Man Again, namely funny
man Tommy Handley) and *Dick Barton Special Agent,* which filled
the early evening slot now long since occupied by *The Archers,*
was the norm.

I joined the local troop, the 151st North London based at our
local church, St Gabriel's in Bounds Green. I was in the Stag
patrol and over my teenage years progressed to Patrol Leader
and then Troop Leader with the usual Scout camps and general
activities.

In 1951 I was chosen to represent the 151, and in turn London
and Great Britain at the World Jamboree in Bad Ischl, Austria.

This was a memorable experience, travelling across war-torn Europe, despite the inconvenience that it pelted with rain for a fortnight. We were forced to build makeshift hammocks with wood and string as a river flowed steadily through our tent.

I enjoyed my two years in the RAF. My initial square bashing at RAF Hednesford, near Cannock, in May/June 1953 included June 2, Queen Elizabeth II's Coronation Day.

On a very cold morning we were on parade at 6 a.m. I remember muttering to a neighbour that it was "fucking freezing". This brought the raucous scream from the drill sergeant: "Jackson, your mouth is like the Mersey Tunnel, never shut."

The commanding officer then attempted what he thought was encouragement: "You must all be very proud. And if you think you are cold, let me tell you it's a lot colder on the top of Everest." At that moment this was total bollocks from an officer who we thought was pissed. We did not know anything about Sir Edmund Hillary and Sherpa Tensing conquering the mighty Everest.

The big consolation was that we were given the rest of the day off to enjoy ourselves and celebrate the Coronation in nearby Cannock. As our pay was four shillings a day we were unable to toast Her Majesty too extravagantly – but several of us were lucky.

We wandered into a pub, where a television set had been hired at great expense to show all the action from London live in glorious black and white, and the landlord took one look at us 18-years-old bucks and declared: "You sing all day, and I'll provide the free drinks." So, we sang.

(It was at this time, with the combination of our small pay packet and the dreadful smell, that I decided smoking was a mug's game. I think I had taken one naughty puff in the woods in Spaxton but I am proud to say I have never smoked one cigarette in my life – and I know I have benefitted from it.)

Generally, the square bashing, with all its marching and discipline was fun. The hardest day came when we were given every injection known to man in the same arm and then forced to shovel sand for hours on end to "ease the pain in the arm". Oh yeah!

From Hednesford I had a pleasant month at Middle Wallop where I was asked if I wanted to go abroad. I volunteered for Hong Kong. Each week the new postings came in and we learned where we were going. When my week arrived, there were no announcements.

A week later two batches came simultaneously. The first group was for Hong Kong but they were handed to the newest bunch, with those of us who had been waiting a week filling the second.

The whole time was spent at RAF Wahn. It was a doddle really. We were billeted in large, comfortable blocks and I shared throughout a room for three with Tom Jobson from Kirkcaldy, and Roger Cusdin from Essex. Two good pals.

We were all fighter plotters which meant doing shifts in the control room, seated at a round table, wearing headphones linked to the pilots from our resident night fighter squadron. When they shouted their position my job was to lean over, grab one of the balls and pull it out to mark the spot. Balls breaking boring, but it could have been a lot worse – like being in the Army!

The time passed quickly as I was able to get myself pass-outs to attend a shorthand course in Hamburg, visit Berlin, and the mountaineering expedition in Switzerland.

The Berlin weekend was an adventure which is difficult to comprehend when visiting now to see our eldest son Nicholas and family in the magnificent German capital city. It was 1954 and Berlin was still isolated within East Germany (the DDR, Deutsche Democratic Republic), and divided into British, American, French and Soviet sectors.

Our journey took us by normal train from Cologne to the edge of the East German border. There all the blinds were pulled down, each compartment was locked and we were not allowed out until we had reached West Berlin.

A group of us stayed at a hostel in the British zone and were

able to roam at will. As we were seven years ahead of the Berlin
Wall going up, we could wander through the Brandenberg Gate.
Nearby stood the burnt-out ruins of the Reichstag, untouched
since the arson attack in 1933.

On our main night we ventured to a nightclub in the
Templehof district of the American zone where each table had a
numbered telephone. The calls from unidentified Frauleins sent
you crazy. On one occasion we discovered the attractive young
lady caller was actually back-to-back with us at the next table.
Great fun!

The taxi back with we drunken airman skirted through the
Soviet zone at one point. Extremely risky as we were all in RAF
uniform.

The week-long shorthand course in Hamburg taught us
no shorthand but allowed us to venture out into a city still
recovering from heavy bombing (as of course was Berlin). At the
famous Planten un Blomen urban park I met Helga Krafft, who
with her friend, Elke, showed a fellow airman from Devon and
me the town over several nights.

Helga was fun and she even invited me to her home to meet
her parents. But when her rather stern father held a snarling
German Shepherd back at the door, and I spotted a picture
of Hitler on the mantelpiece it was obviously time for auf
wiedersehen.

The two years of compulsory military service did more good
than harm. The discipline and comradeship could only help
your development and, overall, hopefully made one a better and
more understanding person. I certainly never suffered from one
moment of it.

At completion I was demobbed and ready for work again.
By law *The Scout* had to offer me my old job back, but I felt it
was time to move on. You can say I had become accustomed to
wearing long trousers!

My demob was celebrated with a trip to Paris with my parents
and sister Gillian. It was the first time I had ever flown, and a

good time was had by all. We stayed at the Hotel Garnier by the Gare St Lazare, to which I returned five years later for a fabulous honeymoon with my beautiful bride Barbara.

I don't think she ever forgave me for the rather sparse room and bathroom down the corridor. But, I believe, we did have our own bidet.

My parents were then living in Birkenhead, as my father had been promoted to deputy manager at Barclays Foreign Branch in Liverpool. I moved in with them and almost immediately found myself on the reporting staff of the twice weekly *Birkenhead Advertiser*.

The editor was a fearsome man named Bill Bothwell – but, by golly, he taught you how to become a proper journalist. He was a tough Glaswegian who had earlier been the chief sub on the *Scottish Daily Express*. He was well known nationally, at least by sports fans, as he did weekly football reports for BBC radio's *Sports Report*. His delivery was precise and clear, despite the revelation that he spoke more words in one minute than anyone else on radio.

His instructions in the office were also precise and clear. You had to walk past his open door each time you entered the small newsroom housing the six-strong editorial staff. If the command "Jack" echoed off all four walls, it was steel helmet time.

There was one occasion when I strutted in, extremely proud of a front page "splash" reporting from an area of Rock Ferry which had become infested by rats. One hysterical woman told me she had seen some as big as Alsatian dogs. Instead of quoting her I wrote it as a fact, I think in my introductory paragraph.

Bothwell went ballistic, suggesting I should find one of these gargantuan rats and bring it to him on a lead. Oh, the innocence, and dopiness, of a young reporter. But you learned – and it never happened again.

Several months into my *Advertiser* career it was announced that the paper was closing (the first of four to fold while I was in harness – was it me?). The rival *Birkenhead News* took two of us on, myself and the news editor Frank Tomlinson.

But I was banished to the Heswall and Neston offices in the deepest Wirral to join a very eccentric, pipe smoking reporter called Brian Danger. After being reduced to filling out wedding notices and door-stepping funerals, I decided it was time to move on.

During my time in Birkenhead I rode everywhere on my Tiger Cub motor bike. (I even ventured to London on it on a couple of occasions.) Regularly on my pillion, to such exotic spots as Bromborough Juvenile Court, was the Birkenhead/Wirral correspondent of the *Liverpool Daily Post and Echo*, Derek Taylor.

Derek later moved to the *News Chronicle* in Manchester, before a chance interview with Brian Epstein, the man who discovered the Beatles, who immediately appointed him press officer with the Famous Four.

Derek toured the world with the Beatles at their height, later stayed on in California to be a disc jockey connected with other famous pop groups, before heavy smoking, drinking and drugs got the better of him.

In the meantime he had married one of my sister's best schoolfriends and they had six children.

My social life in Birkenhead was never dull. I played football regularly as an outsider for Birkenhead Institute Old Boys, attended evening shorthand classes where I was the only male, and went everywhere either by bicycle or my trusty Tiger Cub. Regular visits were made to the famous Riverside dance hall at New Brighton, where traditional jazz was the thing, often with Ken Colyer and his band.

Romantic attachments always seemed to find me venturing "across the water" (in other words, the Mersey) to far flung spots as Bootle and Litherland.

I usually travelled through the Mersey Tunnel, rather than rely on the ferry. Bicycles were permitted then, but let me assure you that while the initial downhill section was a doddle, the uphill stretch, with lorries and buses queueing behind you, was a nightmare. Overtaking was impossible. And then there were occasions when I came a cropper with my front wheels jammed in the tram lines round St George's Square. Thankfully traffic was very light in those days.

First there was a dark-haired beauty called Rita Hopley. Then came the more sophisticated Margaret Morgan, who worked at Liverpool University. With her I often borrowed my parent's old car as we went to the motor racing at Oulton Park and seaside spots like Southport.

By this time I had taken my father's advice to "go west young man" and started the process of trying to get to Canada. It was not easy. It was 1956 and the UK was suffering. The Suez Crisis was looming, conditions at home were poor, and many families were emigrating.

Canada was a popular destination, but all the passenger ships were fully booked. Flying was not considered in those days.

With nothing appearing to be happening Margaret and I, with childhood friends Tim Clark and Monica Reincke who still lived in Bounds Green (Tim was best man at our wedding, and I was best man at theirs), set off on a motoring trip round Wales. We had a lot of laughs, especially at overnight stops where rooms had to be girls in one and men in another. The girls kept their door well and truly locked.

On a phone call to home my father said that he had pulled a few strings with shipping friends who had connections with his bank – and I was sailing to Montreal on the Cunard liner *Saxonia* in four days' time. So it was a rapid return home.

In Canada I had two cousins – Wyn, who left Bradford, Yorkshire, with her family in the 1930s to move to Hamilton, Ontario, and Anne, who made the same journey from Bradford in 1946, to follow Canadian airman Barry Sprague as a "GI bride" to Vancouver.

From Montreal I took the train to Hamilton where I moved in with Wyn and hubby Jack. For work I ventured up to Toronto and walked into newspaper offices and offered my services. It was in the headquarters of Southam Press that a frightening executive greeted me, and before I had uttered a word: "You're English, sit down, what d'you want?"

He liked me and started ringing round their group newspapers that had vacancies. At first, he was hopeful he had fixed me up in faraway Saskatoon, northern Saskatchewan, but that fell through when it was pointed out they needed someone to specialise in baseball.

And then he said: "I know the place for you, the *Orillia Daily Packet and Times*. I'll ring Farmer." (I hadn't a clue what or where he was talking about.) He got through to Farmer Tissington, the editor, found he had a vacancy and my employment went like this: "Okay, how much you paying? 20 dollars a week. No, I like him, make it 25." So I was off to Orillia, 80 miles north of Toronto, for a splendid few months.

On arrival I needed lodgings and was sent to 138 Mississauga Street to link up with the Andrews family – chiropractor Ross (eccentric genius pianist Glenn Gould was a regular patient), wife Evelyn, and baby daughters Cathy and Susan. They made my stay extremely happy with a small room, and I often earned my keep by babysitting the girls.

At the newspaper I soon settled in as the main town reporter/ photographer and thoroughly enjoyed myself covering the court, council meetings and all that goes with life in a small town.

I even covered an ice hockey match, the Orillia Pontiacs against local opposition, but my sports reporting there came to a sudden end when I described how "the Pontiacs pucked off in front of a capacity crowd..." Nobody told me it was called a face-off.

Often at weekends I was left in charge of the bright red *Packet and Times* Dodge station wagon. One very cold winter night I received a late call from the duty policeman to say he had to rush to a possible murder in a nearby township, and could I drive him as his police car had frozen.

I drove at a rather stupid speed on the icy country roads ("you needn't worry about being stopped for speeding tonight" I was told by my passenger). At a house we found that a man had shot himself in an upstairs bedroom, but the first his family knew something was up was when blood came dripping through the light fitting above their dinner table.

The policeman also needed official pictures, so I went upstairs to photograph the remains of the man who had stuck a rifle in his mouth and blasted most of his head off.

I had no problems with this and, in fact, when we had finished we both dined on meaty hamburgers.

Shortly after I had purchased a second-hand Hillman Minx car I met two other Englishmen, Liverpudlian Tony and Londoner Al, who had somehow finished up in Orillia. Together we decided we would drive across North America to Vancouver – over 3,000 miles in a Hillman Minx, three men and all their belongings!!

It was 1958, and what an adventure! Fortunately, Tony was a car mechanic by trade and the front passenger seat of the car was weighed down by his box of tools. It came handy on the very first night in Ontario's Algonquin Park when the fuel pump needed attention.

But on we went, on a route following the shape of a question mark. North to Ottawa and Montreal, then south past Lake Champlain, through the Adirondack Mountains to New York City. There I booked into the YMCA, then scuttled down the back stairs to let in the other two. We were soon discovered, however.

By Washington, DC a new clutch was needed so we had to earn money. I worked as a chef at a burger joint, Californian Kitchens on I Street, while the other two sold sneezeless pepper door-to-door (my first hamburger was returned as uncooked, and no one seemed interested in their pepper).

On to Pittsburgh and Cleveland (where the police towed our car away but fortunately their pound was manned by a sympathetic Irish sergeant), then Chicago and back into Canada and Winnipeg. By this time we were sleeping in the car, but the brave little Hillman was in no state to go further. I sold it for $50.

Here we teamed up with a fourth Englishman who was going our way in a roomier Dodge, and it was off through Regina, Swift Current, Moose Jaw, Saskatoon, Edmonton (told to leave town by the Mounties after being handed tickets for jaywalking), Calgary, Banff, over the Rockies and finally Vancouver.

Once again a cousin came to the rescue and I moved in with Anne and Barrie. No newspaper job was available as one paper had recently folded, and the other two had amalgamated. But I found a job as a treasury clerk with the Canadian Pacific Railroad.

I spent several months writing out cheques for all the staff and generally handling accountancy problems, before saving enough money to "keep going west, young man" and book a sea ticket to New Zealand.

Before that I hitchhiked down to California, with many adventures on the way, and in Los Angeles teamed up with three chaps I met at the YMCA and we rented a house in Santa Monica. Money was short so I sold my blood at a clinic on Wilshire Boulevard and appeared as an extra on two TV shows in Hollywood.

While wandering the huge studios one evening I was welcomed by singer Rosemary Clooney and invited to her impromptu birthday party. There I joined such stars as her husband Jose Ferrer and western singer Tennessee Ernie Ford.

I was cornered by the famous columnist Walter Winchell who exclaimed: "You're English. You're lucky as Winston Churchill is the greatest man who ever lived."

I later joined Anne and Barrie as they drove to Las Vegas (I hit the jackpot in my first casino and was awarded a silver dollar on a special platter, borne by a glamorous blonde) and other spots to meet friends.

And then I joined the Orient liner *Orsova* and sailed to Auckland – met Barbara and the rest of my life is history.

If only we could start all over again!

★★

History is made on a sweltering day in Cape Town.

Above: Rotters 88 at Seoul Olympics. David Williams (*Daily Mail*), Dick Durham (*Daily Star*), Paul Thompson (*Daily Express*), JJ, Chris Boffey (*Today*), Phil Dampier (*Sun*).

Below: With Rotter Hugh Whittow before he became editor of the *Daily Express*.

Hooligan watch.

Above: Feet up after walk to Wembley for fans' guidance before England vs Scotland international hit by London Underground strike.

Left: Keeping close to visiting fans!

Talking to Princess Anne at party celebrating Torvill and Dean's golden triumph in Sarajevo.

Peeping round corner (far right) to spot the winning Bolero ice dancers.

Mirror colleague Ed Vale (left) and *Daily Telegraph's* Guy Rais (right) join JJ in quizzing Robert Maxwell.

Escorting Derby winner Lester Piggott into the Epsom winners' enclosure.

Below: Showing my limited soccer skills to US teenage tennis star
Andrea Jaeger before she reached the Wimbledon singles final in
1983, losing to Martina Navratilova.

Above: Courting Barbara in Auckland in 1958 with
my 1930 Austin Seven.

Barbara and I posing as models for an Auckland Star car
showroom advertisement.

Top: Our wedding day, May 7, 1960.

Bottom: Wedding group with Jackson parents (left) and Johnson parents (right). Sister Gillian bridesmaid next to groom.

Top: Our six at Golden Wedding of my parents, Harold and
Kitty Jackson.

Bottom: Family picture to promote Barbara's appointment as
Sunday People's agony aunt Dear Barbara. Children (l to r)
Catherine, Thomas, Nicholas, Stella – and Ginger the cat.

A complete family gathering at our favourite Rosenhof, Illmitz, Austria. Grandchildren (l to r) William, Ned and Edie, Oscar, Mia, Harry, Jacob, Martha.

Below, left: RAF National Service days. In front of Brandenburg Gate 1954.
Right: The burnt out Reichstag.

Above: Pyjama party jollity at Christmas break at Bad Harzburg 1953.

My Bob-a-Job hedge cutting at Soviet Embassy in 1953 makes my first story in *Daily Mirror*, 16 years before I joined staff.

DAILY MIRROR, Thursday, April 9, 1953   PAGE 5

Bob a job? And Russians pay up

JOHN JACKSON marched smartly up the steps of the closely-guarded Soviet Embassy building in London yesterday and rapped on the big front door. "Bob a job," he said.

And he then set about persuading Mr. Malenkov's diplomats that Ambassador Gromyko's privet hedge needed tidying up.

Minutes later, eighteen-year-old Boy Scout John was snipping and clipping, watched by silent guards and surprised policemen.

And, one blister, a couple of scratches and thirty-five minutes later, John had finished.

After collecting half-a-crown, John, whose home is at Woodside - road, Wood Green, said: "I read about how the Russians were being a lot nicer, so I decided to try. They were very nice. They smiled and shook my hand."

John Jackson—and Mr. Gromyko's hedge

MALAYA PEACE SOON, HE SAYS

COLONEL Arthur Young, retiring Commissioner of Police for Malaya, said yesterday at Manila, on his way home to London, that large-scale Communist activity in Malaya had been reduced to mere nuisance raids, and he was confident the jungle war would end soon.

Six Malay special constables were shot dead by terrorists in the Sungei Siput area of Perak yesterday, cables Reuter.

Above: Picture taken by latecomer *Daily Express*, with shears added in office. (Note uniform sheath knife in those safe old days).

Right: Standing in footprints of Gavrilo Princip where he shot Austrian Archduke Franz Ferdinand in Sarajevo, which led to outbreak of First World War.

After frying an egg on the pavement for newsdesk's
boiling hot day feature.

Discussing with Sir Keith Joseph the merits of having four
children after he upset the nation.

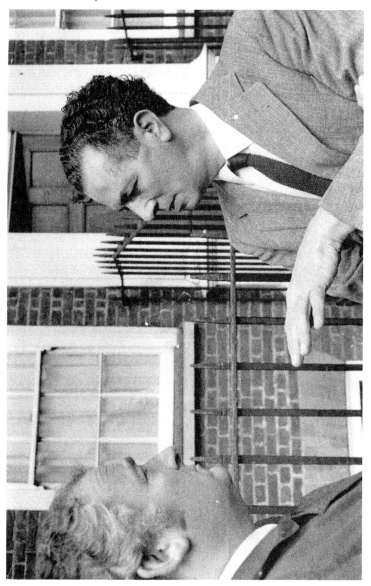

And Wacko Jacko loves the attention!

🐾 SPORT

Wacko Jacko and the Hack Pack

PATRICK COLLINS on our World Cup wordslingers

The Press Centre in Buenos Aires was large, slightly larger than the Royal Albert Hall. Five days before the opening of the 1978 World Cup finals, around 3000 journalists were sitting at typewriters and staring at empty sheets of paper. As I sat and stared with the rest, Jacko tapped me on the shoulder. 'Slow day?' he said. 'Nothing happening? Oh dear! You could always try "Gun-Toting Cops Throw A Ring Of Steel Around This Frightened City". But I think I've done that one already.'

Now Jacko was a tabloid reporter of the old school; a chunky, dapper fellow who knew his market and serviced it brilliantly. He had endured a thousand slow days of his own, but somehow he always found the words to fill them. And, as ever, he wanted to help. So he gave me a story about Scottish fans hitch-hiking down from New York to support their side. 'Very hard trip,' said Jacko. 'Sleeping rough, nowhere to wash and change. They're in a right state. People in Buenos Aires are complaining about the smell. Great story: "BO in BA". Geddit?'

But whimsey, however contrived, was not really his forte. 'You heard this rumour about the Red Brigades' threat to kidnap the Italian squad?' he asked, conversationally. 'I'm checking it out. My office wouldn't thank me if someone nicked a World Cup team and I hadn't told them.' Jacko went off to take on the forces of international terrorism and I returned to the empty sheet of paper.

As any long-serving hack will tell you, World Cups are like that: brief spasms of activity when the football is stunning and the clichés hurl themselves at the typewriter, and long days of gripes, grumbles and groin strains.

By comparison, the players have it easy. They sit around luxury hotels, placing calls to their agents, totting up the profits from their chart-topping theme tune and swapping lies about the size of their salaries. Occasionally they toddle off to the stadium for a football match, safe in the knowledge that if things go wrong, everybody will blame the manager. They neither know nor care about the problems of journalists, in fact they rather despise the breed. As one England footballer remarked after the last World Cup: '"Press" is a four-letter word.'

There was a time when that kind of hostility would have disturbed the sensitive football writer. But no longer. The odd sycophant still remains, to slap a back or giggle at an ingratiating joke, but most hacks adopt the admirable example of their tennis cousins at Wimbledon: We'll tolerate our lot until they're knocked out, then we can get on with the tournament.

Of course, such tolerance is not extended to the manager. Over the past eight years, Bobby Robson has treated the Press with decent courtesy, and he still seems genuinely shocked when he is abused in the grossest terms by men with whom he has shared a late drink or a cordial meal. The excuse they offer carries Mafia overtones: 'It's not personal, Bob. It's business.' And, in a sense, they are right. The persecution of Robson has sold a lot of tabloid newspapers – which is its single justification. How they will miss him when he goes.

By and large, the Robson-baiters tend to keep their own company at the World Cup, dining in small groups and chuckling over the latest malevolent headline dreamed up in London. The loyalists dine at a distant table, with expressions pained and haughty.

The television crowd, haughtiest of all, seek out a superior restaurant, far from these rough fellows. They guzzle Perrier, exchange compliments and list the satellite companies which have solicited their services with six-figure seductions; all loftily rejected. In the hacks' eyes, they are a mite precious, and the tale is told with some relish of how one telly-person, deep in conversation, accepted a large card from a waiter and scribbled his autograph. The waiter was puzzled. 'That, sir, was the menu,' he said.

Telly-men, loyalists and amateur assassins, they all have one prejudice in common; they all regard the news hounds, the Ring of Steel tendency – admirably represented by Jacko and his chums – with the deepest distrust.

Jacko is aware of their feelings, and he cares not a toss. I once saw him hammering a typewriter with demented energy, taking care to cover the paper so that not a word should be revealed. An anxious football hack watched him at work. 'God knows what he's up to now,' he said. 'These people are capable of anything. And we're the ones who have to pick up the pieces'.

Jacko sensed his unease from 30 paces. 'Got a nice little tale here,' he said. 'How many a's are there in Baader-Meinhof?' ∎

ACKNOWLEDGEMENTS

I would like to thank Charles Griffin, the Daily Mirror's cartoonist for permission to use his splendid piece of work showing me off on holiday, which makes our front cover. Also special thanks to Colin Mackenzie for advice, and splendid lunches with his wife Linda, as we wrote our memoirs in tandem during lockdown.

All remaining accolades must go the Jackson family. Son-in-law Eoin Duffy showed all his national newspaper sub-editing skills by suggesting the *Reflections of a Mirror Man* title within seconds as head scratching continued elsewhere. Barbara, the best-read person I know, greatly improved this hack's attempts at fine writing, while our three eldest children – Catherine, Nicholas and Stella – took on an in-house lawyer's duties with my era's descriptive style greeted with reprimands: "Dad, you can't say or do those things these days".

But it is to our youngest, Tom, that I owe the most. A science writer who enjoyed rave reviews worldwide for his book *Chilled*, a page-turning history of refrigeration, and has written more than 100 books over 25 years, became my agent, editor and publisher. Thanks Tom.

Finally more gratitude for Barbara, for her love and devotion over our marriage of 61 years. Without her, reflections could vary.

INDEX

Printed in Great Britain
by Amazon

62480686R00149